KU-205-920

THE COMMUNITY

INTERNATIONAL LIBRARY OF SOCIOLOGY

AND SOCIAL RECONSTRUCTION

Founded by Karl Mannheim

Editor W. J. H. Sprott

A catalogue of books available in the INTERNATIONAL LIBRARY OF
SOCIOLOGY AND SOCIAL RECONSTRUCTION and new books in
preparation for the Library will be found at the end of this volume

THE COMMUNITY

by

René König

Translated from the German by

Edward Fitzgerald

LONDON

ROUTLEDGE & KEGAN PAUL LTD

Translated from the German
GRUNDFORMEN DER GESELLSCHAFT: DIE GEMEINDE
© *Rowohlt Taschenbuch Verlag GmbH, Hamburg*

Published in Great Britain 1968
by Routledge and Kegan Paul Ltd
Broadway House, 68-74 Carter Lane
London, E.C.4

Printed in Great Britain by
Cox and Wyman, Ltd
London, Fakenham and Reading

English translation
© *Routledge & Kegan Paul Ltd 1968*

SBN 7100 3493 8

CONTENTS

BIOGRAPHICAL NOTE

René König is of Franco-German extraction and was born in 1906 into a family of engineers and industrialists in Magdeburg. He first studied Islamic languages and philosophy at Vienna University, and in Vienna he came into touch with the so-called 'Vienna Circle' of scientific logic (above all Moritz Schlick). The study of philosophy, sociology and ethnology in Berlin then followed, where he came under the particular influence of Richard Thurnwald, in whose work *Zeitschrift für Völkerpsychologie und Soziologie* he published a series of critical articles from 1931 on. After completing his Berlin studies (1930) he went to Paris for further studies, and there he came into contact with the second generation of the Durkheim school. He had originally hoped to become a member of the Faculty at Berlin University, but the changed political situation after 1933 caused him to abandon this idea. In 1937 he left Germany for Switzerland, where he became a member of the Faculty at Zurich University. After the war he was appointed to the Chair of Sociology at Cologne University (1949).

After he emigrated from Germany there followed a long period of study in England (1939–40), and then, after the war, in the United States (1952–3, 1955). In 1957 he was invited to return there as a visiting professor (the University of Michigan in the spring of 1957, and the University of California in the summer); he has been teaching regularly in the United States ever since (Columbia University, New York, University of California 1959–60, University of Colorado 1962, University of California 1964–5). After the war he gave lectures at numerous German and other universities (Holland, Spain, France, Italy, Egypt, the Lebanon and Turkey). In this period he was deeply interested in the preparation and development of an international association of sociologists, encouraged by Unesco. In 1948 he was a member of the preparatory committee, in 1949 a member of the inaugural assembly of the International Sociological Association (I.S.A.) in Oslo. In the years 1949 to 1953 he was a member of the Executive Committee of the association, and again in 1956. He was the secretary of the First World Congress of Sociology in 1950. From 1962 to 1966 he was the president of I.S.A. His other activities have included: co-editor since 1953 of *Current Sociology* (Unesco); since 1953, Director of the Sociological Research Institute at the University of Cologne; since 1955 editor of the *Kölner Zeitschrift für Soziologie und Sozialpsychologie*; 1955–59 Vice-Chairman of the German Sociological Association. He is the author or editor of numerous books, many of which have been translated into other languages (French, Dutch, Italian, Spanish, Portuguese, Serbo-Croatian, Japanese).

DEFINITION OF TERMS

There can hardly be any doubt that the local community (*Gemeinde*) is, together with the family, one of the most important basic forms of society. Nevertheless, it must be admitted that – at least in continental Europe – sociological research in this field is remarkably lacking in assurance. The very term itself is used in many different meanings, and is often anything but clear and definite.[1] Sometimes it is taken simply for granted that the meaning of the term is self-evident; or the term is jumbled up more or less arbitrarily with others, with the result that confusion arises, sometimes of an historical, sometimes of a systematic nature. But in this connection we must bear in mind that there is a good deal of very obvious ambiguity, particularly in German (*Gemeinschaft, Gemeinde, Gemeinderschaft*), about the meaning of the expression 'community'. Therefore the possibility arises of a whole series of misunderstandings, which can occasionally lead to very disagreeable objective consequences, as a short glance at the literature on the subject will illustrate. In addition, there is the fundamental confusion which exists between the community (*Gemeinde*) as an administrative unit and the community as a social reality; the former in Germany at least, has almost entirely held the attention, with the result that the latter has been left in an exceptionally ambiguous state. And, finally, the situation is made even more confused by a series of terms, some related closely, others less closely, which are objectively connected but not necessarily identical in meaning, and further by a series of preconceptions which whilst sharing some elements with the sociological conception of the community, do not share them all.

It seems to us a matter of great importance that this conception of community should be clarified, not only for sociology itself, but also for a whole series of other social sciences (for example, economics, economic and legal history, ethnology, folklore, etc.) including 'local administration' whose proper subject is the community. By reason of their own special interests, comumnity policy, political science, jurisprudence, and various branches of economics remain essentially one-sided and have, therefore, limited relationships with the community. Sociology however regards these and other factors *only as aspects of the social reality of the community as an empirical whole and as one of the basic forms of social life, past and present.*

The full implications of this can be recognized only if it is realized that it implies a quite definite decision as to the position of the community in the general framework of social phenomena. This can quite readily be summed up in a brief formula. Whereas we find the opinion quite generally held that the community as a determinative system of social behaviour has, on the whole and with very few exceptions, been replaced by comprehensive social phenomena of a higher order (for example, the national state-society type) this formula implies that despite everything, the community nevertheless represents a reality of its own, which is still in active existence not only in rural areas of advanced industrial societies and in economically underdeveloped societies, but *almost universally.*

The minor proviso implied by the word 'almost' can be explained easily by reference, for example, to the difference between the human family and the community. While it is quite obvious that the family is in origin not only anthropological but also zoological and therefore of really universal significance, one might suppose that the roots of the community do not reach down quite so deep. Further, spatial proximity which we shall meet as an important (though often exaggerated) factor in the relationship of men in a community, appears of less decisive importance as a bond between men than kinship or culture. Very often the neighbourhood factor operates only with and through these other media. This would seem to indicate a lesser universality for the community as a local association by comparison specifically with the family, and with other forms of kinship including the clan, kin and the tribe. On the other hand, many attempts have been made to regard the association of men in a community as on a par with the association of plants and animals in ecological associations. Without exaggerating the importance of this view, we may nevertheless assume that it allows a certain conclusion with regard to the universal scope of the human community as a basic form of social phenomena.

THE COMMUNITY AS A BASIC FORM OF SOCIETY

Although it can certainly be said of the family that, on the basis of its dual biological and social nature, it has shown an extraordinary ability to persist amidst the tremendous changes which have come about in our social life in the course of history, particularly under the influence of modern economic society, it can also be said, at least to some extent, about the community too. Hence we take our stand very definitely against the often-expressed opinion that in view of these developments the community is doomed to disappear. This view is often held, particularly with regard to the 'small community', which is considered in a more or less ambiguous way to be a form of life which is particularly favourable to individual development. We shall soon have cause to note the highly dubious background of this view. For the moment note here that we categorically refuse to admit any fundamental and essential difference between the large and the small community. Of course, there is a very obvious difference between the way of life of a village and that of a big town, but for the moment that is not the point at issue; the point at issue is rather the much more important and *decisive question as to whether in sociology there is really a specific structural 'community' form.* This implies that first of all we must obtain information about the structure of the community; and only after this can further questions be dealt with, such as the expression of specific differences between the large and the small community against this background.

With this, the theme of this book is clearly outlined: our aim is to discover *the structure of the community as a basic form of social life, and at the same time to define the position of this total phenomenon within the framework of social development as a whole both in the past and the present.* This will indicate, amongst other things the almost universal scope of the community; though it must constantly be borne in mind that beyond the community other comprehensive social institutions of a higher order have long since developed. We shall even see that this represents an essential characteristic of the highly-developed industrial societies of the West, whereas the same relationship cannot be shown with the same clarity either in the underdeveloped societies or in primitive societies. Nevertheless, it cannot be ignored that for most people life is still largely lived in the community. Above all it can be said that in his development from childhood to youth and on to maturity, a man first comes into contact with *all social relationships, which extend beyond the narrow limits of the family, in the community*. Although it is not always possible to survey the community (even the small one), despite earlier romantic beliefs, it is nevertheless true that in it *social life takes on the highest possible degree of tangibility*, just as in the family social life produces the greatest volume of intimacy and human warmth, which no other social institution in the later life of man can provide. One might even say that the community is that point at which society as a whole, as a highly complex phenomenon, is directly tangible, whereas without exception all other forms of society rapidly become abstract and are never so directly experienced as in the community.

A few examples will serve to illustrate this. A man can walk to the local market on his own two feet, and there he will experience the most important function of the economy, namely the satisfaction of demand which proceeds by means of supply, demand and price formation in its most obvious form. On the other hand, the 'market' in general is a completely abstract affair which exists everywhere and nowhere. In any case, it cannot be seen. In the morning, at midday, and in the evening, during the rush hours, the operatives of the local economic system can be seen on the streets, hurrying off to their work, or going home from it. But when the process is projected into the larger 'market' this rhythmic inhalation and exhalation of the economy disappears completely, and is replaced by the abstract idea of continual production. At community level this process takes on a completely different appearance.

Now when we consider that, despite all the internal and external mobility of modern highly-developed industrial societies, the majority of human beings still spend the greater part (if not the whole) of their lives in a single community (whether large or small), then we shall realize, without further

4

explanation being necessary, that *the community represents a totality of life not only in its inner extent, but also because for many it is absolutely identical with the totality of life itself.* In this sense the community becomes 'home' in the strictest sense, not only because it embraces the basic and average forms of all social activities, but because in addition it contains an element of nature as certainly as each community is always a part of its social and cultural context. This will not change even in our own age no matter how great the social, economic, political and cultural upheavals to which we have been and are still being subjected.

THE PRECEDENCE OF THE STRUCTURAL QUESTION

The necessary consequence of this view is a preliminary analysis of the structure of the community before the multiple nature of its aspects can be considered. This naturally presupposes a definition of the concept community. At the same time it similarly implies something the reader is not entitled to expect in this book. We have already stressed that the question of size where a community is concerned is of merely secondary importance when dealing with the problems of its structure. It is quite impossible to form any judgement on the importance of this factor until the structural framework in which the phenomenon community exists has been outlined. Thus if this factor is dealt with at all then it is only in order to prevent unjustified and sweeping conclusions. This includes on the one hand, for example, the contention that the small or rural community is particularly simple in its social relationships and therefore easier to survey; and, on the other hand, the equally dubious contention that larger communities, such as towns, and in particular big cities, are socially completely disorganized precisely because a tolerable social order is possible only 'in small groups'. In the former case the inner differentiation of the small community is underestimated; in the latter case the possibilities for the development of small groups in towns, even cities, are similarly underestimated. But all these problems can be dealt with only after an analysis of the structure of the community. Therefore, both in dealing with the small community (usually the field of rural sociology) and the large community (usually

5

the field of urban sociology) *this must take precedence.* It must also take precedence over the sociology of rural-urban relationships which is invariably connected with it. In fact it appears increasingly impossible to make any systematic and effective approach to these central sub-disciplines of sociology without first having satisfactorily decided what the structure of the community actually is. For example, if it were shown that the small community does not in fact show that complete form of integration which is so often uncritically ascribed to it, then quite naturally our attitude to the phenomenon of the big town would change accordingly. Conversely, it might be discovered that within limits big communities can develop an astounding degree of integration, a degree which, under certain circumstances, can be so difficult for smaller communities to achieve because in them antagonisms clash without the benefit of those buffer factors present in the larger community; thus, with insufficient room to manœuvre within the narrow limits of the smaller community, such clashes can cause fatal upheavals in the whole life of the community. But these, and similar questions connected with them, can only be approached with any hope of a successful solution when we have decided first on an unbiased definition of the concept community, and, secondly, when we have made a detailed analysis of its structure. We have now laid the foundations for the central objective of this book.

CHAPTER I

NATURE AND COMMUNITY

THE COMMUNITY AS A BIOTIC ASSOCIATION

If we were to look at our earth from interplanetary space we should see everywhere on its surface vegetable, animal and human life combined into numerous 'communities'; and, seen from that distance, they would all without exception reveal characteristics of 'growth'. Even the lowest forms of life, for example, in the world of a bacteriological life, reveal similar groupings with a more or less definite structure, symbioses, commensal and parasitic relationships of various kinds. Plants show highly variable forms of social association varying from the simplest form of aggregation to the highly complicated form of vegetable life in woodlands. Between the two extremes of lower humus layer with soil bacteria, earthworms, insects, moss and roots, and upper flowering life, there are a whole series of sub-systems. Animals live together in a variety of loose associations: swarms, sleeping groups, breeding groups, colonies, herds and packs, and also in even closer associations such as marriage, the nuclear family, the extended family, the harem and the State, just as human beings do in their communities. Soil bacteria, plants, animals and human beings are all specifically brought together by some uniform 'natural' connection, with the result that one is often inclined to regard elementary forms of human association such as the community as a simple extension of the co-operative living of forms of life, within the framework of their natural characteristics and processes, into the sphere of human society. Occasionally this connection has been stretched further still to include even the sphere of the inorganic in that, for example, a crystal cluster has been regarded as a social form of matter.

When we consider that the communities of man cover almost

the entire habitable surface of the earth, and in some cases even
its largely uninhabitable surface, and that prehistoric man – as
far back as we can see, and certainly including neolithic man –
lived largely in such communities, the preliminary attempt to
include human societies in the general household of nature will
hardly appear surprising. Even the human family is primarily
concerned with its own preservation in a purely natural sense.
There is thus beyond all question an embracing *biotic community*
which compels us to regard basic and elementary forms of
human association as living things.[1] Just as we speak of the
procreation of the human species by the union of the sexes, so
we may, at this level, also speak of a 'social body', or a 'social
organism' of society; and, in the same way, of its 'growth' and
'dying' (senescence). But at the same time we must bear in
mind that in using such and similar expressions we are referring
for the time being exclusively to what is generally biotically
relevant to the phenomenon in question.

This realization is in itself of great interest for the human
sciences, because it is a decisive step forward for them to grasp
that social systems do not exist as part of some divine ordinance,
but as natural phenomena; and that human social systems have a
broad basis in the sphere of vegetable and animal life. But this
realization has narrow limits because it embraces only that
which human associations have in common with all other living
associations, i.e. it does not embrace anything which is specifically socially human; to which, in particular, history and culture
are necessary. It is therefore dangerous to use the term 'community' for vegetable, animal and human associations even
though there are so many common characteristics present. It
is not permissible to smuggle single characteristics of biotic
associations into human social life (for example the factor of
growth, which is so often misused in describing small communities in particular). And where the family is concerned too,
we can quite clearly distinguish between the 'second birth' of
the individual as a social-cultural personality and his physical
birth, even though the one is undoubtedly not possible without
the other.[2]

At the beginning of the thirties these questions were dealt
with at a conference of French scientists to discuss the relationship between animal and human sociology; and it was pointed

out quite rightly that the term 'community' should be used in a different sense in each case, in a wider sense and in a narrower one. The same view was adopted in a discussion on the relationship between vegetable and human sociology, and it was proposed to adopt the Greek word (*koinōnia*) for the wider sense of the word 'community', while for the narrower sense it was agreed to retain the Latin derivative 'society', or the German word *Gesellschaft*. Similarly, for dealing with living communities in general the name 'Biocoenology' (derived from the Greek (*koinos*) was developed; and for the theme under examination itself the analagous term 'bio-coenosis' (which is lately being replaced more and more by the term 'biom'). Thus in this sense the associations of plants and lower animals are bio-coenoses (or phytocoenoses), *while the human communities are societies*, just as the human family finds its most essential function outside the process of procreation.

THE LOCAL BOND OF SOCIAL LIFE

But in so far as man is, above all else, a living thing, understandably he can be subjected to the same considerations as other living things, as, for example, climatology, and, in part also, physical geography, not to speak of biology. In this respect those sciences which deal with man and his spatial environment and which have developed in our day into what is called ecology, are particularly important. They are divided primarily into plant, animal and social (human) ecology. Ecology examines the spatial relationships of living things both to inanimate nature and to their kind; which is sufficient in itself to indicate the extreme importance of the ecological view both for biology in general and in particular for zoology, and sociology. In fact ecology and social research are very closely related to each other. This applies above all to the human community, which is essentially an association of human beings living in spatial proximity and spatially limited, for the time being; so that here too we may speak of a principle of local association applicable to both animal and human sociology. Numerous investigations have shown that the 'territorial' organization of animals and their local association is a widespread social principle.[3] Incidentally we prefer to speak of local association, or area rather than territory, because the latter term indicates the inclusion of several localities, and consequently it is considered in political science to be an essential principle of state national life. With this, however, the clear implication is that with the word 'territory' we have to deal with a dimension which is *superior* to the community. When we mean the spatial extent of the community we shall call it the community area (which approximates to the area amongst animals).

At the moment, however, another problem needs clarification. Regarding bio-coenology in the wider sense, of which ecology forms an essential part, interest used to be concentrated largely on the *one-sided* effect of the locality on the development of the individual plants and plant associations, individual animals and animal associations, and, finally, on the development of human beings and human societies. Such an extreme deterministic attitude has been completely abandoned today; but it is recognized that the development of plant associations is certainly dependent on locality, nevertheless in time the associations themselves affect the locality, *hence the factor of association is of decisive importance.* This is true in the same sense for animals and human beings so that today the following *definition of ecology* has been adopted: 'The science of the conditions of existence and the *interactions* of the living being and its environment.'[4] Thus the relationship between living beings and their environment is regarded as mutual in the general bio-coenotic view also. In addition this factor becomes more and more marked the higher we ascend in the scale of living beings, although the efficiency of lower organisms can be very great indeed; e.g. sulphur bacteria.

THE COMMUNITY AS CULTURE

Whereas at one time there was a general inclination to believe that plants and animals more or less passively suffered their environment, modern developments both in plant and animal sociology have considerably changed this view. This change of view is also important in community sociology, and that is why we propose to touch upon it briefly here. Even plants are in a position to change their environment or habitat, and to develop bio-coenoses which create a new environment, as has already been mentioned. In the animal world too bio-coenoses of a higher order develop, and, in fact, without this the preservation of the species could not in most cases be guaranteed. These associations show a real 'social character' to the extent that they are based on co-operative relations. And finally the surrounding space itself is drawn into the process, just as it is with human communities. Thus we can say – at the present stage of our knowledge – that the parallel between animal and human life is much closer and goes much farther than was previously frequently assumed, although quite early on the French animal psychologist Alfred Espinas regarded even polypus colonies as animate organisms.[5] With the aid of more highly-developed methods of observation[6] quite astonishing insight has often been gained into the frequently highly complicated character of animal social phenomena, which are sometimes hardly less complicated than human communities. Nevertheless, a 'town' of prairie dogs, which – as formerly in Arizona – could extend under certain conditions over a radius of several miles and thereby change environmental conditions very considerably, is still fundamentally different from the corresponding institutions amongst men.

Under the influence of Max Scheler, the Basle zoologist, Adolf Portmann expressed this as follows:

> Whereas the social forms of animals can be changed only by the inherited mutations of the individuals, human social forms are being constantly changed by deliberate decisions, historical transformations, by 'fate' and 'history' . . . . The inherited characteristics which operate throughout this historical conception are always of a broad, formally unstressed, impulsive or intellectual nature; they are characteristics which to a certain extent determine the scope of the performance, the direction of the effort, and also the strength of will and the strength of feeling, but never the content, the indicated forms and the concrete performances of the historical process.[7]

In other words, in his social forms man appears on the scene as the *creator of culture*, whereas the change in environment of animals is necessarily determined by their particular species and therefore remains calculable within a given limit. Everything

human is dependent on 'contingency' particularly in the spatial
extension and development of social life, as was pointed out half
a century ago by the great French geographer P. Vidal de la
Blache, whose influence on the development of social ecology
can hardly be overestimated. There is no other way open to
man, because – unlike the other higher forms of animal life
which are born with highly-developed limbs and are able to
move around freely from the start in the way which is specifically
characteristic of the adults of the species – he has to learn
during the first extra-uterine year how to move in the manner
specific to his kind, whereby socially transmitted culture
develops the process of learning and maturity to new forms.[8]

However, we must stress here and now that we do not agree
with Portmann in all his conclusions, and certainly not where
they contradict his own hypothesis. He quite logically stresses
that the bond between mother and child in the human family is
'natural' to the highest possible degree, but becomes socially
'structured', i.e. significant, only by virtue of social rules, con-
ventions and culture, and not by natural circumstances. But as
soon as he begins to talk of other groups he rather one-sidedly
stresses certain characteristics which human beings are supposed
to share with higher mammals, without paying sufficient attention to the dimensional difference between the animal and the
human world. He writes, for example:

> All our natural aptitudes are appropriate to life in a small
> group; they are in accordance with a form of life in which
> observable conditions, clear and definite relationships, can
> exist between all the members of the group. Our structural
> relationships work best in this social environment, where we
> are best able to estimate our own nature by comparison and
> to act accordingly, and to bring it into a tolerable relation-
> ship with the clearly known advantages and disadvantages of
> the other members of the group.[9]

If it is true in fact that 'man is constantly faced with the task of
developing his social relationships, his sphere of life and his own
personality'[10] then this naturally applies both to the large and
the small group. Thus the above quoted passage must be regarded as a completely arbitrary judgement, and one which, in
addition, is completely at variance with the author's usual

views. Whether the group is large or small, the artificiality of culture remains the same in both cases, as was rightly stressed with regard to the family. But as this misunderstanding can also be met with elsewhere and because, in addition, it has from time to time played a damaging role in community sociology, it had to be touched upon here. The specifically natural can never be more than a marginal value in human social culture, and this is true under all circumstances. Thus a small community is no more 'natural' in this respect than a metropolitan urban centre, even though the dominant social forms and in particular the accepted social patterns, may be different in the two cases.

A passage from the work of the anthropologist Daryll Forde illuminates the fact that even the smallest and most primitive community is a cultural creation in which one can never speak of any directly integrated community of men as in the bio-coenoses: 'It will, I think, be clear that the economic and social activities of any community are the products of long and intricate processes of cultural accumulation and integration, extending far back in time to the emergence of man himself'.[11] If this is true of small primitive communities, i.e. groups without a written culture and without developed technical equipment, then it is naturally true, and to an even greater extent, of the communities of the highly-developed agricultural and industrial societies of the Western world. With this, incidentally, two factors come to the fore which differentiate the human community from all other living associations, namely, technology and economy; the two factors which enable man to change his environment more and more radically.

CHAPTER II

CERTAIN TERMINOLOGICAL DIFFICULTIES

We have already pointed out a very awkward ambiguity which has arisen because of the imprecise use of the term community for vegetable, animal and human groupings. In the previous chapter we also saw one of the consequences of this confusion when the kind of association existing between human beings in a small group was put on a par with associations of higher mammalian groups and at the same time proclaimed to be 'the more natural'. Despite the complexity of the organization involved, associations of animals can never be more than bio-coenoses. If human beings are to be put on the same level then one can only describe man as predator and victim simultaneously, like most other animals.[1] But, in fact, with the development of technology and economy man becomes the cultural master of his environment. But with this the danger of a terminological confusion of things which are independent of each other, is by no means clarified.

COMMUNITY AND ASSOCIATION

Even without falling into biological analogies where the social organism of the community is concerned, there are still a number of ambiguities connected with the terms 'local community' (*Gemeinde*) and community in general (*Gemeinschaft*) in their specifically sociological application. These difficulties are aggravated by the fact that the word community (*Gemeinschaft*) has quite a number of different meanings. First of all, therefore, we must distinguish between the loose use of the term community (*Gemeinschaft*) for all forms of human and non-human groupings, and its specific use as a sociological concept. In the

14

loose application of the term, the word community (*Gemeinschaft*) has become a maid of all work whose use should be banished completely from everyday parlance, since it has really created nothing but confusion. We should like to see it replaced by social relationships. In its more specific use we should then have to draw a distinction between a modern and an older application. The older use itself has a concrete and an abstract significance.[2] Let us first consider the two older aspects, and then the newer applications of the word – naturally within the limits of their relationship to the term local community (*Gemeinde*).

In its concrete application the word originally meant 'the totality of those who own something in common'. Thus in its origin it is, in fact, identical in the older usage with local community (*Gemeinde*), or at least with citizens and associates enjoying full rights, and other actual members of the community who do not enjoy full rights must be distinguished from them (freemen of the community as distinct from inhabitants of the community perhaps). According to Grimm's dictionary: 'Its real development (the word *Gemeinschaft* community) arose in community life (*Gemeindeleben*); at the same time it appears almost as an auxiliary form of *Gemeinde* (community) – as also *Gemeinheit* commonality.' This is also the origin of the word *Gemeindschaft*. In this sense the word community (*Gemeinschaft*) becomes a term for the common land referring to the undivided land which belongs to the entitled citizens. At the same time it is called the community district or area.[3] *It must be stressed that originally both the words community* (Gemeinschaft) *and local community* (Gemeinde) *had a direct relationship to the common land of the community, and only later came in a 'transferred' sense*[4] *to include all other forms of 'common life and existence'.* This latter application is more recent. Grimm's dictionary also says under the heading *Gemeinde* that of all its meanings 'the relation to common land is now the farthest from us, but closest to the origin of the word, if it does not actually represent it'.[5] An intermediate form in abstract use was reintroduced by the Swiss Civil Code in 1907 *Gemeinderschaft*, which is also a form of common family property meaning an undivided heritage usually amongst siblings. The word *Gemeinder* then refers both to this *Gemeinderschaft* and to the word *Gemeinde*, but it has also developed a more independent sense as 'part-owner'.[6] In an abstract sense the word *Gemeinschaft* then develops from this as a juridical term which refers quite generally to the relationship between people who have something in common – property in common, a heritage in common, a household in common, etc.

Thus the word *Gemeinschaft* in German originally had a quite objective meaning, with in each case an exact relationship to material, objective, social and juridical arrangements. It should be stressed specifically that the reference is above all to *a social unity on a definite local basis, i.e. a local group as such,* a factor which makes this term recognizable straight away as a key-term in social ecology. At the same time the fundamental difference between it and the modern form of the word *Gemeinschaft* is also indicated. Here the accent is clearly on the purely personal, spiritual bond in the sense of 'the closest possible form of social relationship'.[7] In German this kind of relationship has often an emphatic, exclusive and particularly intimate sense (*Liebesgemeinschaft* or love relationship, for example), which in extreme cases can dispense with all forms of exterior (institutional) arrangements. At the same time, *Gemeinschaft* (community) in this sense is credited with a particularly intense if not, in fact, the greatest possible degree of integration. Later on we shall consider in great detail this problem of community sociology, both in our theoretical analysis of the term community as well as in our summing-up of the results of certain research into the problems of the community structure.

Although it is quite permissible, and traditional, to use the old term community (*Gemeinschaft*) as synonymous with local community (*Gemeinde*), the same thing with regard to the modern term community (*Gemeinschaft*) must be strictly rejected. But as today this sense is the only current one, consciously or unconsciously, as a result of the general tendency to the personalization of group relationships, the term community (*Gemeinschaft*) should in principle not be used to mean local community (*Gemeinde*) unless explicitly specified. In this sense it *can* be a community (*Gemeinschaft*) but it is not *necessarily* so. This is also true of small local communities (*Gemeinden*). As research has shown, the smallness of a community (*Gemeinde*) is no reason for assuming it is an integrated community in the modern sense. Only too often the outward fact of spatial proximity of a small community (*Gemeinde*) is taken without further ado as an indication of an inner integration (*Gemeinschaft*). But the two things are not necessarily coincident, as experience has frequently shown. We must take care not to fall into sentimental glorifications of the small community. In the old use of the term community (*Gemeinde*) it refers to 'associations of all kinds, both large and small'.[8]

The word community in general (*Gemeinschaft*) should therefore be used to refer to local community (*Gemeinde*) only where definite forms of common property have survived (as is often the case with primitive cultures). And here the matter usually takes on a very ambiguous aspect, as one can easily discover by a glance at the property relationships in the commonality (*Allmende*). The commonality was certainly a community (*Gemeinschaft*) in the sense that a group of old-established inhabitants of a local community (*Gemeinde*) held meadows, woods and water in common possession. But on that account it was not necessarily a community (*Gemeinschaft*) in the more modern sense that all members of the local community (*Gemeinde*) were associates (*Genossen*) working together harmoniously. Those who came in later not only had no rights of commonality, but, quite generally, enjoyed fewer political privileges and this was particularly true where and when the community (*Gemeinde*) showed its authoritative nature most clearly. Now there can be no close association (*Gemeinschaft*) in the modern sense between men whose rights are not equal. In such circumstances the juridical situation very quickly develops into a whole system of varying rights by which three main groups of members are established: full associates, ordinary associates, and protected associates with lesser rights and privileges. In a rural community (*Gemeinde*) the full associates are the landed peasants; the ordinary associates are the smaller peasants enjoying lesser rights than the full associates; finally there are various forms of 'protected associates' with significantly different rights and privileges but more limited ones. In this group belong the dependent members of a household, the so-called 'denizens', the under-tenants, the day labourers, the cottagers, the artisans, *the feofees and* so on. In areas with big estates we also find head-servants and other servants whose position is quickly absorbed in the general class relationships of the village community (*Dorfgemeinschaft*).[9] All these forms (which largely determined the composition of the medieval European village) have survived in part down to the present day; and, in addition, they have been extended by still further and more complicated variations in 'rank' (usually determined socially, not legally). This may help to justify the need for caution in the use of the term community (*Gemeinschaft*) both in general and in the particular case of the local community (*Gemeinde*). The modern community, both large and small, also has its very distinct class and other stratifications, which, under certain circumstances, divide rather than unite. The uncritical use of the term community (*Gemeinschaft*) in the modern sense can be thoroughly confusing because it claims or pretends something which is not really present. In any case the term in its old sense is no longer applicable to the modern Western highly-developed industrial societies with their preponderance of individually-owned property. Thus in the circumstances it would be better not to use the term community in general (*Gemeinschaft*) for the local community (*Gemeinde*).

LINGUISTIC PROBLEMS

In other languages too, the meaning varies. In English, for example, the expression community is equally ambiguous because in one sense it refers to the local community (*Gemeinde*) in it specific meaning, and in another to the community (*Gemeinschaft*) in its more general sense of social relationship. But there is a difference from the German in that the local community (*Gemeinde*) is not understood as a community (*Gemeinschaft*) in a particularly close sense, but refers to various degrees of association. In addition, the term is applicable to societies or associations of any size, from a single pair to human society in general. The effect of this in community sociology is that occasionally the uncritical use of the term tends to efface the exact territorial extent of the community (*Gemeinde*), whereas, sociologically speaking, its limits are almost always very clearly visible. On the other hand, the expression community is used for all forms of association from the most intimate group to the institutional organization.[10] It must be stressed at this point that the very essential local aspect of the German usage plays a lesser role in English. When the reference is to the land the community (*Gemeinde*) hold in

Certain terminological difficulties

common the term used is 'the common', whilst for the local aspect of the community (*Gemeinde*) the expression still largely used today is 'the neighbourhood', or in German *Nachbarschaft*, an expression which is often used in German in the sense that in the old village the full associate peasant is referred to simply as 'the neighbour' (*Nachbar*).

In Italian and in French the terms for community *Gemeinschaft, la communità, la communauté*, come closer to the German term *Gemeinde* (comune, commune), thus largely retaining the old sense; as shown by the French use of the term *commune* for the Paris Commune of 1871. But to express a particularly close form of association (*Gemeinschaft*) in the emphatic sense the French, Italian and English have a special word 'communion'. The *religious ambiguity* of this word should be noted, as we have not encountered it yet.

This ambiguity is also met with quite early on in the German word *Gemeinde* – *Gemeinde der Heiligen* (the communion of Saints), *Gemeinde der Christenheit* (the Christian communion), *Kirchengemeinde* (Communion of the Church), *Pfarrgemeinde* (Parish), and *Kultgemeinde* (religious community).[11] New possibilities of misunderstanding arise when the community (*Gemeinde*) as a Christian communion without hierarchical order is projected (with an obvious confusion between what should be and what is) into the real community (*Gemeinde*) with its vertical authority structure. This has greatly contributed to making an ideology of the term community (*Gemeinde*), which is, for example, particularly obvious in Switzerland. Another contrast in meaning is the community (*Gemeinde*) as a direct human association as against the community as an institutionalized organization, which is also present in the polarity of the prime community (*Urgemeinde*) as an established association (*Gemeinschaft*) and the Church.[12] Sociologically speaking, each concrete community (*Gemeinde*) must include institutionalized organizations, generally of a highly differentiated nature, if it is to survive.

Incidentally, to a certain extent such (religious) ideas play a role, though in a modified form, in certain branches of community socialism, and in particular in its anarchistic form (Godwin, Proudhon, Bakunin, Kropotkin and others), which strive to reintroduce the former regulations of the old community (*Gemeine*) under changed economic conditions and in

19

strong opposition to all hierarchical, authoritative and centralized State relationships;[13] whilst community anarchism seeks to re-establish the ancient liberty of the old Christian fraternity (*Brüdergemeinde*). Although the pure religious origin of these movements still survives, they are all too frequently tinged with utopianism, as E. K. Francis has pointed out in his interesting investigation of the Canadian Mennonites.[14] In this connection one can justifiably wonder whether these Mennonite groups (as they formerly existed in Russia, and as they exist today in Canada and other parts of the world) would still exist if they were not held together by the fact that they also represent national or ethnic minorities, in addition to their religious revivalism. Without denying that common religious beliefs and practices play an important role in the integration of a community, we think, for the reasons indicated, that the religious additional interpretation of the word community (*Gemeinde*) should be kept carefully apart from our specifically sociological interest.

The situation in Spanish is similar to that in English in that the word *communidad* is used in exactly the same way as the English word community, to mean both community in the sense of *Gemeinde* and a general human relationship. Incidentally the word is used for both large and small communities, just as the word *pueblo* is used to include agglomerations ranging in size from a small village to a town of thirty thousand inhabitants and more, but can also mean 'people', thus having a very far-reaching social connotation. Particularly important in Spanish is the difference between *communidad* and *municipio*, whereby the community (*Gemeinde*) is regarded in the one case as a social formation and a system of political self-administration, and in the other as a State administrative unit. In a painstaking analysis of an Andalusian community (*Gemeinde*) of about 2,000 inhabitants the British anthropologist, J. A. Pitt-Rivers, has very clearly illustrated the distinction between the community and the central government; and he rightly connects the existing tension with the anarchist movement in Spain.[15] On the other hand, difficulties which the double meaning of the word *communidad* can lead to, are shown in a more recent work by the Mexican sociologist Lucio Mendieta y Nuñez, in which once again the term community (*Gemeinde*) is confused with community in general *(Gemeinschaft)* in the modern sense. The result, amongst others, is that the sense of locality is once again eliminated from the term community *(Gemeinde)*, because community in general *(Gemeinschaft)* means only a purely personal association. With this he inevitably comes to the conclusion that the community *(Gemeinde)* is a social grouping 'without a definite form and organization'.[16] Accordingly, therefore, he regards the community *(Gemeinde)* as only a 'structural quasi-group'.

A comparison of the various linguistic forms of the term community *(Gemeinde)* reveals not only terminological difficulties but also shows the influence of cultural and historical factors on the development of the word and its meaning. We shall have to deal with this in greater detail later, but first of all we must try to find a definition of the word community *(Gemeinde)* which will circumvent the difficulties indicated above.

CHAPTER III

PRELIMINARY DEFINITION
OF COMMUNITY

ON THE MULTIPLICITY OF DEFINITIONS

In a recent article George A. Hillery Jr. lists no less than ninety-four definitions of the word community (*Gemeinde*), a performance which seems to confirm the impression probably created in the reader's mind by the two previous chapters of this book that we are concerned with a highly controversial matter.[1] In fact, many authors who don't really quite know how to use the word do quote this particular article. Apart from the fact that a good deal could be said as to the reliability of the selection made by Hillery – for example, one could quite easily append to his bibliography at least as many important sources again – we should like to point out for the moment that the list he presents really shows far more correspondences than contradictions; and this is perhaps what his sub-title 'Areas of Agreement' is intended to convey.

In the same way we should like to point out that most controversies have a tendency to resolve themselves provided one keeps to the point. In our opinion real difficulties exist today only in the systematic inclusion of the specific phenomenon community (*Gemeinde*) in the general classification system of sociology, and in particular into the theory of 'social structures'. Here we find an abstract and a concrete definition diametrically opposed to each other. The former is represented, for example, by Leopold von Wiese, who regards the community (*Gemeinde*) as a 'corporate' or body, i.e. as an 'abstract collectivity'.[2] Such a definition will obviously not take us far because it restricts the phenomenon community (*Gemeinde*) to its narrowest aspect as an administrative unit. On the other hand, sociology regards this element, together with others, as projected into the social reality of the community (*Gemeinde*) in its empirical existence, as one of the basic forms of social existence past and present. In this connection the jurist talks of the 'universality (*Allzuständigkeit, Allseitigkeit*) of the effective scope' of the community (*Gemeinde*).[3] But as this expression refers only to the universality of administration and not to that of life, a point which is obvious without further discussion, it does not take us much farther either, though it does not, like Leopold von Wiese's definition, bar the way to specifically sociological analysis. Thus, in the sociological sense, the community (*Gemeinde*) is certainly more than a mere administrative unit, even where this is properly regarded as comprehensive; it rests in the first place on social activities and social relationships, without which all administration would have no basis. Before the community(*Gemeinde*) can be classified into any more extensive relationships – which would raise the question of its genuine scope of effectiveness (self-administration) and that delegated to it by the State – it must first of all be examined as such. We must first investigate the specific social life of the community (*Gemeinde*) before we can decide whether or not we can speak of community self-administration.

THE COMMUNITY AS A SOCIAL TOTALITY

There are various terms current in sociology to describe such a highly complex state of affairs. Marcel Mauss talks of a 'phénomene social total' as against social phenomena which are not total, i.e. those in which men are together for a specific purpose, or a limited number of purposes. The term 'full groups' is also used[4] to describe groups which comprise a variety of functions, social phenomena and processes. But this particular term would first have to be most carefully distinguished from other terms, which, whilst not directly connected with it, refer to a supposed 'autonomy', 'autarchy' or 'self-sufficiency' of the community (*Gemeinde*). These terms refer primarily not to the structure of the community as a many-sided vital phenomenon, but only to its isolation from other relationships; a matter which is not under discussion here. For even if community sociology holds that a given community

(*Gemeinde*) has clearly defined limits, generally speaking, this does not mean that it is therefore isolated, or 'self-sufficient', or whatever similar term one cares to adopt. There was probably no such thing as a self-sufficient community (*Gemeinde*) even in very primitive societies. One always finds at least a minimum of outside trade or exchange, even if only for salt and metals.[5] Fundamentally, the idea of the self-sufficient community (*Gemeinde*) is nothing but a remnant of those ideas of natural right met with in older economic history which have been completely abandoned today. But whilst occasionally a particular community (*Gemeinde*) may be excessively isolated in scientific examination, one reason amongst others is that ethnologists, and cultural or social anthropologists, are accustomed to treat a community (*Gemeinde*) in isolation for quite different reasons, namely because they are primarily interested in the microculture it contains.[6] Whilst the terms used to occasionally give rise to such ideas, as for example is frequently the case in the work of Robert Redfield,[7] it must be pointed out that the way to further social relationships must naturally be left open if the matter is to be regarded realistically. This is true even of primitive cultural spheres, and it is true to an even greater extent of economically highly-developed societies, where the idea of an isolated self-sufficient community (*Gemeinde*) is quite unjustified and is never more than the sentimental delusion of some high-flown folklorist.

However, the term full group can easily lead to such notions, we should therefore prefer the expression 'global society' together with the description 'total social phenomenon'. This seems to us to go farther and at the same time does not exclude by definition the possibility that such a community (*Gemeinde*) may be built on a whole hierarchy of functional spheres, and on a plethora of individual groups and *other* social relationships and forms (including cultural relationships), nor does it suggest the isolation or self-sufficiency of such a community.[8] Accordingly, the old speculative idea that wider and more embracing social or State structures arise out of the amalgamation of individual communities loses ground – just as the same line of thought must be rejected in presenting the relationship of the family, the State or society, though it was often adopted by earlier historians.[9] This idea is completely ruled out by the recognition

24

that during the far greater part of his history man has lived in both large and small communities, and still so lives today; communities which represent the most obvious, the most concrete, and the most observable form of global societies (even in the authoritative sense), and compared with which the old tribal relationships appear far less clearly outlined.

In our analysis of contemporary societies we must also proceed from this fundamental fact, even though in our modern highly-developed industrial societies other types of global societies of a much wider scope may have arisen (regional groupings, federations, national States, supra-national empires, supra-State continental amalgamations, and so on). Indeed communities as living social units have by no means disappeared from our modern social system, provided we realize that the fact of being a global society does not imply any possible isolation, autonomy, autarchy or self-sufficiency on the part of the community. In such cases too the community remains *a more or less large local and social unit in which men co-operate in order to live their economic, social and cultural life together*. Thus from this standpoint it is relatively unimportant whether we are dealing with a hamlet, a village, a small town, a *polis*, a city State, a big town or a metropolitan area. The above-mentioned conditions can be present in each case. As, however, the community as a global society embraces a 'totality' of social relationships, it remains (despite the development of global societies of a higher order which at the same time, usually in the form of the State, claim a monopoly of authority) a decisive sphere of political determination whose decisions are based very directly on a plethora of concrete communally experienced life, whereas in the State, as we have already pointed out, everything necessarily becomes abstract.

SIMPLE AND COMPLEX DEFINITIONS

When we recall the ninety-four definitions listed by Hillery, we must make up our minds from the start that, despite the relative unity which we have pointed out, we must not expect to arrive at any simple definition of the word community (*Gemeinde*). But if we agree to regard the community as a global society in the above-mentioned sense, we shall not find it too difficult to adopt a more complex type of definition, three important elements of which are mentioned by Hillery: local unity, social interaction and common bonds.[10] We shall soon find that we have to incorporate these three elements in our own definition. If we now isolate the special task of finding a definition for our term global society, either agreeing with Gurvitch (cf. 8 above) or going our own way, we shall have to make up our minds that the above three elements cannot be regarded as sufficient to meet all cases. This point is also made by Hillery, in agreement with Sorokin, Zimmermann and Galpin.

With this an old dispute in the sphere of logic arises again, which divides the more or less extensive series of characteristics into 'primary' and 'secondary' categories, of which the former *must* be, and the latter *may* be present. Incidentally we prefer not to deal with this question in case we should arouse new controversy. We will merely point out that we propose to adopt a complex definition, whereby the presence of a certain (limited) number of characteristics will be regarded as the minimum definition. The question of how many characteristics we should confine ourselves to is more or less a matter of judgement, but the tendency will on the whole be upwards, because an 'abundant definition' does no harm. Of course, we must take care that our series does not suddenly include characteristics which contradict the earlier ones. Incidentally, such complex definitions can be greatly extended, as Robert Redfield's book *The Little Community* shows us, *since it is itself really one long extended definition.* The individual chapters provide the chief elements of the definition, whilst each separate chapter develops the auxiliary aspects of the basic elements. An exceptionally close network of terms is developed in this way, whose function as a definition becomes clear only when we see them synoptically in their complex totality. Without wishing to go on record as agreeing in every respect with Redfield we should nevertheless like to point out that we definitely consider his book to be the most thorough attempt which has so far been made to achieve such a complex definition of community.

Following on our previous observations let us now attempt to arrive at a preliminary definition of the term community, one which can subsequently be extended in various directions. A community is first of all a global society of a local unit type embracing an indefinite multiplicity of functional spheres, social groups and other social phenomena, and conditioning innumerable forms of social interaction, joint bonds, and value concepts. Further, apart from numerous forms of inner relationships which may exist in the previously mentioned parts, it will also, and as a matter of course, have its own tangible institutional and organizational external structure. From this alone it is already quite clear that groupings of the type 'family, neighbourhood, community, profession' (such as can be met with again and again) are completely inadmissible since they treat incomparables as though they were on a par. The community is thus under all circumstances a global society, and therefore a term of a superior order to family, neighbourhood, profession, etc., because it includes all these phenomena and groups within itself (together with many others, for instance, social classes). Precisely for this reason it cannot be mentioned in the same breath with them, since on account of its specific structural character it is in a category above them all.

From such a complex definition, which puts local unity, social interactions and common values and ties at the head, it can be seen at once that the administrative aspect of the community is, though not completely effaced, nevertheless pushed so far into the background that it becomes relatively unimportant for the essential definition. In the foreground is the community as a social reality; and that is undoubtedly something quite different from the community as an administrative unit. This principle is quite generally applicable; that is to say, it is independent of any special traditions which may exist in Continental Europe, Great Britain or the United States. A community as an administrative unit need not necessarily be a community as a social unit in the sociological sense. It may be so, but it is not necessarily so. Thus every analysis of a community should begin by offering proof that a social reality of this kind is actually present. Now precisely this has been neglected, for example, in the community investigation conducted by Gerhard Wurzbacher.[11] The German Research Association for Agrarian Policy and Agrarian Sociology evaded the existing difficulties by speaking of 'villages', thus effectively stressing the local character of the subject under analysis,[12] but Wurzbacher lost himself completely and uncritically in the administrative aspect of the

c   27

community. At the same time he assumed without more ado that the political integration of the community in the sociological sense must be in accordance with the demarcation of the particular social structure laid down by the administration; a proceeding which is regarded as 'artificial' even by the administrative sciences. Incidentally, there are numerous indications to suggest that the various hamlets of the community in question represent anything but a social unit, and that they were forced only administratively into a unit of a purely external nature without there being on that account any interaction between the spatially completely separated parts of the community unit as a whole. In addition the various parts are culturally as different as possible in their outlook (almost completely Catholic hamlets on one hand, and Protestant majorities on the other), therefore it must be said that this particular community investigation lacked the three essential characteristics which head both our own definition and that of Hillery (not to speak of others). This casts the whole undertaking in a doubtful light before it has properly begun.[13] The urgency of defining terms before proceeding to any concrete investigation could not be more clearly illustrated. At the same time this should be a challenge to us to continue our efforts to arrive at a satisfactory definition and to separate as clearly as possible the single characteristics from each other.

THE COMMUNITY AS A SOCIAL SYSTEM

Thus as far as we are concerned, the community appears as a 'social system'; that is to say a relationship which is characterized, amongst other things, by the fact that the people concerned are conscious of the relationship, conscious of its limits, and conscious of its differences from other similar relationships. This structural relationship, which is decisive for the survival of any particular community and for its social and cultural identity, is thus independent of the numerous individual phenomena which give it its specific content; an independence which is expressed in the fact that none of the persons concerned ever has any doubt about the individuality of his own community. Apart from that are the many individual features whose interaction makes up the social system, as for example, the particular form of land settlement, the location, the size, the transport system, the distribution of land usage and housing situation within the community, the composition of the population, its increase or decrease, migration, age, sex, race, family size, national origin, language, religion, educational level, rural or urban character; and then the economic system with its branches and its occupations. Much more important, on the other hand, for the identification of the social system of the community are: the communication system, the group formations within the community, the social control and the inner tensions, the power and class stratification, and, finally, the cultural traditions. The social system of a community is thus the structural co-operation of specific social factors which, independent of the many demographic, economic and ecological individual features, independent also of the institutional administrative organization, guarantee the survival of the social reality of the community.

One final point must be mentioned here, and this is connected with the specific sociological estimation of the community as an administrative unit. In view of the facts as set out above, it becomes more or less unimportant whether the community is of 'organic growth' or has been 'artificially organized'. One aspect does not necessarily exclude the other. They are not, as can easily be demonstrated, opposites, but are in homogeneous with each other. As against this, an essential characteristic of all global societies is that they exist for an indefinite length of time (without necessarily persisting through incalculable periods of time). There are no ephemeral global societies; on the contrary, it can be said that such societies develop their own periods of existence. With this relative persistence the distinction between organic growth and 'artificial creation' falls away. A social structure which is artificially created today, for example, a new settlement in a development area, will sooner or later develop its own tradition and appear therefore as an organic growth. On the other hand, all global societies are in many respects necessarily subject to institutionalization whether they are organic growths or not. Implied in this, together with many other similar conclusions, is the fact that community and 'association' are not opposites, but rather 'related structural elements' of social relationships.[14] Thus, for example, the fact that community by-laws are, so to speak, 'borrowed' is completely unimportant for the community structure as a sociological phenomenon. Even artificially created structures such as rural municipalities can develop a traditional character provided they are given sufficient time in which to do so. A structure which may look organic today was perhaps artificially created yesterday; and what is artificially created today will tomorrow appear as though it were organic; for example numerous Kibbutzim in Israel. The point is therefore, at what point in the existence of a community do we examine it. At the same time another question arises, and one to which we shall return later, namely, how long does it take for a tradition to develop? How old is old? These questions are essentially connected with the cultural character of a community and the common ties which prevail in it.

CHAPTER IV

THE COMMUNITY IN THE DEVELOPMENT OF HUMAN SOCIETY

THE PRINCIPLE OF KINSHIP IN HUMAN CULTURE

The community is one of the most important basic social structures in the sense of a global society, but it is neither the only one nor the earliest. Before it, in order of development, were a number of other structures of a preponderantly kinship character (without being families in the sense of the so-called 'nuclear family'). A term often readily used and without any further elaboration is sib, but it is not a particularly good one, because first sibs as groups of blood relationship are quite rare, and secondly they often merge with other forms of kinship, such as the extended family, the clan, the joint family, and so on. Thus we prefer to speak of kinship relations, which allows of other variants. These were undoubtedly dominant with the hunter-food-gathering hordes of the earlier palaeolithic age. Their normal method of obtaining sustenance laid no stress whatever on the land factor, and that was typical. Today this economic form exists only amongst a few nomadic tribes in very backward corners of the earth. Incidentally we can see that they displayed no nomadism of the type which moves freely across the face of the earth, but a nomadism strictly confined to a particular area, as is the case with wild animals. These hunter-food-gathering hordes had very definitely circumscribed hunting grounds and permanent water-holes to which they constantly returned, as, for instance, is the case today with the aborigines in Central Australia. This may be the expression of a general biotic law which links mankind retrospectively with the higher mammals and the animal world in general.

Despite the exiguous character of this life there is no question of any isolation of these bands of nomads. Numerous discoveries from the early and later palaeolithic age indicate the existence of widespread exterior trading on a barter basis dealing primarily in materials for personal adornment (amber, fire-stone, shells and so on). For example, in Switzerland shells have been dug up from prehistoric sites which undoubtedly originated in the Red Sea. We can observe something similar with present-day primitive peoples, so that it is not possible to assume any longer, as at one time certain imaginative investigators did, that a wandering band carried these things from one end of the earth to the other. In fact the many bands, usually small, were certainly in contact with each other, even though the contact may not have been systematic and regular. It is, by the way, very often questionable whether the essential bond which united these groups was kinship. Certainly, such bands often consisted of anything between two and ten families, but on the other hand strangers were constantly being 'adopted' into the band, both as individuals and as groups.[1] However, one can say that before long the feeling of tie by kinship definitely out-weighed any other.

Another remnant of the old economic-history theories (cf. K. Bücher) which are now largely discarded, was the facile assumption that the original economic form was the so-called closed household economy, whereby one family lived in an isolated house in a sort of economic autarchy. This form would thus occupy a place somewhere between the formation of nomadic bands as on economic unit, and the local association of family groups, i.e. the community. In the meantime it has long been recognized that such notions were not based on historical realism, but that they were of a highly synthetic character and influenced by notions of natural law, except that the still older idea of the 'individual search for sustenance' was replaced by that of the equally isolated family group. This naturally does not exclude the existence of settlement groups with a varying degree of density, and sometimes even isolated establishments; but the latter are more the exception than the rule in this development. In addition, before the rise of local communities, an important role was played by a whole series of intermediate phenomena such as small ethnic groups or joint families, based upon a feeling of joint origin. It then often happened that these groups settled down together, but even in this case it was the joint origin which was decisive for their solidarity rather than the joint settlement.

This is perhaps the most important indication that these local communities were neither the only nor the first examples of the global society. And this enables Richard Thurnwald to assert that 'the proximity of settlements was not always a factor which resulted in association'.[2] We shall come up against this problem again when we discuss that type of settlement which Thurnwald calls 'chequered' (*Würfelung*), in which various groups settle down together without there being any social interaction between them. The forms of association based on kinship often persist for a long time even after societies have become established, and, quite independent of the joint settlement, the kinship relations compete with the local association factor. Finally, however:

> independent of the feeling of common origin, the joint settlement as such can act as an associative factor, because the kinship factor is not always decisive for the feeling of solidarity amongst the settlers, but the fact that they are settled together and experience a common fate, a circumstance which then takes on the character of a political association.[3]

This is then known as a 'local group' or a 'settlement community' and its authoritative power structure becomes immediately very conspicuous.

THE PRINCIPLE OF THE SETTLEMENT UNIT IN HUMAN CULTURE

The community has been of paramount importance in the development of human society right down to our own day, not only because it represents a stage of human development, but because a basic principle of human association in general comes into play and creates a global society, namely the 'neighbourhood', exactly as with associations formed on a preponderantly kinship basis. The effect of this neighbourhood factor need not always be in the direction of a harmonious union, it can just as well produce strong rivalries and friction, and even trigger off

33

struggles for power. But apart from the question of whether it produces co-operation or antagonism, the proximity of settlements, just like kinship, can spontaneously produce a wealth of social interaction which would otherwise be inconceivable and from which joint ties, values, myths and cults develop which are essentially local in character. But a word of warning is necessary here: the concept of neighbourhood can be understood in a concrete sense as a definite group or sub-group of people living together, and in the abstract sense as a principle of association. On the other hand, in underdeveloped societies, and also in specifically agrarian societies, we must usually reckon that such communities as local settlement associations will be relatively isolated from each other. But, just as is the case with the nomad bands, this by no means excludes the possibility of relations with other communities. Such relations may even develop into a division of labour as between the communities, and a regular exchange of women and of economic products. Thus, even amongst subsistence economies certain traffic takes place between the various communities. The underdeveloped and isolated areas of Brazil provide a good illustration of this today. A recent investigation conducted in Minas Velhas in the State of Bahia has provided fairly exact information about the volume of trade done with the community by itinerant hawkers. These hawkers set out on tours which last anything from a couple of weeks to several months, combing the immediate and the remote neighbourhood on foot or with mules. This can give us some idea of what conditions must have been like in earlier times.[4] The pre-Columbian Pueblos in the Mesa Verde area in present-day South Colorado provide another example where the basic materials for the production of ornaments were obtained from a great distance – as far as the coast of the Pacific Ocean. Generally speaking, in such cases there is apart from the community, hardly any other global systems of a higher order in existence. Clans, tribes, and also larger regional and territorial groups, something like the religiously-based Amphictyon type in the ancient world, federations of communities (the League of Iroquois for example), and also the 'intercommunion of villages' did not attain such a clear development of social life as the local communities, which also represented the most tangible form of authority. It must further

34

be pointed out that the neighbourhood factor can be effective even with dispersed settlements, as for example in the 'open-country neighbourhoods' of the United States and Canada.[5] However, these presuppose a certain degree of development and availability of communications, and at the same time their existence makes the concept of neighbourhood relative, as in such cases it is not necessarily restricted to a small area. Further, quite considerable changes have come about during the past fifty years; originally the neighbourhood limit was more or less a day's ride on horseback, but with the arrival of the motor-car the extent of this particular neighbourhood form has been greatly increased.

The period in which the local communities came more and more into evidence can be identified with quite astonishing accuracy even though we have to go back a long way into pre-history. After a long time the hunter-food-gathering cultures were replaced by the hunter-gardening cultures; and at the same time more and more intense cultivation of the soil had the effect of establishing a closer connection between the group and the land, though at first in view of the prevailing primitive methods of cultivation, this relationship must have been for a time quite precarious. But the situation changed decisively with the development of improved methods of agriculture – even before the use of draught animals – until in the end combined planter and cattle-breeding cultures appeared; a transformation which was one of the most important ones in the history of human cultural development. Since the end of the last Ice Age and the early palaeolithic age, the system of hunter-food-gathering cultures must have developed steadily, particularly with the appearance of nomadic pastoral cultures and the advance of agricultural techniques. The development of the village communities also belongs to the same period, in our latitudes, in the Middle East (Mesopotamia) and in Egypt. At the same time predatory nomad tribes of herdsmen and hunters constantly harassed the settled peasants and forced them to defend themselves in fortified villages. This, by the way, is quite sufficient in itself to indicate that the closed-house economy as an isolated family economic unit was quite illusory in such times. The evidence of Egypt shows quite clearly that the peasants were accustomed to protect themselves behind thick

walls.[6] The isolated house could not possibly have existed
before the general establishment of the public peace, and
because of this it must have been a comparatively recent
phenomenon. In this very early period we meet with a number
of different community structures, and it is characteristic that at
first it is impossible to distinguish village from town, because the

Egyptian sign
for a town.

fortified town simultaneously protected
peasants, herdsmen, hunters, artisans and
traders. As the population of these places
increased colonies or sister-towns were soon
built, just as was the case later on in Phoenician
times, and above all in the Greek cultural
sphere. In addition there were castles in
whose neighbourhood people settled for
safety. This practice was of great importance in Europe in the
Middle Ages.

THE ANCIENT POLIS

The development closest to our own took place in Ancient
Greece where the first highly-developed form of the community
arose in the so-called *polis*. Originally we must deal with village
settlements (*kōmē*) which withdrew into fortified places during
raids by predatory nomads. With the development of the
monarchy (*basileia*) these fortified places probably developed
into actual castles. This is reflected in an older name for the
town (*ptoliethron*) which means approximately High Town or
Castle Town. In this sense we find in the old Homeric epics the
distinction between *polis* and *asty* which means Lower Town or
Lower Castle, i.e. a town or castle in the plains. In the later
Homeric epics, and in particular in the *Odyssey* this distinction
has disappeared, and the term *polis* is more and more generally
in use, both for rural market places and for the town as such,
or, better, for the Greek City State. It should be noted, however,
that together with this extraordinary and unique development
of the local community, which Aristotle regarded even in his
day as the highest form of 'political' existence, other social basic
forms built up on kinship existed for centuries, as for instance the
patriarchal clan (*patria* or *genos*), the association of clans,
usually called *phratria*, and, finally, the tribes (*phylai*).[7]

36

The community in the development of human society

Indeed, one can say that with the Greek *polis* the local community experienced its all-time peak in the old world, because it was precisely here that the global character of the community was first recognized. At the same time it was developed in contrast not only to the older social basic forms built up on kinship but also to the great empires and States in the Orient, and later in Rome, in which the community as a global society was replaced by global societies of a higher order, though naturally without disappearing in its social reality. Only in Greece were the social community system and the authoritative system of the State identical; and, incidentally, the idea of autonomy or autarchy was attached to the community. But this referred exclusively to the political sovereignty of the *polis*, and had nothing to do with any self-sufficient economy as we understand the idea today. The Greek *polis* not only waged frequent warfare with each other; they also carried on regular trade with each other too. Thus the *polis* was by no means self-sufficient; on the contrary, one could say that the Greeks became a typical trading people very early – approximately in the eighth century before Christ. For example the first minted coins in the Western world were put into circulation in Aegina in the year 650 B.C., and this must naturally have facilitated trading relations.

G. Glotz, the French historian of Greek social history, gives us the following description:

Everywhere, with only a few kilometres in between a mound serves as a frontier post. A small area with its back to a mountain and irrigated by a winding stream, serves as a State. You need only mount to the Acropolis, which is its fortress, and you can survey the whole of this State. This town, these fields, these pastures, these groves and ravines, make up the Fatherland. Founded by the ancestors, every subsequent generation must leave it more beautiful and richer.[8]

What was the Fatherland in the centuries of Greek greatness? The word itself tells us everything. It stands for everything which binds men to each other when they have a common ancestor, the same father . . . Today Greek patriotism strikes us as very provincial. But a feeling of patriotism is all the more intense when the object on which it is concentrated is small. From the day the Ephēbe becomes of age and swears

37

the citizen's oath the *polis* can demand his entire devotion, even his life itself. He surrenders himself with heart and soul, not to an abstraction, but to something concrete, something he has before his eyes every day of the week. The holy soil of the Fatherland is represented for him by the fenced-in property of his own family, by the graves of his ancestors, by the fields whose owners he knows personally. Every one of them, by the mountain in whose woods he fells timber, by the place where he drives the animals out to graze and where he collects wild honey, by the festivals in which he takes part, and by the Acropolis which he ascends in procession. In short, the polis is everything he loves and of which he is proud. And every generation is anxious to leave it more beautiful than it found it.[9]

Before long the Greek *polis* began to found colonies and sister-towns, i.e. new communities, which were more or less systematically laid out from the start.

THE ESTABLISHMENT OF NEW COMMUNITIES

We must stress that communities as global societies have a longer life than any other associations formed for one or few purposes. But in principle new communities could arise again and again, as the Ancient Greek world demonstrated. And apart from the actual foundation of colonies, there were a number of other ways in which such new communities could be founded. In technically undeveloped (i.e. 'primitive') societies, existing communities were often abandoned after a while and re-established elsewhere after a more or less extended migration; because perhaps the original soil was not good enough and the kind of culture insufficiently rational and productive. Occasionally all the inhabitants would leave the original community in a body; as, for instance, at the end of the thirteenth century in pre-Columbian America where the Indians of the great Pueblo culture in the Mesa Verde district moved south-west to escape the great drought. Colonies can also be formed by the actual surplus population emigrating to found new communities. Incidentally this migration and founding of new communities took place in exactly the same way in Germany in the Middle Ages. And, as we know today, it happened in the thirteenth and fourteenth centuries, i.e. long before the Thirty Years War, which is generally exclusively blamed for the disappearance of many communities.[10] In fact, the reasons were many and varied: exhaustion of the soil, the sinking of the water surface as a result of excessive deforestation, emigration, migration to the towns, and also, but less frequently, epidemics and the effects of war. But the fact remains that excessive exploitation of the soil leading to its exhaustion happened more often than is commonly supposed. And then communities were broken up and were spread out, old villages into isolated farms (particularly in Scandinavia). However, these and similar events did not necessarily mean a reduction in population. Both in Northern and Southern Europe the population seems to have copied urban forms of life, very early on and have come together in so called Great Villages, or townlike villages. In fact, towards the late Middle Ages such structures developed quite systematically under the influence of the ruling aristocracy. Occasionally this origin of new communities can be recognized by the geometrical frontiers of the communities in question. All this can be regarded as a confirmation of what was said previously, namely that there is no essential difference between 'organically developed' and 'artificially planned' communities.

THE COMMUNITY AND THE STATE

Today, the position of the community system differs in one important respect from the conditions which existed in the primitive world and in the ancient higher cultures; namely, we must always reckon with the existence, together with the community as a global society, of a series of other and very much more important global societies of which the communities form part, just as formerly individual groups (families, for example) formed part of the communities. One of the most important of these larger global societies is the nation State, and later continental federations and empires. Further, that political autonomy which was so characteristic of the Greek *polis*, has been transferred in the European continent almost entirely to the more extensive global societies (provinces, federated and national States). The only important exception in Europe was

Switzerland, though in the Netherlands and Scandinavia the communities also maintained their independence longer and played a bigger role in public life than elsewhere on the continent, where the importance of the communities, or communes, was very soon reduced by the centralized monarchy and by the local princes. In England 'local government' is still important but the central government exercises only indirect control through the provision of funds, granting of loans, and so on. In England, unlike the big Continental States, there are no 'intermediate and subordinate representatives of the State carrying out the instructions of the central authorities'.[11] In other words, State administration operates through local administration; and in consequence the communities, or municipalities, in England lead a very definite life of their own, the equivalent of which can be found only in Switzerland. But in view of the limited development of the social sciences in Switzerland, the community, or commune, never really became the subject of investigations – at the utmost it was the starting-point for ideological postulates. That special technique of sociology which has become known as the 'community survey' first arose in England, and spread from there to other countries, and in particular to the United States.

The change of emphasis indicated above, which resulted from the rise of higher forms of global societies alongside local communities has had important consequences on the European continent in that, as Max Weber pointed out, the concept community 'has obtained its full significance through its relationship to a political common action extending over a multiplicity of neighbourhoods'.[12] With this, of course, the 'institutional character' of the community as a publicly and legally established corporation comes more strongly to the fore, and introduces the separation of the political study of communities from the sociological concept of community. For example, from the administrative angle things are treated as similar which sociologically are very different indeed; for example, the local community on the one hand, and the 'community associations' on a higher level on the other, associations which are almost exclusively the creations of the modern State. One thing in particular which disappears in these associations is the idea of a limited local unity, which is replaced by something more extensive territorially, whereby the phenomenon of spatial proximity of neigh-

The community in the development of human society

bourhood is largely excluded, although in the strictly sociological sense this phenomenon is inseparable from the idea of community. As these community associations of a higher order are not intended to embrace sub-communities of a more or less related type, they can also not be regarded as on a par with the important geographical concept of 'social area'.

THE INNER DIFFERENTIATION OF THE COMMUNITY

On the other hand, this development has also given a whole series of community activities (community economy, community finances, community administration, community social policy, etc.) a greater significance, a point which should not be underestimated; and this quite irrespective of whether there is a large degree of self-administration, or merely an administration delegated by the State. In both cases the differentiation of modern social life leads to the extension of various institutional functional spheres in the community which are quite clearly separated from each other. With this the character of the community as a global society is heavily underlined, provided that we remain very clear in our minds that the corporate character of the community is, sociologically speaking, not everything, and not even its most important feature. Therefore neither the administrative sciences nor communal practice can do without the help of sociology. The real life of the community derives from a plethora of social relations, ideas, beliefs, organizations, deputations, associations of various kinds, and, above all, from class and prestige structures, and so on. This is reflected in the fact that the evaluation element which derives from the super-corporate, real social life of the community commands greater importance than usual in the administrative regulations of the community, whereby greater importance is attached to local 'customs'. This naturally means that organizations (political parties) and associations in the strict sense of the words are sociologically not necessarily more important within the community than free and spontaneous unions such as clubs and voluntary associations, welfare groups, initiation committees or circles, membership of which can be of such importance for a new member of the community that it can decide whether he is accepted into the community or not; or than informal groups,

41

cliques and so on which may well exercise an intangible but
under certain circumstances permanent and effective influence
on the affairs of the community; or than prominent personalities
enjoying prestige; or those casual friendship groups, groups
formed on the basis of joint interests; or than in small communities, regular meetings of citizens at the pub, and so on. The
sociological investigation of a community pays particular attention to such matters, because they can be of great importance
not only for the social 'prestige' of the community, but also for
the formation of public opinion (and therefore of values) in the
community.

CHAPTER V

THE COMMUNITY AS A GLOBAL SOCIETY ON A LOCAL BASIS

The Principle of Neighbourhood

ON THE TOO NARROW OR TOO WIDE USE OF THE TERM COMMUNITY

When we, as suggested above, term the community a global society on a local basis, then at the same time it must be distinguished both from larger relationships of, say, a regional (area, province) or national character on a territorial basis (commonwealth), and also from smaller phenomena, which do not have the character of global societies. Mistakes are made in both senses and in consequence a good deal of confusion has been created in sociological literature.

We have already stressed the extreme elasticity of the English term community. It can include anything from a relationship of two persons to the total relationship of humanity (the community of mankind). Whilst it is comparatively easy to avoid such senses of the term as are all too wide it is not so easy to deal with the senses which are too restricted because there are many factors in real community life which seem to encourage them. There are at least three possible sources of confusion here. The expression community in English is often used to refer to parts of an actual community, including parts of a village, districts of a town and housing estates; and also mere neighbourhoods. Even where these parts of communities are of a somewhat complex character, they can never be termed global societies, as total social phenomena. Even where urban districts have developed from originally independent communities, their merging clearly indicates that they are no longer independent structures but have become one with a larger unit. Thus this use of the term community contradicts the definition of the word community. In German the expression 'part community' (*Teilgemeinde*), or something similar, should be used for instance in urban sociology.

Occasionally, again in English, the term community is used for small, and relatively ephemeral groups, which can exist on their own or on the margin of larger settlement units. These include temporary housing colonies ranging from the allotment colony in Germany to the African Bidonville, Trailer Camps at a large building site (frequently found in the United States in connection with large-scale building operations such as the Tennessee Valley Authority, or atomic stations); also groups on the outskirts of large- and medium-sized towns; and, finally, quite temporary groups such as the passengers on board a big ocean-going liner, or the members of a temporary camp such as the ones for Japano–Americans during the war which were analysed by Alexander Leighton. But in all these cases the expression community should be used only in a figurative sense, as for example, 'they were a single big family' does not actually mean that they were a family in the ordinary sense. One of the essential factors mentioned above is missing here, namely the requirement that all global societies shall have a certain permanence in time during which they can develop their own time periods. It must be borne in mind that the limits of our examples are to some extent fluid in that the longer a provisional group exists the greater chance it has of developing into a real community in the strict sense of the term.

In German usage especially the term community is applied in another way to concepts which are too narrow. This is almost always the case with such expressions as 'church community', 'school community', 'wood and forest corporation,' and so on. But here, in fact, the reference is either to individual functional spheres of the complex community, for example, school and church, or associations or corporate bodies with a distinct object, such as the utilization of timber. But both are completely different from the concept community in its strict sense, because each community as a global society consists of an indefinite variety of social functional spheres and associations for the pursuit of a definite object. For example, in Swiss–German usage the expression *Schulgemeinde* is not used at all, but the much more appropriate *Schulpflege*, or school administration. In German usage it would, strictly speaking, refer to a 'deputation'. Where the expression *Kirchgemeinde* or church community is concerned, the situation is more difficult, as we have seen previously, because the religious double meaning of the word community is already well established. Incidentally, the word *Gemeinschaft* or communion, would, in accordance with the particular body involved, probably be more suitable than community.

COMMUNITY AND AREA RESEARCH

Whereas the decision is relatively easy where there is a too narrow use of the term community, the situation is considerably more difficult in cases where the use is too wide. This point was raised and dealt with quite recently by the American anthropologist Julian H. Steward, and we shall consider his views after one or two fundamental preliminary observations.

First of all we must dispose of the misunderstanding that the factor of size in a community is of importance for our purposes. There are certainly large and small communities with their appropriate structural differences, but they are all embraced by our central definition, namely that they must be global societies. In certain conditions a community with only 250 inhabitants may well come within this definition, whereas an urban district with thousands, even tens of thousands, of inhabitants, may not. On the other hand, we must bear in mind that even a very large community is limited to a locality, whereby it is clearly distinguishable from all other territorial social formations. Even if it happened to have all functional spheres in common with them, the factor of relative spatial proximity and of territorial unity would still be absent – and that quite apart from the circumstance that there are territorial global societies which are superior to the communities. Community is thus always local community in the strictest sense, using the term here both in its administrative and also in its 'extended' sociological significance, neither of which excludes the fact that a 'community area' (*Gemeindegebiet*) always belongs to a community. But this is quite different from an actual territory, on which there are in principle always a number of communities, even where the polis are

45

concerned, which, at the zenith of ancient community development, began to exceed its boundaries, as was subsequently the
case with the Italian and Swiss city States, and the Free and
Hansa towns in Germany. This spatial limitation of the community is also the preliminary condition for the operation of the
neighbourhood as a principle of association; which extends
over a rather larger area only in such unusual cases as 'the open
country neighbourhood'.

In most cases it is possible to see at a glance whether a given
settlement can be regarded as a community in the sociological
sense. In the case of the small community we mean quite
literally that the circle of those who belong directly together is
determined by the narrow spatial limits of the settlement. One
can literally 'see' the reality of a community, and in all probability this was the case with the Greek *polis* too. It certainly was
so with regard to numerous communities in the late Middle
Ages in Sicily and Italy, communities which had withdrawn to
mountain plateaux. Similar phenomena exist all over the world.
Recently the French sociologist P. Chombart de Lauwe used
aerial photography in order to demonstrate the community unit
visibly and in a most impressive fashion.[1] This method can of
course also be used for larger structures such as big towns and
great cities.[2] In other cases it may well be more difficult to
demonstrate the existence of the actual extent of a community,
hence more detailed proofs will be necessary; such, for example,
as were successfully provided in the Darmstadt investigation,
which regarded both the town itself and its 'hinterland' as a
unit.[3]

Most important conclusions on the regional extent of community investigations have been advanced by J. H. Steward.
His analysis aroused much discussion. Apart from ethnology and
cultural anthropology as such, he regards community sociology
as still defective,[4] in that it neglects to investigate communities
in a wider framework, i.e. area research. In fact we may take it
as an established principle that for a non-ethnologist there can
be no such thing as a community existing for itself alone. The
same is true of the ethnologist as of the pre-historian, particularly
when we regard the phenomenon of widespread trading. For
the advanced industrial societies of our day, the community can
only be a part of a wider relationship. It will then be important

to know how the community fits itself into this wider relationship. The matter will not always be as simple as it is with the relationship of the community to its hinterland. On the other hand it may be necessary, under certain circumstances, to determine the exact limits of the influence exercised by global societies of a higher order on these communities. With this, in principle two possibilities are opened up: in the first place we can regard the structure of a community as representative of the structure of many communities within the larger global society (region, province, nation); or we can regard it as representative of the cultural values of the larger group. In the first case we must deal with certain structural peculiarities and problems which will also crop up in other contexts. This was the procedure adopted by Gadourek in his analysis of the Dutch community Sassenheim, which was taken as representative of many other communities.[5] He demonstrates that this community was unable to achieve any inner unity because of its division into three main religious groups (Catholics, Dutch Reformed Church and Calvinists), and he expresses the belief that this community is a sort of prototype for the community life of Holland in general. It is quite obvious that with this procedure the specific characteristics of Sassenheim itself must to some extent be treated too summarily, though not altogether neglected. In the second case we must deal with definite traits and cultural values in their practical effect on a clearly visible circle of people, who are perhaps typical of a whole region, a sort of sub-culture, like the Liègeois in the 'Château-Gérard' investigation conducted by Turney-High, which also clearly develops the perspective of time and history.[6] In this case it is clear that with the degeneration of the specific (Walloon) language into a mere dialect of the lower classes and of the 'uneducated' in general, the microculture of Château Gérard gradually merges into the larger whole of the Condroz or the Liègeois, and thus becomes subject to all the remote influences which affect these regions. This cultural interest can of course extend farther than a mere sub-culture, and embrace a culture as a whole on the basis of a single community, as so many anthropological community investigations, or community investigations in highly-developed industrial societies carried out by anthropologists, have done, as for example the excellent

The community as a global society on a local basis

Irish community investigation carried out by Conrad M. Arensberg.[7]

THE COMMUNITY AS A MICROCULTURE

Whereas the first form of approach dealt with here has a tendency to confine itself to actual 'problem studies' and to the analysis of special forms of social relationships, the second form leads to an analysis of specific cultures and sub-cultures. Having in a former work[8] stressed the problem character of community investigation, Arensberg switched the accent in a later work to the specific cultural aspect of community investigation, and proceeded to give an excellent abridged description of community types in the sub-cultures of the United States.[9] With this approach the community presented itself as a 'cultural microcosm'. What he demonstrated here within the United States he had already stressed in another connection in relation to the comparative study of various community types in other national societies.[10]

It is certainly correct to regard the community as a microcosm typical of a larger matrix, and at the same time to set community investigation in the larger framework of area investigations, as Steward does. In highly-developed societies there is no such thing as an autonomous community which is in any way self-sufficient and autarchical. Even in the so-called underdeveloped areas the communities are, despite their subsistence economy, connected with larger spheres by innumerable contacts. Only in a very few primitive groups is there any likelihood of relatively isolated and semi-autarchical communities, but even this is problematical. Even if we have to reckon with this possibility we must nevertheless assume in exactly the same way that one of the essential factors of the concept community is that it has clearly defined limits in space within which the neighbourhood relation develops; and that the inhabitants of a community quite clearly feel themselves to be different from the inhabitants of other communities. Although it is true that the community is typical of a more comprehensive culture (i.e. microcosm in the appropriate macrocosm) it is at the same time a specific microculture with its own individuality and its own traditions. Even when many of the functions of a community

48

are taken away and transferred to larger and more extensive bureaucratic State organizations, it still remains a fact that the sphere of community affairs has extended tremendously. This can be seen very clearly in the administrative organization of large towns, which, under certain circumstances, can be even more complicated than that of whole States.

Finally there is another decisive trait which is of great importance to sociologists: even though it is true that there are global societies of a higher order above the community, the fact remains that for the ordinary individual the first acquaintance with social life outside the family is made in his immediate neighbourhood and thus becomes a living reality for him in the community. The importance of this direct experience must not be underestimated, for no analagous experience can be expected from an abstract large-scale bureaucratic organization. With this we have found for the time being a fairly clear answer to the regional and cultural classification of the community. The regional classification will depend above all on the given relationship with the immediate and more distant surroundings, without at the same time ignoring the specific spatial limits of the community. The cultural classification will primarily follow the influence of the cultural behaviour pattern, either of a regional or more extended nature, on the development of the socio-cultural person in the individual, without overlooking the fact that the community is not only a cultural microcosm, but that in itself it definitely represents a microculture or subculture in a related cultural matrix.

THE PRINCIPLE AND PRACTICE OF NEIGHBOURHOOD

The most important reason which leads us to stress community investigation as against the more extended area investigation lies in the fact that the community is above all a local phenomenon dominated by the associative principle of neighbourhood, just as other structures are dominated by the principle of kinship. But the principle of neighbourhood must, as we have already indicated, be distinguished from the concrete and practical neighbourhood; a distinction which is rarely made – to the great disadvantage of terminological clarity. When considering the factor of concrete and practical neighbourhood, investigators usually have the rural community in mind; and there is a general suggestion that this is the only essential form of neighbourhood, and that it is doomed to disappear more and more under urban conditions. In fact, this is a completely unfounded assumption culled from the great reservoir of romantic ideas which invariably crop up when the concept community is discussed. Where the village is concerned the principle of neighbourhood appears at first as the basis of community living. This can, as always in social life, lead to both positive and negative social acts. It is extremely characteristic that in the village the principle of neighbourhood appears only under exceptional circumstances and usually under stress (urgent or heavy labour, natural disasters, accidents, and so on, which demand co-operation), whereas in ordinary circumstances a very definite reserve and distance are more usual (particularly in the rural areas, for there is nothing the peasant hates more in the ordinary way than any outside interference in his own affairs). On the other hand, as Max Weber has already pointed out, it is clear that this principle which operates in any situation of 'joint interest brought about by spatial proximity and temporary or permanent common bonds thereby established' is by no means a specific characteristic of rural communities, but exists in just the same way in small or large towns, although the ways in which the neighbourhood principle expresses itself there may be different. Above all, joint action on the basis of neighbourhood in a rural community is a positive exception to the general rule, even though it does recur from time to time in the same typical forms. And that is precisely true of the town too.

THE VARIETY OF NEIGHBOURHOODS

But this is not the cause of the greatest obstacle to understanding; there is a second circumstance whose fundamental importance is usually even less recognizable than the first. Previously the principle of neighbourhood has been quite generally distinguished from the concrete practical neighbourhood, whose prototype the rural community was then considered to be. In confusing the principle of neighbourhood with concrete neighbourhoods there arises a completely false idea, which more or less underlies many discussions, namely that the village or the small local community forms a neighbourhood association in the sense of a single neighbourhood. In addition the idea usually follows that relationships can be readily surveyed and that there is mutual familiarity. This misunderstanding also derives from a completely romantic idea of the substantive character of the community, and one which ignores all real differences and divisions. But precisely when we regard the community as a global society which embraces not only various functional spheres, but also various sub-groups, prestige groups and social classes, we must assume that parallel to the differentiation in economic interests (peasants, tenants, landworkers, day labourers, officials, employees, artisans, tradesmen, etc.) there is also a neighbourhood differentiation in the sense that even in a relatively small village there are various neighbourhoods constituting forms of close proximity living, in which the members of these various neighbourhood groups are attached to each other by personal and friendly ties. In contrast to the principle of neighbourhood we refer to this concrete and practical neighbourhood as an 'integrated neighbourhood'. Even the village community, as the most important form of the reality of the neighbourhood principle, is invariably made up of a number of concrete or integrated neighbourhoods, held together by kinship or friendship, cliques, a similar class situation, common cultural traits, and so on. These concrete and practical neighbourhoods in small communities are often extremely difficult to distinguish from each other, because they do not lie clearly side by side, thus making it easy to distinguish their limits and mutual borderlines; but they overlap and penetrate each other in the most confusing fashion. The characteristic of being readily observable applies primarily – and perhaps exclusively – to small concrete neighbourhoods, whereas, even with a relatively small village, it does not necessarily mean that it applies to the village community as a whole.

We shall come across this problem again when we deal with the question of 'community integration'. But generally we can already state that the smallness of a community is by no means a guarantee that the fact of living together in close proximity will result in direct neighbourhood integration. In this connection a distinction is made between the purely physical proximity or remoteness, and 'functional distance'.[11] It can very well occur that people who live quite close to each other in an area nevertheless (because of the state of the communications, or some other reason) rarely see or meet each other, and have little if any contact or interaction. In addition, perhaps one can say that when interaction leads to closer familiarity, then those who live nearest to each other have a better chance of establishing mutual friendly relationships. However, proximity is a sort of line beyond which quite different factors begin to operate. On the whole therefore, purely physical proximity seems, in the absence of other factors, to create only quite loose relationships. We can also see that very often cultural affinities or idiosyncrasies can cancel out physical proximity, or succeed in time in replacing neighbourhood relationships which existed previously.

NEIGHBOURHOOD AS A SYSTEM OF INTERACTION

Charles P. Loomis and J. Allan Beegle have dealt with this question in a highly interesting fashion, and came to the following conclusion:

> One should realize that early agrarian sociology was extremely unrealistic in regarding the neighbourhood as synonymous with cliques and groups practising mutual aid. If one regarded only people who live close to each other as belonging to a neighbourhood, and if each neighbour behaved in a neighbourly fashion to others, thus creating a single social system, then cliques and neighbourhood would in fact be identical. But everyone who has lived in rural districts knows quite well that geographical neighbourhoods only rarely create uniform social systems in this sense. In reality most rural neighbourhoods and communities with vigorous interactions between the various families and individuals are built up on several interaction systems. In most villages and neighbourhoods there are frequently bitter feuds and divisions between several social systems. . . . Although these systems exist together in the same small space they nevertheless take different places in the class order and have very little relationship with each other. It is ridiculous to take social systems of

various classes – systems which are inwardly homogeneous but outwardly antagonistic – and force them into a unity known as neighbourhood, and to regard this unity in the same way as a clique, a friendly association, or a mutual-aid group.[12]

The authors are able to illustrate their very penetrating observations in a most convincing fashion.[13] They are dealing with a new settlement in the State of Arkansas. It was observed that immediately after the settlement began the neighbours helped each other in their work and lent each other tools, and visited each other in their homes. These neighbours had quite by accident received plots of land close to each other. The fact that these groups really formed cliques was illustrated by their making decisions in common with regard to remaining members of the settlement or leaving it. Those leaving lived in fact close by each other and revealed a tendency to visit each other frequently. Two years later the same settlement was again investigated, and a completely new inner stratification was revealed; the families which remained now maintained relationships which suited them better, though often they were at a considerable distance from each other. It was possible to recognize these conditions only after sociometry had provided the investigators with the means of laying bare the finer ramifications of mutual relationships in a given social structure of some complexity. With this we can see the inadequacy of all those attempts to give neighbourhood a linear outline. In reality the neighbourhood groups overlap in a most complicated fashion which cannot be easily defined spatially. It is generally true that proximity alone is an important direct factor in the development of social interactions only with newly-formed and perhaps even temporary groupings, provided that we do not regard proximity and remoteness as purely physical, but, as we have already mentioned, in the sense of 'functional distance'. Later on quite different factors begin to operate so that we shall gradually have to get used to the idea of replacing the old and rather naïve idea of neighbourhood by a more precise conception. In this respect it can to some extent be regarded as fortunate that in his investigation of four French co-operative settlements (one in Bordeaux, two in Valence and one in Paris) Albert Meister came to the same conclusions as Loomis in the United States. This allows us to suppose that we are not dealing here with any local peculiarity, but really with a universally valid law. In the case of these four French settlements it was seen that the original neighbourly relationships were subsequently replaced by other relationships based on class considerations.[14]

THE LIMITS OF NEIGHBOURHOOD

The significance of this conclusion is illustrated, amongst other things, by the fact that recently some sociologists have become generally somewhat cautious in their treatment of neighbourhood as a principle of association.[15] Others again are anxious to confine the problem to the town, whether large or small, because they proceed from the assumption that in very small settlements neighbourhood and community are identical, and that accordingly no sub-neighbourhoods could develop, whereas in a town this is often the case. In general one could say that the size of neighbourhoods varies in inverse proportion to the size of the community, so that, for example, in big towns a neighbourhood could consist of perhaps just one block of houses.[16] Apart from the fact that even very small villages can certainly embrace several neighbourhoods – provided that we consider not only the question of proximity, but also the interactions and group structures – the essential feature of modern research seems to us to lie in the fact that today the existence of urban neighbourhoods is being more and more recognized, and these are strongly influenced by the class relationships of urban society – just as in the village.

With the progressive development of the urban character of a settlement, the old communities which merge into the town disappear and become 'quarters' which can no longer be regarded as real neighbourhood groups; but after we have said that even small village communities are generally subdivided into a number of neighbourhoods, it becomes highly problematical whether one may regard a quarter which has grown out of such a community as a normal neighbourhood relationship. On the other hand, it is certainly justifiable to regard it as a specific cultural system which can be very different from the cultural atmosphere of the town as a whole or of other quarters in it. In addition, each quarter, just like the town itself, dissolves into a multiplicity of concrete neighbourhoods, which can take on the most varied forms morphologically. For example, there are neighbourhoods on the same floor of a tenement, or in the tenement as a whole, in one or two houses connected with each other (on the same side of the street, or perhaps including a certain number of houses on the other side of the street), in a street, or in a block, where courtyards which are not too large encourage neighbourliness. The neighbourhood relationships probably go no farther than this, though there is no doubt that the intensity of integration in a neighbourhood can vary considerably.

Here too we must be wary of the sentimental illusion that there is such a thing as a fully homogeneous neighbourhood. Such a phenomenon is, in fact, a very rare exception. Incidentally in the spatial area of every neighbourhood we find elements, often considerable numerically, which take no part in it and are, so to speak, foreign bodies. Often such elements are not even noticed, but in cases of extreme difference they can be removed. Thus it must be stressed that neighbourhood can create not only social attachments, but very often serious social tension too, in that it appears 'as an ecological reflection of institutionalized group likes and dislikes'.[17] There are a number of factors which can strengthen or weaken the intensity of these neighbourhood relationships, for example the fact that a man is born a citizen of the locality or an immigrant, that he is of the same or of different origin (in mixed ethnic groups). Natives, evacuees and refugees also occupy different positions in this respect, as numerous experiences in Germany have proved. Other factors are the same or different religion, the same or different social or economic position, the same or different educational or cultural level, and so on. Neighbourhood relationships are most intense when a number of the above-mentioned factors all combine to operate in the same direction; and conversely they are at their weakest the less this is so. Neighbourhood, however, is only the most general, even though a most important and most decisive condition for the community as a global society on a local basis. Over and above this, the other elements which go to make up a community, without which the factor of neighbourhood cannot become effective, must also be investigated.

55

The community as a global society on a local basis

It is difficult if not impossible to say anything much about the functional spheres of the community in a few words because they are multifarious in the extreme, and because they differ from community to community. But if we regard the community as a global society we can hardly be surprised at this. Even a small community will then embrace a multiplicity of social associations and, within them, social relations, so many in fact that it is impossible to exhaust them all. One can say that the essence of these functional spheres represents an essential part of the whole life of the community (if not the whole) and thus determines its specific character. However, despite this complexity it is quite within the bounds of possibility to make a differentiation which accurately circumscribes the sphere of community sociology. It is quite clear of course that sociology must under no circumstances interfere with the sphere of the administrative sciences. Therefore everything which is connected with institutionalized functions must be removed from the sphere of community sociology, including the administration, educational matters, cultural matters, social policy, public welfare, assistance for young people, health services, planning and building operations, transport and communications, and similar functions attended to by numerous municipal departments (street lighting, sewers, refuse collection, street cleaning, the maintenance of cemeteries and crematoria, etc.). All aspects of community and municipal economy which are purely business affairs must similarly be separated from the sphere of community sociology. On the other hand, the core of community sociology consists of personal relations and connections; in other words, precisely what Loomis calls social systems. It is quite clear of course that these can change specifically according to the functional sphere in which they take place. However, there is nevertheless a very clear distinction between the tasks of the sociologist and that of the community scientist. It should be quite clear that associations formed for a specific purpose have their own particular structure which will change according to whether it is a question of administration in the strict sense or of a specifically economic matter. However, it is not our task here to inquire into the innumerable purposes which involve systematic and continuous activity within the framework of the community. On the other hand, the specific social systems which are set into motion either directly or indirectly in connection with these activities is a matter of great importance to us.

Within this framework we can then make another fundamental distinction, and one which we have already come across, namely the distinction between the more formal and the more informal functional spheres; although we must realize that this particular distinction will cut through the central functional spheres pursuing particular objectives (for example, economic activities, finance, administration, church, education, health services, and so on) which have both a more formal and a more informal aspect. It is quite clear that the former can also be subjected to a sociological examination; for example, there exists today an actual administrative sociology, or a sociology of organized behaviour, an economic sociology, a social psychology of taxation and financial affairs, a sociology of educational institutions. However, all these important branches of investigation have nothing to do with the sociology of the community, which is more interested in throwing light on the social relationships and the supporting structures through which all these and other activities integrate themselves in the community.

In the cases mentioned this task may be difficult because at first it is their objective functionalism which strikes us. In other cases, for example, social bodies, choirs, sports clubs, leisure-time groups, charitable bodies, and, quite generally, voluntary associations, initiation committees and so on, the informal aspect is uppermost, though the specific purpose and functions must not be underestimated. On the other hand institutions for the maintenance of public order, from the police force to the courts, are by definition extremely formal, not only in their purpose but also in their procedure. However, even here there are differences; for example, the police take a different attitude towards youthful excesses according to the character of the neighbourhood in which they take place; and the most upright judge will be inclined to caution when, say, the son of a colleague appears before him. The same thing applies to the transport and communications system, and it is quite astonishing to discover, even in this age of the motor-car and the railway, what a great volume of traffic moves neither on the railways nor the roads, but so to speak on by-ways. Neverthe-less, the volume of traffic which uses the organized transport network, including in particular the daily journeys to and from work, and various other forms of traffic commuting, remains of special importance. However, in all these cases the separation of the phenomena into formal and informal aspects will train our eye to recognize those events which do not take place exclusively along the normal and expected channels, a circumstance which is of especial importance for an understanding of the structure of the community.

In essence further analysis of the functional spheres of the community means a quite simple inventory of all the pheno-mena which could be of interest to the sociologist and thus con-tribute to determining the character of a community. As it is not possible to decide in advance just what is of importance for a community it is not possible to make any definite predictions. In conclusion therefore we have only to point out that all morphological phenomena relating to the population structure with its various characteristics, including criminality, from emigration movements to chronic or temporary unemployment and the measures taken to deal with it, from welfare work for displaced persons to housing and settlement policy, can all be of importance in a given case. The structural constellation will determine what takes the centre of the stage from time to time. We must stress this latter point particularly as a warning against the drawing-up of aimless and thoughtless inventories which try to set down just everything without first considering whether the problems in question have any real relation to the community in question or not.

However, before we deal with all these questions in connec-tion with the structure of the community we must examine in detail the special spatial problems which arise in connection with the community and relate to the general question of neighbourhood. This question of neighbourhood, which is usually credited with excessive importance, is really only a small part-aspect of the spatial problem of the community usually dealt with by the ecologists.

CHAPTER VI

THE SOCIAL ECOLOGY
OF THE COMMUNITY

SOCIOLOGY, SOCIAL ECOLOGY AND SOCIAL GEOGRAPHY

The problems of the spatial distribution of the population in residential areas were dealt with very early on by sociology.[1] However, with the growing interest in community investigation today a more specific line of investigation has branched off from the general sphere of social morphology, namely social ecology. It investigates both large and small communities, though as yet its greatest successes have been obtained in specifically urban sociology, whose most important task before any investigation is to analyse the spatial distribution of the various categories of population and other phenomena relating to the urban community or municipality.

As has often been pointed out, social ecology is closely related to geography on the one hand and sociology on the other, and it may be important to say something about the differences and similarities of these three sciences before we proceed any further in our discussion. Quite recently Maximilien Sorre pointed out that as a result of certain geographical developments the differences between geography and social ecology were becoming fewer, because geography itself had developed into anthropological and social geography.[2] This is certainly to some extent true, but whilst recognizing the essential assistance afforded by geography, we must nevertheless not neglect the differences which do still exist. For example, geography seeks to analyse those phenomena which develop simultaneously in historical fact and in the spatial order. Sociology is of course also interested in such matters, and geography provides it with, so to speak, the morphological substratum. But then sociology, or community sociology, proceeds to deal directly with the inner order of such a group, as formed, for example, by marriage, caste or class structure, power structure, or more horizontally layered voluntary associations and informal bodies, and functional spheres such as economics, authorities, schools and churches. Social ecology on the other hand deals with these phenomena exclusively in relation to their spatial order or distribution and not with the intention of analysing their structure and functions. In this respect the concept of space is primarily social space, whose most important form is the neighbourhood, whereas geography regards space from a very different standpoint. Also on the other hand, social ecology is not in a position to deal completely with the phenomenon, because behind its spatial character there are numerous social structures and social psychological processes which express themselves spatially whilst at the same time contributing towards their interpretation.

SOCIAL STRUCTURE AND SPATIAL ORDER

Even in the primitive world it is obvious that varying social structures produced varying spatial distributions of the population. For example, Marcel Mauss demonstrated many years ago that the two seasonal forms of Eskimo society led to two different forms of spatial order.[3] During the winter the Eskimos live in common houses in extended family relationships, whilst in summer they live in small round tents as single wandering nuclear families. Such spatial changes between summer and winter are very common, and Richard Thurnwald has shown[4] that the inner spatial arrangements of certain houses are socially conditioned and can reflect the structural character of the society in question. The spatial set-up of villages is often an exact reflection of the society which lives in them. For example the division into two of the Pueblo de Taos in northern New Mexico reflects the fundamental structure of the marriage system. Other village forms show still more complicated examples of this nature. The spatial form of a village will also reveal something about its origin; for example, whether it was planned (as a group of houses, as a line of houses, or as two lines of houses along a road) or whether it just grew up (conglomerate village). However, the social ecological conception begins only with specific questions as to its sociological character.

The special spatial analyses of social ecology refer above all to the spatial arrangement of the social strata and their proximity. In the first group of problems there is, for example, the spatial separation of antagonistic groups in the village. Of course this is not always the rule, as is often naïvely supposed; in fact, antagonistic groups often exist side by side and sometimes even mingle, as we have already noted. On the other hand, there is often spatial segregation in a settlement, as between old-established peasants and tenants on the one hand and immigrant workers who moved in later; as, for example, in the French community of 'Nouville'.[5] There is, of course, a local unity, interactions and common ties; but within this whole framework the community dissolves into two, or in certain circumstances more, ecological sub-units. These can, of course, sometimes form completely distinct hamlets.

These phenomena can be seen in greater variety in larger communities. But it still remains a definite fact that each community is built up out of a multiplicity of neighbourhoods, even though to some extent the concept of neighbourhood experienced a decisive modification, and perhaps clarification, because it was confined to the smallest neighbourhood groups. On the other hand, the larger and spatially separated sub-districts of a community are termed 'natural areas'.

Formerly, for example in the work of the American pioneer of urban sociology Robert E. Park, the terms neighbourhood and natural area were used indifferently; and this was responsible for a series of subsequent difficulties which we will deal with later.[6] The concept of natural area refers both to individual distribution areas of certain groups of the population (working class, middle class, upper class) and to sub-districts of a community having the character of a quarter and often developed from villages or towns which have been included in the whole and in which a population of a more or less homogeneous character is living. Finally it refers to several ecologically separate functional spheres such as business centres, banking districts, newspaper districts, governmental districts, amusement districts, and so on.[7] These natural areas vary in size; they begin beyond the actual neighbourhood, in which relationships of personal intimacy predominate, perhaps in a larger block, or complex of blocks, and proceed over quarters in the strict sense of the term to the town without its Hinterland, and even to the town with its Hinterland; the metropolitan area. The next step leads to regional formations which are completely independent of the community as such and represent a sphere of investigation of their own.[8] With this it has become very questionable whether the neighbourhood really represents such a natural area, and whether perhaps the latter begins only on a larger scale, for example with quarters, which are themselves built up on a multiplicity of neighbourhoods.

Conversely, the concept of natural area must be kept carefully separated from that of community, with which it sometimes tends to coalesce – as we find in the work of Robert E. Park, who refers to town quarters as local communities.[9] Both possibilities of misunderstanding can cause a good deal of confusion. Sometimes, for example, they suggest that the natural areas are characterized by social relationships of personal attachment in the same way as the neighbourhood; and on the other hand they permit the false assumption that these formations are global societies in the same way as communities are. It must also be pointed out that what we refer to as quarters have only in very rare instances a real specific individuality (as the origin of the word and its actual significance both suggest), and they have usually developed for purely administrative reasons. Chombart de Lauwe has also pointed out that one must distinguish 'the small quarter' from the quarter in the real sense of the term.[10] By the small quarter we mean what the average man calls 'my quarter'. This is fundamentally larger than the direct neighbourhood, and is also characterized by a multiplicity of highly personal relationships. On the other hand, it is usually smaller than a quarter in the historical and cultural sense of an amalgamated village or urban community, or an administrative unit.

Similar results were obtained by Quoist when investigating a poor quarter in the town of Rouen. It was seen that the part of the town in question, far from representing a natural area, was formed from a whole series of sub-quarters in the same

The social ecology of the community

sense as we have seen with Chombart de Louwe. The composition of the population was very mixed, whilst at the same time there were concentrations of relationships on the one hand, and carefully preserved isolationary tendencies on the other; for example, where there were groups of dockers on the one hand, and groups of minor employees on the other.[11] Such and similar experiences suggest that matters are perhaps rather more complicated than they looked at first.

THE QUESTIONABLE NATURAL AREA

In this sense the concept natural area has been questioned more and more in recent years[12] because it was said, with a certain amount of exaggeration, that quarters and sub-districts of a community represented real bodies in their own right.[13] This can be interpreted in various ways. The easiest opinion to refute is that which regards them as representing social relationships in the sense of a neighbourhood, when we understand neighbourhood as a complex of personal social relationships, and under such circumstances a quarter is undoubtedly too large to allow of such relationships. More difficult to refute is the urban conception of the natural area which soon developed from the original use of this expression by Robert E. Park, to whom it originally meant 'areas of population segregation',[14] i.e. an area whose character is determined by the fact that a separate population group lives in it. In the United States this refers chiefly to ethnic origin or to colour (black or yellow). But even with ethnic groups the discrimination is against certain groups only, for example, Jews, Italians (Sicilians), Greeks, Poles, Irish, and so on. This exists in Europe to a lesser extent too. Now and again it was necessary to measure the composition of the population in such districts more accurately, particularly in marginal districts where the dominating factor was not immediately obvious. With this the statistical method arose as a matter of course, and was then soon extended to other characteristics, for example, population density, rent levels, land values, and so on. It was then supposed that specific characteristics of a particular quarter could be deduced from the combination of such characteristics.[15] This is undoubtedly an error

63

because it involves a completely illegitimate hypostatic treatment of statistical indices.

Amongst many other factors we should like to stress the following which arose very prominently during an investigation we ourselves carried out: the statistically recorded homogeneity of certain population traits invariably disappeared as soon as a microanalysis of the quarter was carried out, house by house, block by block, or street by street. In an investigation of Zurich, the first town quarter (together with the unusable statistical division into districts) was first of all divided up into 132 sub-districts averaging thirteen buildings each. As these districts were too small to produce useful results in any classification of the residential population, a second analysis combined them into 'zones' each having a structure as uniform as possible. Naturally, these zones did not have the same homogeneous traits as the groups of buildings from which they were formed, but nevertheless their structure was surprisingly uniform. But precisely here there were such great deviations, both up and down, of certain statistical averages that they could no longer be explained by the usual statistical variations. For example, the built-up nature of the zones varied from 2 buildings per hectare (2·47 acres) to 33, or an average of 12, whilst the density of the population varied from 8 per hectare to 353, with an average for the whole district of 117. At the same time the surplus of females varied from 64 to 100 to 49 to 100 with an average of 57 for the whole district. Similar variations were also revealed in relation to numerous other characteristics. From this it emerges quite clearly that the characteristics set up for most quarters are exclusively statistical concepts which must be carefully distinguished from the actually existing social relationships. Quite apart from the fact as to whether this division into sub-districts and zones as used by Leutenegger[16] in his Zurich investigation is correct, one thing can be deduced with certainty from his work, namely that the socially relevant units must necessarily be much smaller than quarters if they are to take proper heed of the real social relationships existing. Only in this way can we hope to realize the postulate formulated by Paul Hatt, namely that as against the logical and statistical construction, which may very well be valuable for administrative purposes, we must work out a formula 'which embraces a series of spatial and social factors, operating decisively on all the inhabitants of a culturally and geographically clearly defined district'.[17]

The situation here is completely analogous to that in another branch of sociological investigation, namely the analysis of social classes. In this case average income figures tell us very little, because the same outlook can be found in different income brackets, whilst different outlooks can be found in the same income brackets. It is still frequently suggested that certain series of characteristics must be in accordance with a clear separation of a social class as though it were a caste. In addition there is the danger of creating a vicious circle by adopting a series of statistical features intended in the first place to characterize a certain social grouping, then using them in order to carry out an investigation, and finally extracting from the results precisely what was put into the series of statistical features in the first place. This danger has been largely overcome today in the sociology of social classes, but it still crops up here and there in the question of natural areas.

THE SPATIAL SOCIAL ORDERS

On the other hand, we must admit that, irrespective of these qualifications, there are at least certain extreme examples of districts, usually very clearly definable, both in the social class theory and in social ecology where extremely poverty-stricken slum districts, and, on the other hand, extremely wealthy districts, really form relative units of spatial social orders[18] which do, in the above-mentioned sense, 'operate decisively on all the inhabitants'. We are referring here only to the completely different aspects of the neighbourhood in the two extreme examples mentioned. In the exclusively wealthy quarters there will be very little real neighbourly relationship because none of the inhabitants is in need of anything which could be borrowed or otherwise obtained from the others. And 'people who don't belong' are just ignored even if they do happen to live in the same neighbourhood. They are simply not integrated, and the others keep them very clearly at arm's length. On the other hand like seeks like irrespective of whether the residential neighbourhood is the same or not. Thus here, as has already been stressed,[19] the contact is usually negative, because private relationships easily outdo neighbourly relationships, and this is necessarily so on account of the particular character of such a district as a wealthy one. On the other hand, the situation in the poor or slum district is very different; there the given situation enforces relationships, both good and bad. In such a district the inhabitants are constantly in need of neighbourly assistance, because in many cases they are unable to help themselves, and are not in a position, as the wealthy are, to employ servants.

However, one must certainly be very careful when dealing with such matters, as an illuminating discussion amongst criminologists in the United States has recently shown. Under the influence of the early social ecologists such as Park, later ecologists like Clifford R. Shaw and Henry D. McKay developed a sort of ecological theory of juvenile delinquency[20] which purported to show by statistical methods that juvenile delinquency was greater in the slums bordering the business quarters of large towns than elsewhere. This seemed to suggest a sort of ecological determinism in criminality. But subsequently a number of considerations were put forward[21] which suggested that the problem must be approached with much greater differentiation. For one thing it was pointed out that the police tend to act far more vigorously in slum neighbourhoods than in wealthy ones, and consequently the available statistics are unreliable. Further it must be said that even in the worst slums the overwhelming majority of young people are not delinquents although they come under precisely the same influences as those who are. This alone shows clearly that there must be other influences at work which produce delinquency; for example, broken marriages, abnormal family conditions, unhappy lives, the formation of gangs with criminal tendencies, and so on. In addition there is also a relationship to the total structure of society, as Robert K. Merton, following Emile Durkheim, pointed out in a very significant contribution to a discussion of the problem.[22] At the same time this is an indication that we are dealing essentially with structural and specifically sociological problems here, and not with any statistical averages, which at the utmost do no more than suggest that certain phenomena may arise in greater numbers in certain circumstances, but never provide any certainty on the point. Certainty, on the other hand, can be obtained only from the specific relations of facts, whereby the character of the social sub-structures and total structures plays a decisive role.

What has been said here of individual extreme cases also applies in the same way to those quarters which represent actual functional spheres, for example, a business and shopping area; the town centre, the City, with the notable difference between its workaday population and its actual inhabitants; an amusement district, a theatre district, government quarters, and so on. In addition there are the cases of ethnic and racial discrimination; for example, the still very radical dividing-line between black and white in the United States. On the other hand there are also cases of clearly mixed racial populations (mostly of Chinese inhabitants). Finally it must be admitted that with all 'medium' cases, between the two extremes, the decision is not easy to take, just as when dealing with social class, even the most detailed and involved statistical indices are not a great deal of help.

DIFFICULTIES OF DRAWING THE LINE

Without exaggerating either in one direction or the other, it must nevertheless be admitted that in addition to the actual neighbourhood in urban communities, there are also natural areas of various kinds, though when we go into details it is not possible to claim that they can be easily distinguished from each other in exactly the same way according to one or more characteristics. Above all, it must be stressed that it will never be possible to analyse a town thoroughly and completely according to such natural areas. Apart from the extremes of poor and rich districts, and from certain relatively few functional spheres, which tend to separate themselves spatially, we hardly ever find exactly circumscribed sub-sections of a community beginning, for example, at one street and ending at another. At the utmost we can sense certain more or less vague cultural atmospheres, which perhaps become a little more clearly defined – particularly in Europe – when there is a certain tension between the old part of a town and the new, where the separation is often clearly marked by the existence of ancient city walls; or in relatively independent urban districts, in which a community has been administratively amalgamated with a larger town, but continues to live on independently, at least culturally, whilst its own political, social, economic and geographical life has long ceased to exist. This is shown quite clearly in an investigation conducted by Hansjürg Beck into one of the suburban communities of Zurich, where even the newly arrived inhabitants are conscious that they are living in a particular kind of cultural sphere.[23] We should like to draw this to the attention of the more radical critics of the concept of the natural area. In conclusion there is another serious point at which the importance of the natural area expresses itself very clearly, despite all the critics.

We must, namely, bear in mind the fact that under certain circumstances the political limits of a community are by no means identical with its sociological limits. In such cases the natural areas formed by economic or social relationships clearly ignore politically-drawn lines of demarcation; a point that was clearly illustrated by the Darmstadt investigation. Such a situation often gives rise to community political problems of a quite special nature, particularly when a town extends into a predominantly rural hinterland which then develops into working-class housing estates thus experiencing what the Americans call 'rurbanization', i.e. the transformation of formerly rural areas by the influx of a new kind of residential population which works in the town but does not live there. The French talk in this respect of the *banlieue*. Thus today in the case of many urban communities we can observe processes of urbanization taking place beyond the community limits, whilst for the inhabitants of the town the transformation process has long been completed. To the extent that the town offers facilities which the hinterland does not possess, and whose inhabitants therefore make use of them (from swimming baths and sports grounds to hospitals, schools and universities), this develops into a direct financial problem which calls for some financial arrangement between the urban community and the surrounding smaller communities, whose inhabitants earn their living in the town and make use of the facilities it affords, but pay rates in their residential community. From the purely sociological standpoint this situation in which the political community is often not identical with its real (social) extent also gives rise to a multiplicity of other problems. Thus to some extent the natural areas under discussion really do exist, though the expression must be used with great caution, particularly with regard to the 'dominating influences' to which we have also referred.[24]

THE STRONG AND THE WEAK SENSE OF THE
CONCEPT OF NEIGHBOURHOOD

A little while ago an important distinction was introduced with regard to the term neighbourhood, and one which is of great significance for the questions we are discussing here. This comes from Ruth Glass's investigation into the community of Middlesbrough, which was in many respects illuminating. On the one hand there is a weak sense of the term neighbourhood as a group in a certain locality and distinct from other groups of a similar nature by certain characteristics of the district and its inhabitants. The meaning is just as weak when it is used to refer to people who merely live near each other. The term neighbourhood in its stronger sense must be clearly distinguished. In this sense we mean that a group also exhibits 'a neighbourly relationship', that is to say, a group having social interactions expressed in a multiplicity of social contacts.[25] The fact of personal familiarity is thus reduced to the neighbourhood in the latter sense, whereas the interactions and relationships both in larger urban areas and in communities as a whole are very definitely of a more general nature. When the communities are small this distinction undoubtedly becomes very relative. We should however like to stress, on the basis of our personal experience in a whole series of investigations, that a lack of personal familiarity can be observed even in the case of exceptionally small communities. Therefore it would in fact be advisable to attach the trait of personal familiarity exclusively to the small neighbourhood in the strong sense of the term. Up to the present this has not been done in the literature on the subject, and as a result we have had endlessly repeated assertions concerning the so-called close neighbourly bonds which allegedly exist in the village as against the town, whilst no one seems to have asked whether all the people even in a small village actually know each other; whether perhaps whole categories of people can sometimes be there and notoriously not known, as in former days the outsiders, and today the commuters; and whether perhaps there is the phenomenon of people recognized only by deliberately ignoring them, for in small villages enmities can be very intense indeed and have cruel consequences. We shall find ourselves faced with these problems again when we deal with the problem of community integration.

When we bear in mind what has already been said on the point, it is already very clear that there are far fewer integrated neighbourhoods than is commonly supposed, whilst, judged from purely ecological standpoints, such as similar living conditions, rents, living space, and so on, there would seem to be far more local sub-groups in the community in any given sub-group of the population occupying any more or less cohesive area. But these are precisely not groups as such. The above-mentioned investigation conducted by Ruth Glass also showed that real neighbourhoods were formed above all in the poorer quarters, and incidentally the population size of these quarters played no role.[26] This usually means that small wealthy quarters show little tendency to form integrated neighbourhoods, whereas, on the other hand, the usually overpopulated and spatially large poorer quarters in big towns reveal a very definite and intensive neighbourly behaviour on the part of their inhabitants. Thus once again we are faced with exactly the opposite of the stereotyped assertions about the lack of neighbourliness in large towns.

A second distinction was added to this distinction between neighbourhood in the weak and the strong sense of the term. This second distinction separates neighbourhood in the sense of neighbourly interactions into manifest and latent interactions (where in both cases we are dealing with narrow circles only). It turned out that in certain individual cases a latent readiness to show neighbourliness could be present whilst at the same time, for various personal reasons, actual integration of the neighbourhood is avoided.[27]

It should be noted here that the English usage of the term varies: the expression neighbourhood is still used to mean larger districts, whilst for the smaller spatial unit there is the term 'residential area', or, better, 'residential cells'.[28] We, however, should like to see the expression neighbourhood

limited to small and very small units which are in fact characterized by a closer social relationship. Every extension of the use
of the term beyond this merely leads to sentimental illusions, or
confuses ecological-statistical characteristics and combinations
of characteristics with relationships of practical social interaction (latent or manifest). For the rest, we may assume that a
community is a jointly functioning relationship even though not
all the people in it actually know each other, in exactly the same
way as – to use a simile introduced by Arensberg – one can
speak of a colony of bees without necessarily having to prove
that each separate bee has rubbed wings with each other bee in
the hive.[29]

Conversely, we may assume that actual neighbourhoods offer
at least a considerably greatei chance for the development of
living interaction units. This has often led to an attempt to
associate some kind of administrative order with such integrated
neighbourhoods; sometimes in a favourable, sometimes in an
unfavourable manner. For example, the concierge system which
was introduced into Napoleonic France served to control and
spy on the neighbourhood, in exactly the same way as the Nazi
Block-Overseer system did in Germany under National
Socialism. The following quotation is a typical example of the
latter system in operation, and the stilted swollen style is almost
as illuminating as the content itself:

> The construction of the party and many of its subordinate
> organizations on the principle of neighbourhood penetrates
> as a magnetic field of political education into the multiplicity
> of our locally determined existence, and from this simple basis
> it creates a determining power which is overwhelming. Its
> effect begins with the outward uniform direction of action and
> behaviour; then it goes deeper and gets things going until
> finally it dissolves and transforms opinions. When its effect
> has reached such a profundity then the public demand
> becomes unavoidable and impossible to evade: a public
> behaviour of the neighbourhood is then in course of develop-
> ment which not only releases forces which are ready for action
> and reduces the great and minor evils of laziness and meanness,
> but creates a basis for new orders. With this process, which
> verges on the miraculous, something else is proved too. The

mobilization of those forces which are dormant in the neighbourhood relationship and which make for unity is made
possible even where the blood relationship of kinship no
longer exists; namely in the population flood of great
industrial concentrations. It is, in fact, precisely the direct
operation of the executive power when people are together in
everyday life which makes the neighbourly relationship
politically tangible.[30]

These involved and turgid sentences do give an excellent idea of
the work of the Nazi Block-Overseer, and they are meant not
theoretically but in grim earnest, and translated into plain
language they mean delation, denunciation, spying and the
intervention of the Gestapo.

THE EXTENT OF THE NEIGHBOURHOOD

The most important question which now arises out of all these
matters is: *how far does the neighbourhood really extend?* The fact
that it is based primarily on unorganized, i.e. informal, personal
relationships, tells us at once that it must be very limited in its
extent. On the basis of many experiences in many different
places and cultural situations we are inclined to accept the
opinion that the neighbourhood is in some way parallel to the
local environment which can be surveyed with the eye. In this
sense a recent investigation conducted in Liverpool suggests
that only 'visual wholes' should be treated as neighbourhoods.[31]
The fact that in the blocks investigated in a large working-class
housing estate, the poorer inhabitants had closer neighbourly
relationships than the better off, who preferred to stress their
desire for privacy, although in the last resort the whole population belonged to the lower and the upper lower classes,[32]
suggests that perhaps another factor beyond mere class status
must be looked for. It seems to us that the need for spatial
proximity is accompanied by the opposite need for an 'arm's-
length' distance; with the result that when people live too close
together and too near to each other, hedges and fences are set up
to keep out inquisitive and prying glances. It may also be that
people with rising educational levels always react more sensitively to violations of this arm's-length distance, and therefore

regard physical proximity as involving the danger of undesirable personal familiarity, which they promptly reject. As however, on the other hand, spatial proximity is often regarded with favour and the opportunities of social relationships it provides are readily used, the question arises as to whether there is a certain optimal distance between too near and too far, at which point neighbourly relationships would be unobjectionable and would operate in a manner favourably regarded by all concerned.

As quite clearly no neighbourly relationships can develop beyond the limit of visual wholes, the limit for 'too far' seems fairly clear. But what does lack of distance, too close a physical relationship of living mean? The investigation conducted in Liverpool seems to suggest that the question of origin plays a role, since people who had moved into the housing estate from the suburbs reacted more sensitively to the close proximity than did those who had moved into it from overpopulated slum areas. Probably other factors play a role too. We should like to mention just one point which seems important for any estimate of neighbourly relationships: although most of the inhabitants seemed to value neighbourly relationships they were sceptical of any too personal or too familiar relationships. Therefore although one may certainly regard the neighbourhood as a 'primary group' in the sense adopted by Charles H. Cooley, one should at the same time bear in mind that there seems to be a more or less definite aversion to all very personal relationships in all too close a proximity. At the same time there is probably a very strong desire to be able to choose whom one is prepared to accept as a partner in such relationships, without at the same time being compelled by the layout of the housing estate to be on top of the neighbour all the time. This is a point which all those architects and planners, who tend to assume naïvely that only the architectural layout of a housing estate can encourage people to establish neighbourly relationships with each other, should bear in mind. The other influences which may well make themselves felt are, for example, of a familiar nature. An investigation conducted in Sheffield showed that bread should be borrowed from neighbours, whilst in the case of serious illness the number of cases in which neighbours were called in sank, whilst the number of cases in which recourse was had to relatives increased very considerably (by about sixfold).

73

The social ecology of the community

Persons who would be called on for help in greater or lesser household emergencies (153 housewives).[33]

Percentages

Persons whose help was sought	Lack of Bread %	Serious Sickness %
Neighbours	63·4	48·3
Relatives and Others	6·5	41·1
		5·3
No one	30·1	5·3
Total	100·0	100·0

Numerous investigations conducted by Loomis and Beegle produced similar results. This could perhaps mean that personal relationships are more easily adopted in neighbourhoods where the inhabitants are additionally bound by ties of kinship. Influences operating against the establishment of neighbourly relationships can, in certain circumstances, include age differences, particularly in a more or less homogeneous environment; and then the difference between respectable people and the others; and, quite generally, the differences between the various sub-groups of the lower classes. For example, the investigations in Liverpool and Sheffield suggested that many causes for the favourable or unfavourable development of neighbourly relationships must be sought for in the sphere of the environmental total society and not in the neighbourly relationship itself.[34]

Nevertheless the microanalysis of such neighbourhood relationships naturally remains of the greatest importance because they help us to understand the weight of various factors, and a general idea of their range. In this connection the distinction between physical and functional distance established by Leon Festinger and his collaborators seems to us of particular importance. Physical distance creates at the utmost only 'passive contacts'. If people live at a distance from each other the chance of even such passive contacts is greatly reduced; when the opposite is the case then the chance increases rapidly. The functional distance on the other hand is determined by the architectural layout of the neighbourhood, or, alternatively, by the position within the framework of the building complex. These two forms can go parallel with each other or stand in

74

The social ecology of the community

opposition; for example, where the physical distance is the same, the functional distance can be greater or less.[35] However, the investigators themselves stressed that the conditions of their investigation were to some extent extreme, in that they were dealing with unusually homogeneous housing estates. Later on they admitted that cultural affinities might well play a role in addition to purely spatial factors,[36] so that even here the purely spatial element was subject to a certain qualification. From this we may conclude that the concept of 'functional distance' includes a whole series of other elements in addition to the spatial factor; for example, elements of a structural nature, which in the last resort determine the character of the neighbourhood. It is noteworthy that whenever an attempt is made to go into the problem in detail, the factor of spatial proximity, which at first seems all important, becomes in reality more and more uncertain in its effectiveness.

The far-reaching significance of the functional interpretation of social space in the community was really first pointed out by W. Lloyd Warner in his wide-scale investigation *Yankee City*, in which certain classes were described with locality names ('those from Hill Street') just as the Zurichberg is described as 'Dividend Hill', where in the same way an amalgamation of local phenomena with cultural and class phenomena is indicated. Conversely, *Yankee City* also referred to the lower groups with similar locality names ('Riverbrookers' for example).[37] Generally speaking, however, Lloyd Warner is interested only in larger zones, without going into the actual problems of neighbourhood,[38] and he closely follows the procedure adopted by Robert and Helen Lynd in their books *Middletown* and *Middletown in Transition*.[39] The most important difference lies in the way in which the social classes are dealt with. The method adopted by the Lynds is more descriptive, whereas Lloyd Warner proceeds more theoretically and uses statistical methods of measurement.

CHAPTER VII

ATTEMPT AT A COMMUNITY TYPOLOGY

The question of the spatial layout of community life embraces only one aspect of the problem, though a very important one. Over and above this our attention must turn to the totality of the contemporary life of a community, in that together with the interlocking influences of its various vital and functional spheres we must also seek to reveal the *constellation* which is characteristic of the particular community in question. This would mean an actual structural investigation, whereby at the same time and as a supplement, the necessity of a typological investigation also becomes clear, one which would permit a classification of the communities. With this we finally arrive at a threefold aspect of community sociology: *ecological, structural* and *typological*.[1] Attention will always be concentrated on the present in accordance with sociology as a science of contemporary life. In addition, of course, the present is the only time dimension which is open to direct empirical investigation.

THE HISTORICAL CONDITIONS FOR A COMMUNITY TYPOLOGY

It is a matter of course that contemporary analyses are frequently impossible without preliminary and far-reaching historical investigation, because the problems which dominate the present day can often be traced far back into the past, and should be so traced.[2] This question regarding the extent of our subject matter, the community, in time, is exactly parallel to the question which was raised earlier as to the extent of the community in space and in the general culture of global societies of, for example, a national type. We therefore find ourselves under a direct obligation to include the historical dimension of our phenomena in our investigation. Space and time are also inseparable in the sphere of culture. Both Steward and Arensberg have recently stressed this viewpoint again; and, methodologically speaking, it is not without its consequences, as we shall see later.[3] However, we should like to point out that for a long time now this viewpoint has been opposed in various quarters. The history of the establishment of a community, for example, can be of particular value to us, a point which is hardly surprising after all that has been said about the spatial development of the community. The demographic history of a community is of similar importance, in so far as we must stress that the fundamental concepts of ecology such as 'invasion', 'succession', and 'concentration' of certain population groups, and their possible 'segregation', etc., and the development of 'sedimentary layers' are all of temporal significance.[4]

If in the course of a community investigation we catch a momentary picture of its contemporary life, that is certainly an important contribution to any understanding of the social structure of such a community and to its typological classification. However, when this procedure is adopted the investigator may well miss precisely the most essential factor in the process, as we know nothing about the course along which it has developed. This remains like a concealed action in a drama. Just as the audience would be unable to understand the drama as a whole without knowledge of this concealed action, so we too must break through the walls of the contemporary action and go back into the past. In addition to a descriptive and statistical contemporary analysis and the combination of various statistical inventories taken at various moments of time such as are provided regularly by the population censuses, we need some insight into the actual process of those occurrences which have formed the specific traits of our community.

New territory was definitely opened up in Germany recently by an investigation *Mines and Communities* conducted by Kurt Utermann.[5] Helmuth Croon then dealt in detail and in a highly interesting fashion with the methodological problems which resulted from it.[6] At the same time an interesting light was cast on the problem of integration in the community. In particular, the development of the mining towns in the Ruhr district, with

77

the clash between the established population and the vigorous influx of immigrants, provided us in the first place with a picture of communities with a very varied demographic population (including ethnic differences with the influx of Polish miners) settling down side by side and mingling together, and developing a local unity, local interactions and a joint aim. Nevertheless, these communities are far removed from forming a 'whole'. First of all they present us with a typical picture of ethnic and occupational interchange. We can safely say that at the beginning of such a process the old community is literally overwhelmed by the influx of immigrant miners. However, the original tension, though it still persists today amongst the older generation, shows a progressive tendency to disappear, or at least to decline in intensity. We may say therefore that in such cases there may one day be a community integration, though this cannot be taken for granted. This integration may reach various stages and develop through various stages, provided that no new disturbances from outside crop up. Utermann speaks in a felicitous phrase of the 'attainable' unification of forces brought about under the given circumstances.

An interesting parallel to this German investigation can be found in the United States, in a study by Herman K. Lantz entitled *Coal Town*, which deals with a mining community in the Middle West. This study also sets out to record the stormy developments of the past fifty years as retained in the memory of people still living. This particular community was founded in 1804 by white hill-billies from the Southern States, that is to say by already established Americans of English, Scottish and Irish extraction. For almost a century this community was a subsistence economy living its life more or less isolated from the main current of American developments, and maintaining old beliefs and old customs. But at the turn of the century this quiet existence came to a sudden end when a group of six brothers arrived in the neighbourhood and began to mine the coal which for some time had been known to be there. Exactly the same situation now arose as in the Ruhr district; labour was necessary and it was not available on the spot, and the result was that masses of miners, most of them recent immigrants of continental origin, began to stream into the place: Poles, Lithuanians, Croats, Serbs, even a few Montenegrins; and finally a mass of Italians. A community now grew up which was characterized by great social differences and social distances. The main division was, of course, between the newcomers and the old-established inhabitants, but within these two main groups there were still further divisions into social classes. All this must be borne in mind if the present situation in the community is to be understood. As a matter of fact, the clash between the subsistence economy of the old-established inhabitants and the industrial economy of the newcomers did not produce say a 'third force' which had any interest in the community as such or in the perpetuation of its 'cultural identity'. This sealed the fate of the community when the first of the pits was closed down in 1948 and the second in 1956.[7]

An examination of the historical factors involved is of the greatest possible importance for any understanding of such developments, since they have built up the structure of the community, formed its individual characteristics, and developed its specific type. For this reason the exploration of the historical background of any given situation is an essential preliminary to any draft of a community typology. Thus the historical extension of community studies does not in the least endanger community sociology, but, on the contrary, provides a very welcome extension which opens up new sources, methodological included, for community investigation. For example, Turney-High would never have arrived at any understanding of the essential processes of contemporary development of the Belgian community of Château-Gérard if he had not first established the fact that this community took its rise from a very unusual sub-culture of romanized Kelts which had persisted with extraordinary obstinacy for centuries. The process of senescence taking place in that community today lies not only in the excessive ageing of the population, but in the decline of the ancient tongue into a dialect. The upper classes no longer use it but prefer to model themselves on Brussels and Paris, and only the lower classes still retain it. The peculiar structure of this community as it exists today becomes apparent only when it is seen against the background of the whole past.

With such a precedent the relationships of the given community to its environment in general must of course be examined as such, because from this angle the existing social structure of a given community is often seen in a new and instructive light (immigration, emigration). Incidentally it is at this point that the investigation of a community, as a local unit under the influence of its past history, verges directly on area or regional surveys, and in respect of both the relationship of the community to its hinterland and its more far-reaching regional relationships, though the latter begin to play a role where almost exclusively urban large-scale metropolitan communities are concerned. These relationships are often very complicated.[8] However, it is sometimes astonishing to observe the influence even an exceptionally small town can exercise on its environment, as shown by the French investigation of the small Alsatian community of Pfaffenhoffen.[9]

It is necessary to point out here that so far these relationships of a community to its environment have been very one-sidedly investigated, either purely economically or from the angle of the migration from the countryside to the towns. But apart from this extremely important process of migration, there are other factors in the relationships of the rural communities themselves. Such factors can also be of great importance to the structure of the community, because they exercise a great influence on the development of the relationship between its old-established inhabitants and the new immigrants and the commuters. Thus under the impression that the dramatic aspects of migration from the countryside to the town are more significant, the movements in the rural areas themselves have been completely neglected, though it should be pointed out that this is perhaps a relatively new phenomenon developing parallel with the recent tendency of industry towards decentralization and its establishment in rural areas, a process which can be seen most clearly in Switzerland.[10] We think that it would be possible to show the existence of similar processes in Sweden, where from the beginning industry showed a tendency to establish itself in the rural areas in the first place. It must be stressed here that the latter traits very clearly distinguish those community investigations such as social anthropologists carry out with regard to people in a low stage of technical development, from those which sociologists carry out in relatively highly-developed industrial societies.

The former communities will often be relatively isolated

(though not necessarily self-sufficient), whilst the latter – despite the fact that they are sometimes relatively isolated – are always characterized by the fact that they are part of global societies of a higher order; at least of regional economic type, or even a national society. Even when in this case the community is pre-served as a global society, the relationships to the environ-mental world (natural area, region) and to other communities of various kinds must necessarily exercise a dominant influence, whereas with primitive communities this is not even approxi-mately the case, and sometimes not at all. But this should not, and does not, mean that social anthropological investigations and sociological community investigations cannot be of mutual assistance and provide mutual enlightenment. On the contrary: in view of the great importance which the comparative method possesses today, both types of investigation are closely dependent on each other; and, in fact, more and more investigators are now combining the two approaches in their work. With this, sociological community investigation as a contemporary science comes face to face with the same problem as sociology as a whole: the highly developed industrial societies to which the investigators themselves belong are particularly difficult to understand precisely because we are so involved in them. Our own standpoint is part and parcel of that life and therefore we often overlook the specific nature of its being. Conversely, we usually find it easier to understand other cultures of a lower level of technical development (to which all the technically and economically underdeveloped countries belong), precisely because of the differences between their culture and our own. The inevitable consequence of this state of affairs was the development of the comparative method, which succeeds in revealing the specific peculiarities of our highly-developed industrial civilization only by way of community investigations amongst primitive peoples and those who are semi-cultured. The value of such a comparison of primitive communities and those of more developed societies characterized by the presence of global societies of a higher order should not be under-estimated.

THE ECONOMIC CONDITIONS FOR
COMMUNITY TYPOLOGY

With this the economic factor begins to loom larger and larger. Although its main treatment belongs to the economic sciences, nevertheless the existing form of economic activity greatly influences the social relationships of a community. Further, one of the fundamental characteristics of the concept community is that it is, amongst other things, a group working economically together. As such it in time creates its own environment; particularly since the transition from the hunter-food-gathering culture to the earliest forms of settled agriculture, as a result of which not only did economic activity extend but the local communities became spatially fixed. This process is perhaps identical to the already mentioned transition from the palaeolithic to the Neolithic age. Its essential characteristics include not only the spatial settlement of society and the greater development of its structure, but also at the same time the increase in material riches and the greater development of its technique for transforming its environment. With this it is obvious that the economy, and the culture which belongs to it, must increasingly affect the character of the community itself, so that from the typological angle the structure of the community must be considered in essential relation with the dominant economic form. At the same time this means that the physical conditions of life determine every cultural development and cultural form, even in their highest aspects as abstractions and sublimations. But they do this, as Daryll Forde points out, not as 'determinants' but only as a category of raw material for cultural operations.[11] This applies in the same way both to a more geographically and a more economically slanted determinism. Thus if we wish to classify the communities as local global societies according to the dominant economic type, then we must always proceed so that the cultural determinants are visible at the same time. A general glance at existing typologies will show us that this has often been done already. Unfortunately however it very soon transpires that the nearer we come to reality the economic factor is usually so obtrusive that the existing typologies are much too one-sided for our purpose.

The most important contrast that arises here, and which

unites the geographical, economic, social and cultural viewpoints in the required way, is the contrast between largely
agrarian communities on the one hand, and industrial communities on the other. In addition we have the other contrast
between rural and urban communities, but here we must raise a
warning voice against the error frequently committed, of presenting the two pairs of contrasts as though they were necessarily parallel. On the contrary, they cut across each other,
because the problem of the urban community is only partly
attached to the industrial economic form; quite apart from the
fact that together with the industrial economic form, other
economic and other functions connected with the modern
economic system can be concentrated in the towns and be more
typical of them than industry (trade, transport, banking, insurance, administration, community and central administration,
government, cultural institutions, etc.). According to the
different cultural environments, we find typical industrial
villages (in Sweden and Russia), and towns with largely
agrarian populations (in Italy, Sicily and Spain).

As a result of the extreme complexity of these relationships,
today no less than three branches of sociological investigation
occupy themselves with these specific problems, namely,
agrarian sociology, urban sociology and – if one cares to regard
it as a separate branch of investigation – rural-urban sociology,
which is particularly highly developed in the United States. But
in all these spheres the community is the centre of attention, and
the interest of the actual community investigations is not so
much concentrated exclusively on economic questions as on the
cultural form which the social relationships between the individual and the sub-groups take on within communities of a
certain type.[12] This is expressed, amongst other things, by the
fact that the general category formation and classification
systems of community investigation work rather with usually
very obvious cultural differences of the type which divides
'community and society' (Tönnies), rural and urban cultural
styles, popular culture and bourgeois-urban society, traditional
and progressive society, and so on. On the other hand agrarian
sociology, which is more interested in concrete detail, and urban
sociology, and rural-urban sociology which amalgamates the two
standpoints, seek for ever finer and more detailed systems of

classification. Although community investigation gains a great deal from such finer and more detailed systems of terminology, which – as we shall soon see – usually serve economic ideas, its primary interest nevertheless remains concentrated on the cultural characteristics of community life and on its inner structure; and it is still a moot point whether these vary in the same way as the purely economic classification characteristics, and whether perhaps precisely here factors other than economic ones begin to operate (professional structure, social class stratification, power and influence structures, and so on), or perhaps such factors in combination with the economic characteristics. We must also stress that the cultural characteristics of a community need not necessarily change at the same time as changes take place in the composition of its socio-economic groupings. For example, a small rural community can continue to represent peasant culture even long after it has become an industrial community. In fact in Switzerland, for example, this is quite frequently the case, and it has led to a sort of idealization of peasant culture and peasant community ideas so that you still find small communities at a high stage of industrialization which behave, think and perhaps vote in a peasant fashion.

THE CULTURAL BASIS OF TYPOLOGIES

It is a matter of course that the classificatory characteristics of the community vary very considerably according to the particular conditions prevailing in a given country or part of a country (region). Consequently it is probably quite impossible to work out a system which would apply to all countries and regions in the same way. This difficulty is greatly increased by the fact that many different sciences are interested in the creation of such a typology (apart from sociology there are economy, demography, communal sciences, geography and national planning), all of which have their own, usually very abstract, guiding principles. In addition, there is a morphological classification according to physiognomic-cultural characteristics which combines some of the above-mentioned aspects with historic-political, regional or cultural and geographical aspects. This latter viewpoint appears to predominate even in the pre-scientific everyday, but as experience shows, even scientific attempts at classification are dependent on such views, which accounts, in fact, for the difficulties mentioned. For example, American attempts of this nature are quite clearly affected by the special conditions prevailing in the Middle West; German attempts by the special conditions of the German village -- quite apart from internal-German regional differences – which are again quite different from the conditions prevailing in the Italian, and, in particular, the South Italian village.

In this connection the Austrian Hans Bobek has quite recently expressed doubt as to whether a 'strict comparability' extending beyond all these 'physiognomic characteristics', is – though desirable in itself – really absolutely necessary.[13] This attitude seems very realistic to us. Even so, the question still remains as to 'within what limits comparability must be required'. Bobek expresses the opinion that we shall have to be content with comparability within given national limits, and not attempt to extend it to international comparisons. However, in view of existing difficulties we regard even this as very optimistic, and we would therefore prefer a more regionally based system, i.e. a system which one could neutrally refer to as 'area research'. This, of course, leads in the last resort to a classification based more on socio-cultural lines, of the type specifically represented today by Arensberg. But to some extent the dilemma remains, and in exactly the same way as it does in social ecology, since the necessity for quantitative comparisons and the formation of 'marginal values' cannot be ignored. In this connection we should have to fall back again on inner-State comparison because at least it can rely on approximately analogous research methods for the whole country, something which, for the moment at least, is not the case with international comparison – quite apart from the culturally conditioned differences of evaluation of various basic factors. In conclusion we should like to stress that the structural viewpoint also demands such a typology.

For all the reasons which have been mentioned, the typologies developed by community sociology in the United States are of no use to us, or only in a very general way, as is the case with Sorokin and Zimmermann.[14] They distinguish the primitive original community, the village community in the European sense, the American village (including the purely agrarian type, and the non-agrarian village of various sizes which, according to circumstances, offers limited, semi-developed and fully developed amenities), the industrial village, the suburban village, and, finally, the larger 'open-country' neighbourhood already mentioned. Over and above this series there is also a series of classifications relating to the urban community, and Louis Wirth enumerates the following examples: industry, trade, mining, recreation, university and government town. In addition, an industrial town will vary according to whether it depends on one single industry or a number of industries. Suburbs are different from satellite towns; residential suburbs are different from industrial suburbs; a large town with an urban hinterland (a metropolitan area) is different from a town without such a hinterland; and an old town is different from a new, and so on.[15]

EARLIER TYPOLOGICAL ATTEMPTS

Undoubtedly, a classification of European communities will have to be guided by other characteristics, and these will, incidentally, vary from land to land. Max Weber was the first to make such an attempt for Germany, and it was remarkable for being multidimensional, though it is true that it confined itself to urban communities. Weber distinguished three dimensions: the economic, the political and the historical-class-status, because, in his view, the town considered as a community is bound up, as far as the West is concerned, with the existence of privileges deriving from class status – in this case the privileges of the full citizen or *Bürger*. These factors are undoubtedly of great importance, but at the same time it must be stressed that the actual sociological dimension is missing in this kind of typology! This is not only the great weakness of his classification of urban types, but it also produces a lack of cohesion in the many sociological characteristics which do appear in the actual working out of the scheme.[16]

Werner Sombart's derivative classification ignores the sociological viewpoint with the result that he too cannot refine his 'more complex' concept of the town. The subject of the civic community has for him no importance in itself but only 'in the framework of a factually defined combination . . . of e.g. the

86

cultural sphere of economics or politics'.[17] As will be shown, he fails to differentiate adequately here as well. This is also true of Leopold von Wiese's attempt at a sociology of the rural settlement. He claims that his chief concern is a 'truly sociological exploration' of forms of settlement, but he misses the individuality of the subject community from the first because he limits himself to the 'social processes denoting the category of settlements in question'. In this way the formal character of the village is lost sight of as a structural problem, as his typology loses by its highly external enumeration: 1, the isolated farm; 2, isolated groups of farms; 3, the estate with house and farm; 4, the village. He completely overlooks the fact that totally incomparable things are treated on the same plane – probably on the basis of the really primitive attempt to proceed mechanically from the simpler to the more complex. Moreover it is not clear whether isolated farms as primitive settlements are extremely rare (existing only in Norway) or whether they merely represent a hangover from an earlier stage in economic history.[18]

Whereas in the various attempts at classification made by rural sociologists in the U.S.A.,[19] rural political points of view are emphasized, in the German works the purely economic point of view has remained paramount. This applies just as much to the earlier as to the later observers.

LATER ATTEMPTS AT TYPOLOGY

Paul Hesse[20] distinguishes as follows: industrial communities and centres of administration, workers' communities and settlements, worker-peasant communities, petty peasant communities, peasant communities. This is reached by a combination of a total of six marked groups; for example, the amount of land attached to a household is expressed as a percentage by setting the landless households or those with an area of half a hectare at the most against the total amount of land attached to all the households; professionally employed people in farming and forestry are compared with the total of employed people; the non-agricultural element, in particular the degree of industrialization, is expressed by the total number of persons engaged in non-agricultural employment compared with the number of local persons; the extent of temporary emigration from the area is expressed by the number of people who leave to find work compared with the total number of local workers, and by imported labour measured against the workers in local non-agricultural jobs; the weight of home industry and small lots is set against the agricultural and forestry concerns greater than half a hectare; the proportion of landed estates and large concerns of all degrees is measured against the total of agricultural and forestry concerns. The further subdivisions are then arrived at only in economic and not in social terms, so that the industrial communities and administrative centres can be subdivided among: extractive industries such as mining and quarrying; communities concerned with the production of iron and non-ferrous metals, with the processing of iron, steel and non-ferrous metals, with heavy and light engineering, precision engineering and optics, electrical technology; those concerned with the food, recreation and tourist industries; those with the building and allied industries, the wood and allied trades, etc. To be particularly appreciated as comparatively positive in this attempt is the aim to establish 'marginal values'. It is also true that this classification can be of the greatest use to agricultural policy. No doubt too there are some sociological ideas hidden in it; but they are overshadowed by the economic ones.

The situation is similar with another attempt at the classification of community types, carried out this time by Heinz A. Finke,[21] although it certainly goes rather further than the one just dealt with. It claims specifically to enumerate 'social community types'. Here, too, economic production is in the foreground. The main divisions are drawn first horizontally according to the social characteristics of the population as independent existences, co-operating members of the family working for the family, labourers, officials, and employees; and then vertically, according to the economic position of the population, in economic compartments, with the main stress on the share of the agricultural population. Purely sociologically speaking there is also a parallel division according to other characteristics: stability, structural disturbance, structural change,[22] to which we shall return later in connection with social change in the community. However, here too, unfortunately, the economic viewpoint is predominant.

Attempt at a community typology

M. Schwind has also given us another interesting typology.[23] In the beginning he too proceeds from the social status of the gainfully-employed person, whereby he very correctly stresses the extreme vagueness of the category 'independent occupation', which embraces the large-scale merchant as well as the hawker, the itinerant musician as well as the large-scale landowner. This category is quite useless from the sociological standpoint, and therefore it must be further subdivided, with the assistance of occupational statistics and the placing of the population into economic compartments. This procedure allows us to see quite clearly, particularly where peasant communities are concerned, which is the more prominent in the category, the peasant, the artisan or the man following an independent occupation. The independent occupations belonging to agriculture must also be subdivided into a scale ranging from the large-scale landowner to the small plot-holder. Any attempt at a typology without regard for the problem of these independent existences will result in communities dominated on the one hand by workmen or officials or employees, or by both categories, and on the other by independent existences. In the first case it is easy to typify, but in the second it is not. The independent occupations must therefore be subjected to a further analysis. In this way we shall be able to distinguish between: purely peasant communities (the independent occupations almost always represent only peasants, and account for between 30 per cent and 50 per cent of all gainfully employed persons); worker-peasant communities in which the original sociological core has been swamped by workers (45 per cent to 60 per cent of all persons gainfully employed are workers, not only in agriculture but also in local industry); rich-peasant communities, because alongside the estate owner and one or two rich peasants the overwhelming majority of those gainfully employed (up to 95 per cent) are agricultural labourers; industrial communities in which the factory owners take the place of the few rich peasants. The army of workers is also very large, although remnants of the peasantry are still visible, artisans, small traders, and employees; artisan-worker communities, where the independent occupations are not so much peasants as artisans and small traders; worker-official communities ('official' here also includes employees) where the better-off social groups increase numerically;

and communities of officials where this group represents over 30 per cent of the whole. As its originator points out, this classification also has its exceptions which refer in particular to transitional stages of unclear classification. He also mentions the not unimportant type of 'charitable community', with hospitals, old people's homes and convalescence homes, whereby the type of independent non-employed person essentially determines the social structure; and, incidentally, creates community problems of a quite specific character. To these could also be added school communities including boarding schools, in which the same groups probably appear, though with much lower age limits.

A typology which is quite noticeably sociologically developed is that of Hans Linde,[24] although his interest is not primarily sociological, but very clearly economic with special relation to 'the needs of almost all branches of the administration, and of public, economic and political life, particularly at the higher levels, which necessarily lack a direct view of all the smaller units involved, but which need this information daily for a conscientious estimate of numerous processes'. But beyond this, Linde's conception of the 'social structure' of the community remains strangely empty of actual sociological content. The reason for this is, on the one hand, that obviously under the influence of Leopold von Wiese – he proceeds exclusively from the 'inter-human relationships', which from the start prevents all access to the actual structural character of the community; and, on the other, the purely economic interpretation of the concept 'structure', which he understands as 'the practical demonstration of gainfully-employed persons according to their legal position in their profession'. Although he regrets this, and observes: 'There can be no question whatever of the specific social laws of development of a community in this narrow but widely-used interpretation',[25] he himself gives no more, or, at least, very little more. At the utmost he calls for a classification according to property, wealth, income, number of children, education; but in the absence of statistical data he nevertheless comes to the conclusion that these problems can be solved only by 'monographic treatment', whereby every possibility of a typology is once again rendered illusory. This is all the more surprising because Linde himself has elsewhere taken important steps towards an understanding of the social structure of the village, and sees clearly that the community is not an 'organic' but 'only a topographical relationship', i.e. an 'agglomerative association of heterogeneous sub-masses or groups'.[26]

In an Austrian attempt at a typology of the community, both Hans Bobek and Robert Ofner show that they are firmly convinced of the importance of the sociological factor. Bobek even occasionally reproaches Ofner because his characteristics reveal 'too little inner relationship', so that their application might well illuminate the community complex from a different aspect, but without any thorough penetration in the sense of structural understanding.[27] For the first time we have an undoubtedly purely sociological argument here, and it is completely in accordance with the central interests of community sociology. Ofner himself proceeds from what sounds like a thoroughly sociological definition of the community, which he regards as: 'a group of the population living within the smallest spatial unit of the State, working, taking part in the administration, and, with its whole life, impressing its character on that particular piece of land'.[28] His sociological slant is also expressed in the fact that his first characteristic is the gainfully-employed as a type-formative element, and only then does he go on to the economic grouping. Also sociological is the attention he pays to the commuting process as a third type-formative element (though this is also to be met with elsewhere). In addition there are (fourthly) the 'social stratification', and (fifthly) the pensioners and the size of the community. Judging from this series and from his actual observations we have to admit that Ofner does come quite close to a sociological type study of the community. However, in carrying out his work he does not live up to his own demands, even when Bobek observes (against Linde) that one cannot abandon 'non-statistical characteristics' altogether, whilst Linde himself stresses that 'one should not place an excessive accent' on 'the evidence of types exclusively based on statistical material',[29] an observation with which we entirely agree.

Therefore this should lead all the more to a step which has long been recognized as necessary in sociology. But how rarely this is taken can be seen very clearly in this latter case too. Instead of dealing thoroughly with questions relating to the social stratification of the community, and thus getting a view

G

of the social structure, Ofner, too, contents himself, when dealing with 'non-statistical' characteristics, with a mentioning of types, such as mountain-peasant type, or settlement kind (scattered or homogeneous settlement). With the exception of the very informatively presented commuter problem, and despite his separation of the occupational elements from the economic groupings, he himself falls into the very naïve division into land and forestry, trade, industry and services (commerce, transport, public services and liberal professions), which merely nullifies the intended differentiation. And similarly, in dealing with the elements of 'social stratification' he falls into the highly doubtful distinction of independent occupations, and co-operating members of the family and non-independent occupations[30]. Bobek also condemns this, though he lays the chief blame for it at the door of Austrian official statistics, which make no attempt to differentiate between these extremely complex concepts.[31] But when in conclusion Ofner expresses the belief that with this characteristic he can represent the vertical arrangement as well as the horizontal layering of the gain-fully-employed inhabitants[32] the sociologist must definitely disagree with him. In view of the complexity of the problem of social stratification in the community the division mentioned cannot provide even a preliminary approach to the actual situation.

THE SOCIO-CULTURAL PROBLEM OF COMMUNITY TYPOLOGY

Interesting as all these attempts have been, and correct as many of their conclusions undoubtedly are, they nevertheless – quite apart from the excessive stress placed on the economic standpoint – remain to some extent up in the air, because they lack a concrete sociological community investigation as a basis. This is still lacking in Germany despite one or two very noteworthy beginnings.[33] It is particularly obvious that in addition to the actual structure problem, neither the question of value nor the question of joint ties has really been dealt with so far, though it is precisely here that the structure problem really becomes concrete. We must particularly stress that we cannot accept the conclusions of the folklorists as any sort of substitute since they miss the point both methodologically and practically and are completely distorted by the ideology of the sentimentalized village community concept. And just as painfully obvious is the lack of a real historical viewpoint, which would make it possible in the first place to understand the present constellation; because similar structures may well have developed under quite different circumstances, and this, together with the present constellation, can open up quite different future perspectives. Such a standpoint should be of particular importance with regard to national planning.

To sum up, typological attempts such as those previously mentioned can serve only as a provisional solution as long as no more far-reaching material is available. The situation is no better in the United States, as August B. Hollingshead has pointed out,[34] although there experience in actual structural analysis is much greater than in Europe.

However, using such categories, Herbert Kötter has succeeded quite well in characterizing certain communities in the hinterland of Darmstadt, producing at the same time an interesting arrangement of trades and industry, one which is certainly of sociological importance precisely because it takes the historical standpoint into account; to wit, according to its earlier or later emergence from the old household economy; according to the progressive division of labour, and, finally, according to its involvement in a market which quite clearly extends beyond the community.[35] However, we certainly cannot agree with him when he declares that a typology according to sociological standpoints can never be more than a 'second step' after the economic typology. In the first place this fails to take into consideration the fact that totally different structural types can exist with similar economic constitutions; such as agriculture in a purely peasant community, or in a community dependent on a landed estate. In accordance with the various ruling structures the culture in the two communities is fundamentally different. And secondly, we must also reckon with the possibility that the cultural characteristics do not change 'with possible changes of the economic composition',[36] from which the phenomenon we have called 'ideological peasant behaviour' develops; which is neither a sociological nor an economic phenomenon, but a purely political one.

Precisely in the investigations of Kötter we can see very clearly that beyond an independent agrarian sociology on the one hand, and an urban sociology on the other, there is a rural-urban sociology, which should certainly be taken into account in any attempt to create a community typology. It is no longer true, as Oswald Spengler thought, that the village stands more or less on the outskirts of the field of development. On the contrary, with the development of modern industry new impulses have revealed themselves here too, compelling us to abandon quite a number of our earlier ideas. Fundamentally these go back as far as the reform of agricultural technique since the eighteenth century. Whereas at the end of the nineteenth century industrialization and urbanization went more or less hand in hand, this has changed fundamentally during the past fifty years or so. Industry has often moved into rural areas, with the result that problems of industrialization are arising there against a quite different background, whilst urbanization, which often, but not always, arose as a consequence of industrialization, has to some extent become independent of the town – paradoxical as this may sound.[37] Incidentally, this circumstance has probably contributed more than any other to thrusting the special peculiarity of the sociological urban problem as a special cultural type very forcibly into the foreground by comparison with the economic, transport, industrial and other problems of the town. The urban style of living is to be met with everywhere today, even in the countryside; and in the clash between town and country there would seem to be a great deal more at stake than two types of settlement, or two types of economic systems. Therefore, in a number of community investigations suggested and carried out by us we used the expression 'cultural clash'.[38] Incidentally, it seems strange that agrarian sociologists, who are extremely interested in the economic process, always confine themselves to the relationship between town and country when they deal with the problem of commuting. Yet the pendulum movement in the countryside itself between the individual villages has exercised an unusually powerful influence on the community structure, though it has gone unnoticed because attention has been directed so exclusively to the prevailing kind of economic activity. We must reckon in principle with the possibility that though agricultural activity remains unchanged there are people working in every village today who are unknown in the community as such, and are neither integrated with it nor interested in its affairs. As a result of this, unusual political problems arise, since it leads to the permanent under-representation of these groups when community affairs are being settled, and underlines the lack of political interest amongst the 'sub-peasant' strata at the present time.

THE SOCIO-CULTURAL PROBLEM IN
THE TYPOLOGY OF URBAN COMMUNITIES

It is interesting to note that the cultural aspect of the whole question has always bulked larger in urban and big-town sociology; and much more recognizably too, as we can see from the voluminous and detailed work of Elizabeth Pfeil. Alexander Rüstow expresses this very trenchantly when he writes: 'All highly-developed culture is urban culture.'[39] We feel that the typology of the urban community points in the same direction, and the urban communities are being 'more and more recognized as functional types', which has been clear since Lewis Mumford, although his analysis, with its strong critical accents and often utopian and constructed viewpoints, is frequently unobjective. [40] Similar ideas led to a typology of urban communities, according to their achievement of a higher level of living of a regional, national or continental type.[41] At the same time this is seen in conjunction with the occupational structure and the social structure, which are both the condition and the consequence of the exercise of function. With this the concept of the urban community was at last separated from the primitive concept of purely numerical magnitude which previously prevailed. In this way six types were evolved: (a) the central towns, Type I, the focus of central function for a hinterland; Type II – has in addition industries operating for external markets; (b) incomplete central towns, Type III, with industry; Type IV, with industry and external trade (business towns); (c) Industrial towns, Type V, with manufacturing industries; Type VI, with raw-material industries. It should be stressed that this typology is also strongly economically slanted, although it does take into consideration the demand that further progress should then be made towards actual sociological standpoints. Further, it is economically incomplete because it incorrectly neglects important activities which are of particular significance where large towns are concerned, such as banks, stock exchanges and insurance companies. However, all non-economic functions are completely ignored, such as towns peopled by the retired, tourist and convalescence centres, purely cultural centres, university towns and so on. Perhaps if economic divisions are to be used in evolving a typology of urban communities, it would be a good idea to take economic divisions which are also sociologically relevant. The Australian economist Colin Clark has done this in dividing the productive economy into a primary section, consisting of agriculture and forestry, fisheries and hunting; a secondary section, consisting of mining, industry, building, and public utilities such as gas and electricity; and a tertiary section, consisting of everything else, and including in particular, trade, finance, transport, administration, the 'non-material production' of the liberal professions, and personal services.[42] As this division also includes structural insights into the development of our modern class society, it would be easy to amalgamate the economic with the social structural and the latter then with the cultural.

THE INTEGRATIONAL TYPE AS A CLASSIFICATION CHARACTERISTIC

But here too, the fact remains that the angle for a useful typology of the urban community can be attained only after the concrete development of urban sociology. Only then perhaps could we dare to accept evidence which utilizes the process of urban integration and its variants as characteristics for the classification of urban communities. Then, beyond the undoubtedly very essential, although not completely adequate economic classificatory characteristics, we should begin to see sociological characteristics for a typology of the urban community. But at the same time these have a very tangible cultural content, because a community can develop satisfactorily only when there are common values which determine its life.

On the basis of the concept of the 'moral integration' of the urban community Robert C. Angell[43] has made the problem the subject of an unusually illuminating and penetrating investigation which undoubtedly represents one of the most decisive steps forward in community sociology since the founder days. The concepts which are taken as the centre of this investigation are really different from all that went before, although they are founded and thoroughly prepared in the tradition of American community investigation. The moral integration of the urban community as illustrated, say, by the fairly high statistics of criminality, and by other negative social actions, and the causes which influence it positively or negatively, were measured against the compatibility of the prevailing social norms; against the adequacy of the prevailing social norms, and against the efficacy of the measures and processes which operate towards the compatibility and adequacy of these norms. With regard to the latter point, the mobility rate of the population proved of decisive importance, because where the population is most highly mobile no common ideas of value can develop. Therefore it is important whether the institutions such as schools and churches, which make an important contribution to the formation of character, are community-based or not.

In addition, the function of the local newspaper is of the greatest importance in the community and has a great influence on its integration, as Morris Janowitz has already pointed out.[44] Finally, the effectiveness of the leaders of the community plays a decisive role, from which it may be postulated that these functions should not be left to a small group of notoriously overworked specialists, but spread out over the widest possible circle of co-operating people who represent a certain standard of value in the various occupations and strata of the population.[45]

We owe an interesting development of these problems recently to a group of investigators in Vienna, which concentrated its attention particularly on housing conditions, needs and desires. Before long this investigation developed into a community investigation proper, and in this connection Leopold Rosenmayr developed a highly interesting socio-cultural structural analysis of the Vienna municipality (community) based on these housing desires. It was seen, for example, that the Viennese does not care to live on the outskirts of the town like citizens of most big towns do. There were various causes for this, some of them purely ecological; for example, the fact that the Vienna Woods penetrate practically into the town. But the socio-cultural conditions were even more important. For example, to live in the centre of the town is considered *de rigeur*, illustrated by the fact that the 'cultural gathering' is the centre of thought, as in Paris.[46]

CHAPTER VIII

THE STRUCTURAL ASPECT OF
THE COMMUNITY

Once such questions have been settled, as to how human beings of various kinds are spatially distributed in a community, how they are bound up with their neighbours, and what they live on, then the problem of the social structure of the community presents itself with increased urgency.

THE STRUCTURE OF THE COMMUNITY AND THE
SPONTANEITY OF INFORMAL GROUPS

This raises once again the question as to whether the community as a social formation really has something we can call a 'structure'. If we regard the community as a 'global society' then the answer is, of course, in the affirmative. The real difficulty of the question lies not in this very simple decision, but rather in the subsequent fact that, as G. Gurvitch clearly stresses, all global societies are not merely structural formations, but that their vital totality completely overwhelms their structures, and that they thus become involved in actions which have no structural reference whatsoever. In other words, when we approach the problem of community structure our task can be carried out only within the framework of the everyday life and presence of the community. The term 'everyday' means not only that the average life of the average citizen must be dealt with seriously, but also that community life is not confined to its institutional framework, i.e. within the specific structure, for example, in its class system, but often very definitely beyond it in a totality of life aspects. For example, Robert and Helen Lynd point out in their investigation of Middletown that although the whole life of Middletown is determined by the division into 'business class' and 'working class', and that this division extends

99

The structural aspect of the community

right into its most intimate recesses, e.g. who may marry whom, what a man does during the day from the moment he gets up in the morning, which church he belongs to, what make of car he drives, and whether his wife and children are active members of certain clubs, and so on; on the other hand, such a structural division can create only approximate values in individual cases, because in the last resort life is lived by the individual and not by the abstract group.[1] They then point out that in addition to the more formal groupings which make up the structure of a community, highly informal groups spring up spontaneously on various occasions; groups which, despite their institutional and organizational amorphism, sometimes persist for decades and are in a position to develop their own traditions. These groups are just as important, if not more so, for community sociology as the more formal groups or associations whose members co-operate within the framework of fixed institutions (factories, administration, authorities, tribunals, churches, associations, and so on).[2]

Our approach to the community structure must therefore develop along two lines; first through an investigation of the more informal aspect of this phenomenon, which expresses itself in numerous ways contributing to the richness of community life. Then we shall turn to those phenomena of a higher structural character, such as social groups and classes, together with more formal associations and institutions. With this we shall fully meet the justifiable requirement of Gurvitch that the global social system of the community must be embedded in the inherent totality of community life aspects. Incidentally, we consider this to be of much greater importance to the matter in hand than the question of A. B. Hollingshead as to whether we are to regard the structural elements of the social classes or castes as realities or merely as statistical constructions.[3] Quite justifiably he points to the relation between this problem and the problems of the perceptive value of ecological indices. But just as these problems can be relatively easily solved by harking back to smaller units which, so to speak, are 'closer' to life itself, so we can overcome the difficulty of the class attachment of men in a given society by studying their behaviour, not in great statistical averages, but in the actions of small and very small groups, which act together or against each other, interact, and perhaps for shorter or longer periods seize the leadership, whilst others remain in apathetic lethargy.

It is interesting to note that in this respect modern community sociology proceeds along exactly the same lines as modern industrial sociology; just as both branches of investigation have often developed under one head.[4] Recognition of this fact strikes us as of great importance particularly for the communal sciences if they are to completely understand the developmental impulses which arise spontaneously within the community. Thus, in another connection it has been stressed that developmental impulses in 'underdeveloped' areas, are brought about not only from the outside (or at least not sufficiently when the outer stimulus does not correspond with an inner readiness) but can just as spontaneously arise from within by a sort of 'creative adjustment' within the framework of the society in question.[5] Similarly we believe that a very careful distinction must be made between the formal organizations and the informal activity centres if we are really to understand the formation of political intention in a community.

LEADER GROUPS AND CLIQUES IN THE COMMUNITY

It is well known that the influence of informal leader groups in underdeveloped countries promotes the development of new techniques and new economic procedures. Thus the persons in question must have a high standing in the community, though – and this is typical – not necessarily the highest. For example, a community investigation in the Weserland in Germany showed that the people who displayed initiative were not necessarily those designated by 'office', though they certainly enjoyed a high reputation in the community and at the same time maintained connections with the outer world.[6] In our investigation in a co-operative village in the Saar-Pfalz it was seen that the activity of the community, which was organized in numerous co-operatives, did not spring at all from any institutionalized co-operative will, even of a minority in the village, but sprang exclusively from the initiative of the mayor, of a local prosperous peasant, and of the auditor of the co-operatives. These three individuals did not work together as officials, as executors of the formal administrative organization of the community, but as a small clique, or group, with its own particular and very definite ideas concerning the possibilities of this community for development. The completely informal character of their association was still further emphasized by the fact that although the mayor, who is again in office today, was deposed by the National Socialists in 1933, his successor did not dare to undertake any action at all without first consulting him as a private citizen. In 1945 the old mayor was restored to office and he promptly proceeded to carry out all the plans he had worked out in his enforced period of official idleness.[7]

In the same way Renate Pflaum showed the case of a community in the border district of the Westerwald, that at the local council elections it was not those organized in this or that party who had the advantage, but that, on the contrary, the parties had to win over the leading men in the community in order to put them forward as candidates.[8] Very aptly the parties referred to these men as the 'social activists'. Renate Pflaum continues her report as follows: 'The social control exercised by public opinion compels the party group, if it wishes to be successful, to adapt itself to existing conditions and to adopt the standards set up by the village ethos'.[9] And further: 'They therefore do not try to put the tried and trusted party official on the local council, but the man who has proved himself in years of daily living and working in the community to be a capable and helpful neighbour, an interested fellow citizen and a representative of the interests of the community'.[10] This also corresponds with the following table which illustrates opinions as to the likelihood of the exercise of influence on community affairs.[11] The influence is:

	Communal Affairs %	Governmental Affairs %
Possible	53·3	27·5
Impossible	42	63
No opinion	4·7	9·5

This clearly shows that most people think this influence is more significant in community affairs. When questions were put as to the reason for this, the majority cited personal connections:[12]

	%
By personal relations to elected officials	46·1
Through the Municipal Official personally	6·7
Through a political party	5·6
By letters	24·8
By elections	6·7
Miscellaneous and no opinion	10·1
Total	100·0

With this the importance of informal activities on the community is underlined once again.

It should be particularly noted that these informal cliques and groups were not investigated in the first place in small communities, where one would naturally have expected something of the sort, but actually in a small New England town of 17,000 inhabitants, the Yankee City which has already been mentioned. It was here that W. Lloyd Warner and his collaborators first established the concept as such, and then developed various ways in which to recognize its reality.[13] In relation to the class structure of this community it is interesting to note that nothing so firmly determines a man's position in the local community – apart from his membership of a particular family – than his membership of one or more of such cliques. As against the more structural nature of the social classes, it is shown here how to some extent real life breaks through the rigid class limits in that the cliques permit successful people a relationship with those higher in the social scale, and thus improves their prospects of rising. Here again, living processes take place in these small associations which extend far beyond the normal structure of class relationships.

Charles P. Loomis carried out similar investigations in smaller communities, supporting them with rich empirical data. At the same time he treated small cliques, informal friendship groups, and groups of relatives, or of people who under certain circumstances gave mutual assistance, as on a par. Incidentally, it was he who first raised the question of what was really decisive in this question of spatial proximity: the neighbourhood or the small groups cited.[14] He also records an extremely useful means for detecting and exposing these groups; namely through the mutual visits which their members regularly

pay each other. Further, the connection between clique formation and leadership functions in community affairs is particularly
obvious here. Finally he stresses very definitely that these small
groups are by no means specifically small community phenomena, but can be found in exactly the same way in larger towns
and communities.

In this connection we should like to draw attention to the
fact that not very long ago it was discovered what crises and
difficulties can be caused in a community when for some reason
or other this informal leadership breaks down. For example, in
Yankee City considerable tension developed in a local boot and
shoe factory because both the owner and manager no longer
lived in the community and was therefore in a position to
evade its control. Formerly he had been subject not merely to
the law 'but also to the far more compelling informal control
by the traditions of the community', with the result that
the mutual responsibility of factory owner on the one hand
and of the community on the other did not allow abnormal
tension to develop in the first place. But as soon as the social
structure of the factory extended beyond the limits of the community this relationship was of necessity fundamentally
changed. We can clearly observe the distinction here between
the economic and the social orders. The factory in question was
always dependent on the market; so much for the economic
factor. But now the social organization of the whole changed.
The higher factory hierarchy transferred itself to the great
administrative centres of industry, from where the regional or
national concerns which had developed are now controlled.
Further, labour relations were no longer determined by personal negotiations, but by negotiations between employers'
associations and labour unions, which are also usually outside
the community and often centralized. In such circumstances
factory workers can very easily feel that they are helplessly subject to 'anonymous' powers.[15] Apart from anything else, it is
made clear that despite the increase of his organizational and
practical power, a manager in large-scale undertakings loses the
informal personal prestige with the workers, with the result that
established labour relations in the community are thereby
jeopardized. On the other hand, it stresses the importance and
influence of the old-type factory owner who lived in the com-

munity – perhaps even grew up in it – and who after his death was still held up as an example of generosity and competence, and compared favourably with his successors; though during his own lifetime he may have been anything but an angel.[16] We must stress that this loss of prestige is a phenomenon which is not confined to industry, but is to be similarly found in the *élite* of the State administration.

Renate Pflaum is undoubtedly right when she points out in the German community investigation already mentioned[17] that political events take place not only on a national level but also and in the same way in the sphere of community and municipal administration (questions of road building, and so on). However, this does not as yet deal with the real problem. The question is this: where do the decisive impulses come from in the community sphere: from the formal administration, from the 'masses of the citizens', or perhaps from elsewhere after all? Of course, in the first place administrative and public rules and regulations are decisive, but at the same time it may very well be (in accordance with our whole procedure) that these factors – under certain circumstances, in exactly the same way as the traditional class structure – remain relatively unimportant when it comes to the real point, or limp along behind the real developments, and are even taken into tow by other forces and used in their interests.

During a community investigation conducted by Hansjürg Beck in a suburb of Zurich, it turned out, for example, that the purchases of land which started a rapid process of urbanization in a community which had previously been purely rural, were carried out by two people who were not members of the community and who came not from the town itself but from its rural hinterland. 'Misled by their rural origin, people treated them without prejudice or reserve, and took them, so to speak, into the village community; thus opening the door to their activities.' In face of this the local (peasant) administration (which at that time had no permanent paid positions, and was run exclusively by part-time volunteers who were paid only compensation for loss of time, etc.) proved too feeble; a certain official apathy set in and things were let slide so that in the end the incorporation of the municipality into the town of Zurich became inevitable.[18] This very characteristic development shows very clearly how the actual impulses for far-reaching developments can come from informal groups.

The investigation conducted by Renate Pflaum reveals, or at least suggests, the existence of similar problems, though they are not actually deduced.[19] At one point it is stated outright that there are no cliques in the investigated community,[20] whilst a few lines further on it is said that 'the leading groups in the individual spheres greatly overlap', so that the degree of the actual overlapping 'results in a connected, interlocking group'. In reality the investigation indirectly conjures up a picture of the overwhelming dominance of a small clique, to whose existence and significance only the investigators seem blind. Similarly, Charles P. Loomis has criticized 'the blind spot' in the eye of the agrarian sociologists,[21] who have so long ignored such phenomena. We must emphasize that one of the causes of this blindness both in Europe and in the United States is the ideology which regards the village community as 'a circle of fellows closely welded by destiny'. Any kind of uninhibited cliquism naturally seems quite out of place in such a community so therefore the existence of cliques is simply denied – on the old principle that 'nothing exists which ought not to exist'. However, a more realistic approach provides us with a very different picture, to which we shall return shortly when discussing class relationships. The fact is that an acknowledgement of the existence of such cliques is of decisive importance for any understanding of the relationship between rural and urban communities, and also to the disorganization of urban communities (particularly those of medium size), and to the serious consequences for a community by the desertion of its '*élite*', a phenomenon which we shall also discuss later.

Unlike the European attitude, these problems became the centre of vehement discussion in the United States during the past two decades, once industrial sociology had become aware of the importance of informal groups. Here too a preconceived ideology barred the way to understanding; in this case the 'American belief' in a society without cliques and classes, though this prejudice was soon destroyed by the realism of the sociologists. Incidentally, community sociology greatly contributed to a recognition of the real situation, because, of course, this realization came quite logically as a fulfilment of the postulate that the totality of the everyday reality of a community must be investigated objectively. Thus in their investigation of 'Middletown' the classic representatives of the new community investigations, Robert and Helen Lynd, stressed the great extent to which the functioning of the administration is affected by all kinds of background activities,[22] although, in the spirit of the age, they perhaps over-dramatize it by using the expression 'political machinery'. In using this expression they were probably thinking more of 'professional politicians' than the actual informal leadership and influential groups – as we can see from their remark that the professional politicians do not belong to 'the inner circle' of business people. Apart from this, however, they describe a series of informal associations in Middletown – beyond the business people, who are apparently not particularly interested in politics. It is also interesting to observe the various influences of other informal groups, for example, those with charitable objectives, on both working people and business people. Where working people are concerned this activity is more or less restricted to direct neighbourly assistance, whereas with business people the preference is for semi-personal contributions on specific occasions (Christmas, Thanksgiving Day). For the rest, the criss-cross activities of the numerous small groups in Middletown show how the fundamental structure of the class order develops in a vast network of mutual relationships, sometimes tending in the same direction as the fundamental structure, but just as often in a contrary direction, but in any case always tending to loosen the rigid system; growing up around it freely, and frequently taking a completely independent line.

Without dealing with all such investigations we should nevertheless like to mention two of the more recent investigations by Floyd Hunter, which make a clear distinction between the execution of a previously adopted policy and its original formulation. Whereas the former lies primarily in the hands of the formal bureaucracy, i.e. the administrative, police, educational and economic institutions, the latter lies chiefly in the hands of various informal groups in the community.[23] The question remaining is only how and through what 'channels' the agreed formulation is brought to the attention of the community. The family is not a particularly suitable instrument for the purpose;

the church is rather more so; but best of all are voluntary associations of all possible kinds in which the relationships are frequently very informal.

This is true not only of the Anglo-Saxon countries with their highly-developed club system, but also of Germany and other countries. This is clearly shown by the previously mentioned investigation into a Swiss suburban community in Zurich, which showed us the formation of a community or citizen's association at the direct instigation of the land speculators with a view to politically supporting the intentions of its founders, and obtaining the necessary public backing.[24] On the other hand, in the same community the voluntary fire brigade, for example, remained a bulwark of the old peasant ideas. Even though a certain number of agricultural labourers and townsmen were admitted, the leadership remained purely peasant, and revealed a strong cliquism amongst the old-established peasantry.[25] Thus this group represented a powerful centre for the formation of conservative ideas, despite the fact that its members came together for the very practical reason that in general peasant farmhouses present a greater fire risk than town dwellings. However, after the introduction of electric light, and the general architectural improvement of farmhouses, the voluntary fire brigade began to lose cohesion so that today its influence as a centre for the maintenance of conservative ideas is declining and its functions are becoming more of a social nature.

The German Westerwald community investigation previously mentioned also stresses that 'subordinate functions', chiefly of a social and local nature, play a big influence in the voluntary fire brigade there.[26] The same thing applies to other associations; even to the Carnival association, which bring the majority of the inhabitants together annually in a village festival. The specific political function of these associations as channels for influencing village opinion is also clearly visible, and they are described as 'a training ground for socially-active personalities'.[27] However, we must confess to some astonishment at the investigator's contention that 'neither the economic position, the religion, the birthplace, nor the membership of any definite socially privileged group plays such an important role as do personal interest, personal character, and willingness to play an active part',[28] whereas – as a glance at the statistics

reveals – working people are almost grotesquely under-repre-
sented as association leaders compared with the 'independents'
(farmers plus artisans). And when we are then told:

> The association leaders are often at the same time leaders of
> other fields of social life, whether in the local council, a co-
> operative or a party group, or, though less often, in a church
> group. The prestige which a leader obtains by his activity in
> such associations, and his reputation and importance as a
> capable man, can smooth his path to other leading positions.[29]

We can clearly see the political function of these groups, which
certainly have a much less formal character than the administration or the political parties. At the same time it becomes clear
that the mass of the citizens, i.e. the working people who represent 40 per cent of all gainfully employed persons, and are thus
the largest single group in the community in question, are not
represented in this way.

The final matter of interest is the identity of the people
behind the more prominently active association members; the
people who invariably refuse office in these associations on the
ground that they are 'too busy', but who are nevertheless
the only real powers behind the scenes in any given community
because they propose their own friends and associates for these
offices. The various office holders may then be regarded as their
mouthpieces. The way to understand these conditions is
through a careful analysis of the various very informal 'committees', 'study commissions', 'preparatory commissions', 'initiative committees' and so on, through which the influence of
the real powers that be in a community makes itself felt.[30]

An investigation carried out by Roland L. Warren into
'citizen activities' in the town of Stuttgart provides us with a
preliminary glimpse of the function and behaviour of such
groups in South-West Germany. Under citizen activities in the
community are included 'honorary, non-party and voluntary
activity directed to the good of the community as a whole'.[31]
This investigation shows very clearly that there are far more
groups of this type active in Germany than was supposed. On
the other hand, it also reveals a very strong authoritarian
attitude on the part of the authorities, who, apart from election
periods, 'do not allow themselves to be greatly disturbed by

public criticism'.[32] The most intensely active groups are those which represent certain very definite interests, and, in addition, specialized expert committees. It is characteristic – a point to which we shall return when we discuss community integration later – that the integrating activities of these groups are by no means merely local and communal, but 'vertical', exactly as the division of labour between the chief institutions of municipal life, so that 'the strongly marked demarcation lines' between the individual spheres of activity positively prevent the develop-ment of an expressly citizen activity. The result is a monopoly wielded by experts and authorities, 'whilst laymen are allegedly not competent for such functions'.[33] Here again we realize how important a knowledge of the historical conditions under which the community has developed is for an understanding of all these phenomena. In the case of Stuttgart we have a mixture of absolutist authoritarianism and a democratic system of citizen-ship. The latter is responsible for the great number of these groups, and the former for their ineffectiveness except where associations with very definite interests are concerned.

THE AUTHORITARIAN STRUCTURE AND THE RELATIONSHIPS OF POWER IN A COMMUNITY

The decisive point is: irrespective of whether the community as a global society is the only form of government (as a more or less institutionalized power) or whether it has other forms of global society above it (regional, provincial, federal or national in character), equally irrespective of whether the executive power of the community is autonomous in the real sense or merely 'delegated' from the State, the fact remains that the community itself represents a very important power centre in which certain persons can count on the obedience of others, and in which control over economic resources is available to such persons without this relationship being always formally reflected institutionally. Apart from those associations which represent a very definite interest (pressure groups) and therefore exercise an interested influence on affairs, there are numerous other power constellations which are not formally provided for in the official structure. It should be remembered, of course, that there are also numerous similar power relationships elsewhere; for example, in the economic system, where the theoretical freedom of the working class is often coupled with very practical dependence. However, the community remains the place where such power relationships of an informal nature are more clearly visible.

Accordingly we are in complete agreement with George C. Homans when he ascribes the social disorganization in the New England community of 'Hilltown' to the emigration of 'the old families', who were the real holders of power in the community. In practice this means that social interests retrogress, and thus also the social interactions of the inner system (feelings), the clarity and generality of social standards, and, finally, the leadership which is based on these standards. In so far as the effectiveness of social control depends on the maintenance of the above sequence, then in the last resort, this too must lose both its direction and its intensity.[34] We can therefore say that community policy represents the interests of the citizens of the community; but the question which now arises is: which circle of persons constitutes the citizens of the community at different times?[35] This question can be answered also in the community sphere by the well-known theory of Robert Michels that even where there is a 'democratic constitution' (in the sense of a formal institutionalized structure) the actual exercise of power remains oligarchic, and – as we must now add – usually extremely 'informal', so that the actual holders of power cannot always be readily identified.

Purely theoretically the consequence of this is that all those who pursue an active policy are 'men of power'; but not all men of power in the sense of a formal institutional dominance are therefore active politicians and thus the real wielders of power. In addition it must be stressed that this fluid system of power can function only in a socially accepted authoritarian order in which the number of those who formulate the policy to be carried out is incomparably fewer than the number of those who actually represent the executive.[36] In the case in question the executive is the formal administrative system. Let us ignore the resultant practical consequences of a planning, educational and municipal character, and stress only that a recognition of this very real situation does not in the least mean resignation, but, on the contrary, presupposes the necessity of building up

The structural aspect of the community

corresponding control institutions based on an adequate recognition of the facts; for example by an intensified development of general citizenship activity. Any adequate sociological understanding of the community structure requires that the background of these power relationships should be laid bare; and this is a task which has been receiving close attention on the part of community sociology in recent years.

We had decided to inquire first of all into the real processes of the exercise of power in the community, which are constantly in flux, and then to examine their structural suppositions. We will now consider the purely structural factor. Cliques and classes are completely separate from each other; nevertheless class-like formations can develop from cliques once these succeed in persuading the community to recognize their pretensions. However, such cases are rare, as H. H. Turney-High points out in his Belgian community investigation.[37] On the other hand, cliques often reveal class structures behind them, although the cliques themselves can display (and usually do) more vitality and more mobility than the class structure itself. In this respect organized associations are of particular interest, because they are naturally more rigid than cliques. It is highly illuminating to observe how the distribution of offices in such associations reflects the class structure behind them.

In an investigation of the English community Gosforth, W. M. Williams provides us with a very thorough review of these associations. His study indicates that a man's position in the class system predisposes him to the occupation of certain offices in the associations. At the same time the position occupied in the association is favourable to the prestige of the occupier. The investigator provides us with a table showing the class distribution of the members of twenty-three various associations,[38] and a table showing the class position of the individual officials (President, Vice-President, Secretary, Treasurer, and so on) and of the members.[39]

The first table shows us that there are very few associations whose members come from one class, or even from a few of the classes listed; whereas this is outstandingly true of the cliques whose existence is recorded. Only two associations consist of members of three classes only. On the other hand, there are also

1 GOSFORTH SHOW
2 WRESTLING ACADEMY
3 ANGLING CLUB
4 CHURCH COUNCIL
5 PARISH COUNCIL
6 BRITISH LEGION
7 WOMEN'S INSTITUTE
8 CONSERVATIVE CLUB
9 DRAMATIC ASSOC
10 PUBLIC HALL COMM.
11 FURTHER EDUC COMM.
12 READING ROOM COMM.
13 EVENING CLASSES
14 READING ROOM COMM.
15 MENS CRICKET
16 LADIES' CRICKET
17 TENNIS CLUB
18 FOOTBALL CLUB
19 BEAGLES & FOX HUNTING
20 MOTHERS UNION
21 G.F.S.
22 SPORTS COMMITTEE
23 SCHOOL OUTING COMM.
═══ OFFICIALS.

Class membership of committee members of formal and informal associations in Gosforth. From W. M. Williams *The Sociology of an English Village: Gosforth.* London 1956.

CLASS	PRESIDENT.	CHAIRMAN.	VICE-PRESIDENT & VICE-CHAIRMAN.	SECRETARY.	TREASURER.	COMMITTEE MEMBERS.
UPPER UPPER	○○○○○ ○○○○	○○○○ ○○○○ ○○○ ○ ○	○○○○○ ○	○		○○○○○○ ○○ ○
LOWER UPPER		○ ○○	○			○○○ ○○·○
INTERMEDIATE		○○○	○ ○	○○○	○	○○ ○○○ ○
UPPER MEDIAL		○ ○	○	○○○○	○○○○○ ○	○○○○○○○○○○ ○○○ ○○ ○○○○○ ○
MEDIAL	○	○○○	○ ○	○○○○ ○○○○	○○○○ ○○○○ ○○ ○	○○○○○○○○○○○ ○○○○○○○○○○○ ○○○○○○○○○○ ○○○○○○○○ ○○ ○○○○○○○○
LOWER MEDIAL			○○○○ ○	○○○○ ○○ ○	○	○○○○○○○○○○ ○○○○○○○○○○ ○○○○○○○○○○ ○○○○○○○○○○ ○○○○○○○○○○
LOWER						○ ○

○ = I PERSON

Distribution of members of the different social classes in Gosforth. From W. M. Williams *The Sociology of an English Village: Gosforth.* London 1956.

only two associations who have members culled from all seven of the classes listed. But the situation is very different indeed when we examine the leadership structure of these associations. We then see that with one exception all the presidents of these associations belong to the upper class. This one exception is, characteristically, the president of the theatrical association, who happens to be a member of the middle class. The lower classes are practically excluded from office, and there are only two of them who are committee members; the rest do not occupy any official positions whatsoever. In view of what these tables illustrate we may well begin to question the pious assumptions with regard to the alleged integrational effects of voluntary associations on community life.

THE PROBLEM OF SOCIAL STRATIFICATION
(CASTES AND CLASSES)

In any attempt to recognize the true nature of any community structure the decisive inquiry must be concerned with the social stratification of the community into castes and classes. Although this is a problem which certainly extends beyond the confines of the community, since it applies to all global societies as such, we can nevertheless study it in the community in a comparatively pure culture; particularly when the communities are not very large, since in this case we are not under the same obligation to prove the existence of social classes by complicated procedures in the first place, because we are able to recognize them immediately in the mutual relations between the members of the community, in the uniformity and differentiation of their behaviour, in the way in which they greet each other, talk to each other, regard each other, seek each other's company – or avoid it. Quite a number of American community studies are available which refer in particular to the class structure of the community.

It might, of course, be objected that the one aspect of stratification, i.e. by caste, is valueless for European conditions, seeing that such differences of birth as black and white play no role. However, it must not be forgotten that there are a great number of caste concepts still in existence, at least in European class ideology.[40] Further, it cannot be denied that the European class system is much more rigid than that of the United States, so that, in fact, it represents a phenomenon lying somewhere between class and caste. The caste characteristics would obviously be most evident when, say, a certain upper group in a community, on the basis of tacit understanding, operates a completely exclusive connubium of a caste character. As far-reaching problems relating to wealth (landed and industrial possessions) are usually involved, such phenomena are, indeed, of the greatest importance for the community structure. In general, though, problems of class structure are of much greater importance than those of caste so that we may confine our attention to the former. However, it should be pointed out that E. Digby Baltzell was able to show very clearly in an investigation of the upper layer of Philadelphia (which possessed its riches even before the Civil War) how a 'provincial aristocracy' can gradually develop by intermarriage with very definite caste characteristics – particularly where its exclusiveness is concerned – so that it is very different from the prosperous strata developing on a national basis.[41]

At the same time, it should be pointed out that in another respect the various books which have been written about the colour problem in the United States on a community level, or in the form of community investigations (such as those of John Dollard),[42] Hortense Powdermaker,[43] Allison Davis, Burleigh B. Gardner and Mary R. Gardner,[44] St. Clair Drake and Horace R. Cayton[45] and many others) have contributed a great deal to an understanding of community structure, since their chief subject is precisely the investigation of the influence exercised by the behaviour of people under the conditions of the double structure of class and caste, which is so typical of the mixed communities in the Southern States. However, the attitude of Black and White can be understood only in the mutual relationship of the two groups, though within each separate group class differentiations create additional problems. Although on a community basis the two groups are ecologically strictly separated, nevertheless regular interaction is inevitable between them, as well as the development of joint relationships, because the Negroes are progressively adopting an American scale of values. Further, investigations conducted and initiated by John Dollard have studied the psychological effects of these structural problems; naturally, the interaction of Negroes and Whites provided an extremely fruitful basis for the operation of the frustration-aggression pattern,* which in this case is caused largely by the structure of the Black-White mixed communities

---

* Described briefly, this means that the constant exclusion from certain social activities by the environment of those concerned must produce an increasingly aggressive reaction. The same pattern has been adopted with success to explain the attitude of the middle classes to the lower classes, and the latter's reaction to it. Examples of this will follow in the text.

of the Southern States. The sociological theory of learning has also received interesting impulses from this course.

THE CLASS PROBLEM IN THE COMMUNITY

Despite all this, however, the fact remains that the actual class problem is generally speaking more relevant to the formation of the community structure. The inner paradox of this problem has been summed up very succinctly by W. Lloyd Warner, in a way which is particularly illuminating as regards conditions in the United States. He says that on the one hand there is the democratic postulate that all men are equal, whereas on the other there is an attitude, which those who adopt it dare admit only indirectly, which assumes that men are fundamentally unequal; that a few are greatly superior to the many; and that the rest are inferior to them.[46] In 'Yankee City' he shows how life there is determined by a complicated system of rank and prestige, which is itself in the last resort determined structurally. An important mediatory role is played by associations of all kinds. Perhaps the most astonishing thing in all these investigations is the revelation that all members of a particular community are well aware of all the imponderables operating in the whole extraordinarily complicated system. In a very penetrating investigation of the community 'Elmtown', A. B. Hollingshead shows that even the adolescent youth is very well aware that although 'there are not supposed to be any classes; but there are'.[47] At the same time he demonstrates that the formation of cliques amongst the young people takes place well within the framework of the prestige groups of the adults, in that the influence of class prejudices is seen to be stronger even than the influence of parents.[48] Further, the interests of the various classes are just as manifestly different amongst the young people as amongst adults, even in a community of only 6,200 inhabitants. In such circumstances it is therefore quite out of the question to speak seriously of any community of feeling and judgement.[49] We shall return to this subject when we discuss community integration.

In order to avoid misunderstanding let it be said immediately that the inner divisions of a community have nothing to do with its size. In other words, it cannot be said, for example, that a small village community shows a tendency towards equality, whereas in towns, and in particular the large ones, the tendency is towards greater human inequalities. In every respect the facts reveal exactly the contrary, because the large towns of our highly-developed industrial societies develop altogether new kinds of differentiation beyond the problem of classes, whereas in the villages, on the contrary, the old class pattern persists practically unchanged. Even in such a small and uncomplicated community as 'Plainville' with its 275 inhabitants, which James West has described for us in such a penetrating fashion, the existence of social classes leads to deep divisions between the various groups in the population and greatly influences the behaviour of individuals.[50] Quite recently a similarly small community (280 inhabitants) in the province of Drenthe in the Netherlands was very carefully studied, with particular attention paid to the class structure. Although everyone in this community insisted 'we are all equal', and pointed out that class differences were very much greater in neighbouring (larger) communities, and in particular in the town of Groningen, the facts nevertheless demonstrated that despite its smallness this community had a very definite class stratification, which, according to the evidence of the historians and of the inhabitants themselves, was formerly even more definitive and binding than it is today.[51] The existence of a wide division between independent peasants possessing considerable land which has been in their families for a long time, and leaseholders is quite a common phenomenon in Europe; whilst the agricultural labourers and the few people of rank represent two quite different social groups again. Even when the equality of all is constantly stressed, the groups nevertheless separate on every possible occasion; and, in addition, the young people of the various groups marry only into their own class.[52] However, it is interesting to note that before the onset of puberty the children of all the social groups play together indiscriminately. Different behaviour is also expected of the various groups, a difference which extends even into their consumer habits.

Other studies have produced very similar results; for example, the investigation into Château Gérard.[53] Thanks to its clarity and logic this class system (only 4·84 per cent of the entire population remained unclassified or unclassifiable) can readily be compared with that of Lloyd Warner. The criteria of the structural differentiation at Château Gérard were obtained by discussions with Belgian informants; and this is a matter of importance, since otherwise the American author of the investigation might have introduced inaccurate points of view. Incidentally, in this case too the combination of class characteristics and ethnic characteristics is very illuminating; we find, for example, that in the heart of Walloon districts the Flemings primarily belong to the lower classes. Here too it is taken for granted that membership of this or that class must produce a difference of behaviour, including in this particular case a difference in the use of language too. The old upper layer of the community originally spoke Walloon, but then it gradually began to model itself on Paris and Brussels and to emigrate to other Belgian towns, with the result that only the middle and lower classes remained loyal to the old language, and because of this it gradually degenerated from a language into a dialect, which is now spoken only by 'uneducated' people. The Flemish lower group is unaffected by this particular development.

A similar problem of cultural division which runs to some extent parallel with the class structure can also be seen in the English village of Gosforth, a community which is particularly interesting to us because it is rather small, having only 723 inhabitants. Here too it is possible to classify almost all the inhabitants quite clearly.[54] The upper class is characterized in a typically English fashion according to birth, wealth and education. The latter division is very clearly marked in that the members of the upper class speak what might be described as 'Standard English', which is very different from the local dialect; this clearly demonstrates the inner homogeneity of this upper class and its separation from the other classes. On the other hand, trade, profession or occupation is not so decisive, as can be seen from the respective positions of the two doctors in the village. According to their profession both should belong to the upper class, but particular circumstances relegates the one to the lower upper class. Whereas the upper class is extremely homogeneous this is not true of the lower upper class, which consists of a number of families which are, for a variety of reasons, highly respected but not highly enough to make them members of the upper class. It is interesting to note that the investigator finds an intermediate class between the two upper classes and the three middle classes; an intermediate class which is neither fish, fowl nor good red herring. One of the families which belongs to this intermediate class has come into the community from outside. A characteristic feature is also the general attitude of the upper classes to the lowest class, whose members are usually referred to in very uncomplimentary ways. As this particular class has no material possessions it can only be classified by its behaviour. Incidentally, the members of this class are well aware of their reputation in the community, and this provokes extremely aggressive reactions, including on suitable occasions the use of obscene language. Here we see another example of the reality of the frustration-aggression pattern though in quite different conditions from those which exist in the Southern States of America. Further, the situation offers us an excellent example of the vicious circle – the 'self-fulfilling prophecy', as Robert K. Merton has called it. Under the influence of the contempt expressed for it by the upper classes, the lowest class becomes resentful, rough and aggressive in its behaviour, whereupon this behaviour is immediately taken by the upper classes as a confirmation of its own opinions of the lowest class in the first place.

THE DIFFICULTIES OF CLASS CLASSIFICATION

Occasionally it has been objected that these so-called social classes, which decisively (if not exclusively) determine the structure of the community, are sometimes regarded as tangible realities in the same way as ecologists once regarded their ecological units and sub-units.[55] However, with few exceptions, this is not really so, though, admittedly the choice of language sometimes suggests that it is. Fundamentally, ideas of this sort would lead us back to a substantialist interpretation of these social groups. However, social classes are not in the least stable, but are, in fact, highly dynamic units with very different degrees of structural formation. It is a fact, as any community investigation can easily prove, that practically every member of a community has a tendency to classify himself, and others, in relation to others. The characteristics may therefore be very varied and in part highly complicated; and they may be more or less formal, such as the distinction between established local citizens and inhabitants of lower status, which may possibly involve differences in rights too; or the distinction between old-established residents, newcomers, commuters, and – in post-war Germany – the distinction between old-established inhabitants and evacuees and refugees. There may be one intermediate group (or more) difficult to classify. In particular the existence of such class evaluations in the minds of the citizens of a community can be seen in the division between an absolutely upper class and an equally absolutely lowest class, which is often regarded as a source of criminal tendencies, even when this is quite untrue.

Such differentiations defeat without further ceremony all opposing ideological systems which repeatedly assert that, of course essentially, all men are equal. This differentiation between the extremes does not correspond with two species of human beings, at least in so far as no caste relationships or ethnological minorities are present. In these cases the existing structural differences will become more pronounced because of social prejudices which exacerbate the separation of the classes into true discrimination. However, it is made particularly clear here that we are dealing only with 'points of view', and only with perspectives of a complex system. But as our opinions determine our actions, very definite behaviour patterns result from these opinions, and impress their stamp on the power structure of the community. The difficulties of mastering these problems and making them clear to everyone lie in the fact that in most cases the deciding factor is not 'social position', 'profession', 'trade', 'occupation', 'income', or anything else as tangible, but an extremely complicated amalgam of given situation, self-estimation and appraisal by others. Certainly origin, birth, long-standing citizenship, profession or occupation, wealth (and whether it has been in existence for one or two generations), education, place of residence, and so on, represent contributory factors. But apart from such matters, there are innumerable traditional ideas and standards which are equally important and which naturally greatly complicate the problem, as also these concepts are extraordinarily variable by regions.[56]

The structural aspect of the community

When we speak of social classes on a community level we must stipulate that generally speaking two very different factors combine, namely, (1) a stratification on the basis of objective facts, which determines the whole level of life and also the separation of the various classes from each other. In the global societies, such as the nation, which are superior to the community, this stratification is usually relatively uniform (sometimes developing even further as an accompanying feature of certain economic systems which are more than national). (2) A stratification on the basis of subjective factors which determine the rank and prestige of the citizen over and above his economic status. Of course, these two factors do largely conform, but not altogether; and that is precisely the point. In the present connection we are dealing exclusively with the latter system of stratification. And when we deal with the more objective stratication factors we will find that they are always seen only through the preconceived notions which the members of the community already hold. This, of course, does not exclude the possibility of an analysis of social classes on a totally different basis; but it must be stressed that all general class analyses at a community level are to some extent unreliable because the class borderlines often shift; because, according to the nature of the community, quite different groups can appear from time to time as the prestige classes; and, finally, because class status is determined only by the community evaluation of rank and prestige and is by no means given from the start. At the same time in all cases concrete behaviour plays a central role, and this is taken as the essential preliminary for the differentiation of classes and groupings in a community.

In such a situation the historical preliminary conditions of a given social tradition will naturally make their influence felt, with the result that it is not only very difficult to compare various societies, but also to transfer essential categories which may be valid for one society to the other (or even from one region to another, as we have already seen in our discussion of community typology). At the moment when we are interested in estimates and standards of value any comparison becomes extremely difficult. On the other hand, the structure and the integrational type of a community develop only with these standards of value. This is perhaps the biggest dilemma in which community sociology finds itself today. The structure of the community is determined more by certain standards of value, which are translated into reality by social control and thus become forms of settled behaviour, rather than by the prevailing economic forms. To quote Theodor Geiger, who investigated these problems in a Danish middle-sized town (a community of about 100,000 inhabitants) : 'It is no longer true to say that a given person takes this or that rank in the general evaluation on account of his social status; on the contrary, the individual social strata are characterized, amongst other things, by their various social ideas and scales of value".[57]

In his investigation of Gosforth, W. M. Williams has paid close attention not only to the way individual classes describe themselves,[58] but also to the way in which they describe the other classes.[59] His survey is of particular value because it really does approach completeness. The language differentiations used to express these 'social perspectives' are most amusing and diverting. It is, of course, quite obvious that such very subtle shades of opinion must exercise a big influence on everyday life, because they determine the relationship of people to each other. In his investigation of Plainville James West makes a somewhat similar attempt which is particularly important because it refers to a very small community. Here too, we are shown not only a complicated class system as such, but, over and above that, a supplementary differentiation according to 'social perspectives'. The objective class structure itself is based on the nature of landed property (in the prairie with good land, in the hills with poor land), on the standards of technical equipment on the individual farms, on origin, wealth and general standards of morality (honesty and sobriety, particularly with regard to the consumption of alcohol). In addition, as a subjective characteristic, comes the question of 'behaviour', which is an extremely complicated criterion, because everything which has previously been mentioned now mingles, and because it leads to an infinite variety of situations in which the accepted prestige order expresses itself. But having said this we must immediately add that this outlook is characteristic only of the upper group; the other groups may well have a totally different viewpoint, particularly when they pass judgement on the various other classes.

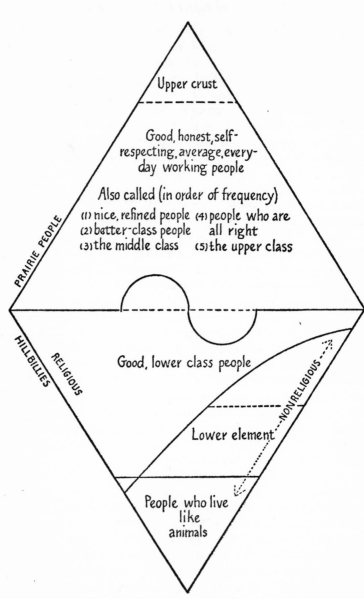

Plainville class scheme. From James West *Plainville U.S.A.*
New York, 1945, *page 117.*

(Reprinted with kind permission from Columbia University Press)

The structural aspect of the community

All these questions would be of relatively minor importance for understanding the structure of a given community, but for the fact that the problem of social control, i.e. the prevailing standards, whose observance is regarded as 'right', is closely connected with them. For example, according to George C. Homans: The closer an individual or a sub-group approaches to the realization of general group standards in all his, or its, activities, the higher is the social rank of this individual or of this sub-group.[60] The observance of the given standards by this individual or this sub-group represents social control,[61] from which it follows that class order and the system of values – at least on a community level – cannot be separated from each other. We must be quite clear in our minds that the form of social control usually exclusively considered, although it is an essential form of regulation where social behaviour is concerned, is the standard of justice which arises very late indeed in development and even then affects only a very small part of our social behaviour. The much more comprehensive part of social control and the part which is far more important for our everyday existence, is, on the other hand, of a more informal nature, and it becomes effective through the various forms of habit and custom and also through gossip, rumour and various forms of public opinion whose determination is an essential function of the community structure. Thus as a general rule the uppermost group in society most clearly represents the traditional values of a community, and the lower we go in the social scale the greater become the deviations, parallel with – to quote Robert C. Angell – 'the incompatibility' of social standards, which can definitely influence the integration of the community. This is invariably the case, for example, when an old-established community is infiltrated by a new population, perhaps of immigrants, evacuees or refugees, whose standard of values differs from that upheld in the community. If this influx is not on a large scale, then the interlopers either have to conform, or find themselves pushed out to the periphery of the community, where they persist as 'marginal existences'. But if the influx is on a larger scale, perhaps very large, then the whole social system of the community under certain circumstances may well be deeply affected.

At this point we can observe the significance of social change for the community, which means essentially that the standards of value of a community (which are not in themselves fixed, but are in 'fluid balance') are so decisively changed by influences from within and outside that integration cannot develop, or at the very least strong conflicts of loyalty arise between differently aligned standards of value. Modern sociological investigation has paid special attention to this process; particularly Robert and Helen Lynd in their study of *Middletown in Tradition* (1937) in which they investigated the effects of the 1929 economic crisis. But we also meet similar ideas in the investigations already mentioned dealing with the mixed colour communities in the Southern States; as well as in Robert Redfield's double investigation of the Chan Kom community in Mexico.[62] Both in Europe and in the United States a very special form of social change is often important, namely the rural-urban relationship (exemplified in the Darmstadt study in Germany) though it is by no means an isolated aspect of this question. The same is true of the agrarian-industrial contrast, which G. Wurzbacher had particularly in mind. However, the development has, as has already been frequently pointed out, gone far beyond this point, which – as Conrad M. Arensberg showed only recently[63] – is connected with the centralistic system of the railway age, but which must change rapidly in the age of the motor-car, which is not bound to any rigid lines. As the population becomes more mobile so the rigid barriers between town and country break down, and other problems of social change arise; for example in the immediate post-war period, the refugee question presented many difficult problems in a number of countries (Israel, India, Germany), problems we shall consider in greater detail later on when we come to the question of community integration. A great deal of work in this respect has already been done by that branch of sociological investigation which deals with the under-developed countries.

CHAPTER IX

THE INTEGRATION OF THE COMMUNITY

The problem of community integration has come up again and again throughout this book, though so far we have not considered it closely. However, now that we have broached the community structural problem, the question of integration becomes the real central point of our subject. On the other hand, we have not neglected it too long, because a whole series of preliminary questions had first to be cleared up before we could directly approach the question of community integration.

THE FUNDAMENTAL PREJUDICE OF THE 'WHOLISTIC' APPROACH

In our view the decisive mistake made in most of the earlier studies was that the problem was approached in the wrong order; that is to say the integration of the community was put forward first as though that were a matter of course, and all other problems were examined from this essential pre-condition. This was due in part to general historical–philosophical ideas such as those of Ferdinand Tönnies, who held that the whole development of social humanity fulfilled itself from the community to society. In this respect the word community means, amongst other things, a properly integrated living together, a state in which men 'remain attached despite all divisions', whereas in society no inner unity is ever possible. Tönnies illustrates his point by the contrast between organic and 'mechanical' development. To some extent similar ideas arise though in a less pretentious form when 'small' communities are credited with such homogeneity, which is denied the town, and particularly the big town, whose character is alleged to be fundamentally different. The most important representative of this viewpoint today is Robert Redfield, whose debt to Tönnies is so obvious that it goes practically without saying. In his book *Small Community* he regards it directly in the sense of an 'integral whole', and throughout the book he stresses his 'wholist' and 'seeing the matter as a whole' approach.[1] We take Redfield as the particular representative of this outlook because his outlook really is based on empirical experience with his subject, and not on purely literary documentation or on ideologically coloured preconceived opinions – like the outlook of most of the German theoreticians.[2] Despite the undeniable realism which is often visible in his work and that of his pupils, we must, in view of everything we have already said here, divorce ourselves from him and his ideas.

A few years ago a highly interesting discussion took place between Robert Redfield and Oscar Lewis, who re-investigated the Mexican community of Tepoztlán on the basis of the investigation made seventeen years earlier by Redfield, and came to quite opposite conclusions.[3] As the opinions of Lewis coincide largely with our own we propose to deal with them briefly here, and also with Redfield's reply. Redfield's book describes Tepoztlán as a well-balanced and harmoniously integrated community – which goes far to explain the great interest the book aroused on publication.[4] Incidentally, we do not propose to assume, as Lewis does, that Redfield started his investigations with the preconceived antithesis borrowed from Tönnies: 'folk culture' and 'urban culture', and therefore unconsciously looked for it in his material.[5] He may very well have been fascinated and carried away by this form of life, and, as he says himself,[6] have developed the pair of concepts only afterwards. If this is so, he is certainly not the first fugitive from industrialism who has been carried away by the infinite charm of the Mexican landscape and its Spanish–Indian culture. However, we feel that the problem lies deeper. A very important point that strikes us at once is that in all probability – as Lewis suggests – Redfield completely failed to understand the economic situation, because – like most European analysts of the village – he just overlooked the existence of a sub-peasant population owning no property at all. This alone would effectively prevent his ever getting the problem of integration properly focused.

And this is much more important than the question of whether the community had fundamentally changed in the intervening seventeen years. Of course, such changes had occurred, and Lewis himself points them out. But this does not affect the essential point, which is, as we have indicated above, of a structural nature. This community also revealed tensions originating from the earliest colonial period, and quite powerful enough to ensure that there could be no integration. Perhaps integration will develop at some time in the future once the new Mexican culture which is arising from the revolution has had a chance to form and set. At present, however, there is no trace of it.

In view of this situation it is interesting to see what Redfield himself had to say to Lewis. His reaction revealed the naïveté of his attitude with shattering clarity. His argument boils down quite simply to the observation that one investigator stresses 'this' whilst the other stresses 'that',[7] that there are many parallels for his pair of concepts, folk and urban culture; and that one must, like Tönnies, see them in relation to individual phenomena as 'complementary concepts' and 'in combination'.[8] Tönnies himself also uses this rather unimpressive argument.[9] It fails to recognize that the whole preliminary assumption is false, and that we are not dealing with a categorization of this or that type, but with a structural question, which must be settled before any conclusion concerning integration or non-integration can be arrived at. Then, in particular, comes the property question and this is essentially connected with the class system, then comes the population pressure, which it is impossible to evade, and, finally, the other factors which cause tension, distrust and reserve, even though they may not express themselves in open acts of violence. We may, in fact, conclude that Redfield's answer to Lewis is no answer at all, but merely an indirect admission that he has not yet grasped the real problem.

INTEGRATION NOT A MATTER OF SIZE

If we stand by our definition that a community is a local group in which men react to each other, work together, linked by common bonds, then we can only say that to burden it with the further condition that the community must therefore be an integral 'whole' is going too far. The social reality of interaction between men linked by common bonds does not exclude the existence of powerful inner tensions, definite power groupings, and even a lack of inner homogeneity, which can, under certain circumstances, break into open conflict. Incidentally we must insist here that the chances of such inner conflicts are, under certain circumstances, much greater in a small community than in a larger one, precisely because the members of the smaller community are closer to each other. Where conflicts arise in a small community the only way to avoid them is usually by leaving the community altogether, or by being content to lead a marginal existence; whereas in a town it is much easier to establish a 'defensive distance' which makes it possible to avoid acute conflicts, or at least to ameliorate them. On the other hand, of course, we are certainly not saying that the small community in Redfield's sense can never be an integral whole. To do this would be to fall victim to the same prejudice, but in reverse.

The only rational solution of this problem seems to us as follows: a small community in Redfield's sense can be an integrated whole, but it need not necessarily be so; and certainly not on the grounds of its small size. If in our efforts to define the community, the question of the difference between primary and secondary characteristics is ever to be of any importance then that is the case here. For the time being no conclusions relating to the quality or the inner structure of this conception as an integral whole can be drawn from our assumption that the community is a social co-operating group on a local basis and with a common standard of values – that is to say, if we are to speak of the community at all in the sociological sense. Even when the in-group out-group relationship begins to operate, in that those who live and work together begin to develop their own joint aims and standards of value in contrast to other communities of a similar nature, we must still reckon with the fact that internally there will be a strong power gradient between the different groups and any suggestion of integral homogeneity must be illusory. This can be seen very clearly in the mixed-colour communities in the Southern States of America, where the two groups which make up the community are strictly separated by an insuperable barrier of colour, notwithstanding the fact that today both groups, Whites and Negroes, accept the same standard of values, namely the standard of the White middle classes. On the other hand we must add that this does not necessarily exclude such an integral homogeneity in some distant future. We shall return to this question later, and for the moment it is sufficient to say that we must not presume such a development by definition, as Tönnies, Redfield and all those of similar opinions invariably do. This is true not only of the 'bigger' communities, where it is regarded more or less as a matter of course, but particularly of the smaller communities – as can be seen from numerous examples.

BIOTIC COMMUNITY AND SPATIAL INTEGRATION

The most elementary explanatory method for such a direct inner homogeneity of life is undoubtedly to treat the human community as though it were a biotic association. Although one might have a certain right to assume this with regard to the family as a reproductive group, the assumption is pushed *ad absurdum* immediately by the fundamentally more complex cultural level of the local association compared with pure kinship groups. But when we remember that in the sociological sense even the family is a specific cultural phenomenon in that the upbringing of offspring amongst human beings on the basis of their particular biological situation does not proceed according to purely natural factors, but is dependent on 'tradition', then, *a fortiori*, the untenability of the biological analogy should become quite clear. Incidentally, in the same way this excludes the supposition that small communities of human beings are in some way 'more right' than big communities – as we have already seen in our first chapter – merely because higher mammals also live in such small groups. Although it is certainly true that no human communities could exist without a general biotic association, we must nevertheless not forget the specific characteristic of human communities, namely that as the local form of social association, they are and will remain simultaneously and essentially cultural.

But when it is admitted that the biotic association does not perhaps suffice to ensure the integral homogeneity of the community there is still, secondarily, the spatial factor, which is so often strongly underlined. Here, however, it can be shown on the basis of numerous investigations that the spatial factor in itself also does not necessarily create such an integral homogeneity. In fact research seems fairly generally to suggest that on its own the spatial factor operates only in exceptional circumstances towards integration, for example in the case of new settlements. And even here it seems to operate so strongly only because at first there is no opportunity for adopting other methods of social co-operation. But one way or the other it is frequently seen that the spatial factor is soon displaced, at least partially, by other factors, for example by so-called cultural affinities.

Of course, occasionally the existing spatial circumstances remain so obvious that one is involuntarily tempted to argue from the outer homogeneity to an inner homogeneity. Consider, for example, the case of a village of the rock inhabiting Indians in the Canyon de Chelly in Arizona, or in the Mesa Verde, where the oval hollowings out in the rocks act as a kind of framework which not only determines the architectural shape of the village but also its inner relationship. On the other hand, however, we regularly find various *kiwas* (underground cult chambers) in these troglodyte villages, and hence we conclude that the existence of a multiplicity of cults must have created an inner differentiation, which, similarly, must tend to separate rather than to unify. Or consider the late medieval Italian and Sicilian communities which lived high up in the rocky hills, and whose houses were crowded so closely together that one might suppose the situation sufficient guarantee for a completely integrated homogeneity. But, in fact, we know that precisely these communities were rent by a vehement party and faction system; so much so that there was sometimes an open state of war within the community, and each house was transformed into a fortress, as, for example, in San Gimignano in Tuscany. Just like the biotic association, the spatial factor is an analogy which must not be pushed too far. The same is also true of certain tendencies in modern architectural layout and town planning, whose originators believe that the spatial and architectural layout provided is in itself sufficient to guarantee the new communities an inner social fulfilment. From what we already know of the extremely problematical influence of the spatial factor in the social association of human beings this is undoubtedly an illusion.

THE OUTER AND INNER SYSTEM OF THE COMMUNITY

Thus if neither the biotic association nor the spatial factor are in themselves sufficient to guarantee integral homogeneity, then nothing remains but to look for this homogeneity within the framework of social and spiritual association as such. As however no community exists in a vacuum, we must first examine its spatial relationships, and in general its relationship to its environment, before we can consider the question of its inner homogeneity. Following the example of George C. Homans we shall call the first the 'external system' and the second the 'internal system'. In accordance with our previous definition of community, the external system is easy to define; it is nothing but the essence of all the activities, interactivities and connections by means of which the group maintains itself in its environment. Certainly, this is only one side of the question; and the total social system needs the addition of the internal system. However, it is important to keep the two systems separate from each other at first, as their mutual relationship is by no means as clear as has sometimes been assumed. Returning to the problem of spatial proximity once more, we should be inclined to say that under certain circumstances the spatial form does create social connections (so much for the external system), but that subsequently other factors come into operation and overcome the purely spatial factors (so much for the internal system). As Homan has indicated, the same state of affairs can be expressed differently and more generally. Are we to say that a community which masters its environment simply 'adapts' itself to this environment? The word 'adaptation' itself is, in fact, ambiguous. Is it to be understood only in the sense that the specific characteristics of the group are determined by its environment? Clearly not, because, as we have seen, these characteristics do not come only from outside, but also, and in exactly the same way, from within. It can therefore happen that whilst a group with its specific characteristics survives in its environment, that environment itself changes in time; and in this case the passive adaptation turns into a socio-cultural creative adaptation.[10]

Thus in the first aspect the group is under pressure from without, and in the second it reacts to this pressure. But precisely here inner differentiations become visible, and they need not necessarily develop in line with the pressure from without. In the words of Homans we may regard 'the external system as a group attitude which allows the group to survive in its environment; and the internal system on the other hand as a group attitude which is the expression of mutual feelings developed by the members of the group in the course of their living together'.[11] With this a standard of values and a group culture arise simultaneously, and create an inner gradient to the extent that the expected attitude of the one is regarded as representing the group relationship, whilst the attitude of the other is not. For example, we are told in *Plainville* that the upper class is 'good', 'honest' and 'respectable', whilst the lower class consists of people 'who live like animals'.[12] With the projection of the activities of members of a community to cultural standards a ranking system appears within which the one member will better attain the expected standards than the other. But under certain circumstances this distance and its extension can decide the question of integration or non-integration, because conflicts of standards now arise which can develop into social conflicts if they have not arisen from them. This was ultimately the standpoint from which Robert C. Angell developed his typology of communities. The essential difference between our view and those of Angell, and to some extent those of Homans, lies in the fact that for us this whole problem begins immediately with the small community, as we shall now see in a series of examples.

NON-INTEGRATED GROUPINGS IN THE VILLAGE

Recently in Germany Hans Linde and H. Tenhumberg discussed this problem, and Tenhumberg described the whole situation of the village in its environment as 'a settlement in which the common life of the inhabitants was led on the basis of some form of agricultural activity naturally associated in the form of a community'. The word community here is to be understood as Tönnies understood it. From this Tenhumberg then developed the concept of an 'unconscious association of the whole village', something which is supposed to indicate the temperature of the internal system in direct reaction to the conditions of the external system. With this, of course, two questions are raised, one historical, the other systematic. The former would have to provide proof that in fact the integration of the community did at one time come about in the form of an 'unconscious association'. The latter, on the other hand, would have to develop the concept of a quasi-natural association as a direct reaction to the specific environmental situation of peasant agricultural activity.

We are not in a position to go into the matter thoroughly here, but we can say that this concept of the unconscious association is just as untenable as that of a biotic association or of an association determined simply and solely by the spatial factor. All it does is to continue on a new stage of consciousness, namely that of spiritual association, the old idea of organic growth, which, as we have already seen, either underestimates or even completely ignores, the decisive factor of human communities, namely the factor of culture and the specific standard of values. Of course, this does not exclude the possibility that sometimes a small community may form such an unconscious association. But far from being the rule, it is, in fact, a very rare exception, and will probably remain in existence only for short periods. It is easy to see why this is so: wherever a total social system develops we find such great inner differentiation, including standards of value, that it would be altogether senseless to talk of any unconscious association.

Apart from this systematic question, the historical question which remains to be answered is: 'whether this leading idea of the unconscious association of the whole village ever had a real social and political background at any period of time open to our knowledge?'[13] With this Linde has really summed up the whole problem very clearly indeed. Without attempting to go back to the history of the village community in primeval times, we can nevertheless say that quite early on its structure evinced very clear factors which make such an unconscious association impossible. Thus this concept reflects either a sentimental wish-dream or a special aspect of the national socialist theory of the 'master race', as displayed very clearly in the work of Gunther Ipsen, who regarded the lower strata of the old village, i.e. the landless inhabitants (hands, day labourers, and so on) as the antithesis of the old long-established peasant families, as 'the ultimate social stratum of definite village poverty . . . as the self-productive misery of anti-racial selection' – to fall back into the jargon of the National-Socialist era.[14] From Ipsen's standpoint, of course, these strata did not come into question for 'true association' such as he had in mind. Thus this conception of the community is revealed as the ideology of the landed classes, and therefore as very narrowly limited. First of all, never at any time did the village community consist only of landed peasants, but always contained such elements as rural artisans and other tradesmen; and secondly, the community of old-established landholding peasants are paralleled by a community of mere inhabitants which very early on showed all the characteristics of differentiated composition. Now although it is quite certain that many of these outsiders ultimately succeeded in obtaining the same privileges as the old-established group, at the same time conditions continually brought in more and more outsiders with lesser rights than the old-established inhabitants – from the Middle Ages down to the present day. And this went on irrespective of the internal changes which took place in agriculture, such as the transition from the ox to the horse as a draught animal – whose importance Linde indicates. The increased volume of work to be performed required supplementary hands, and 'the additional smallholdings as the social source of the production of hands thus founded a semi, or sub-peasant stratum.'[15] The given structural conditions produced this group which was far from integrated into the village community; it was in fact so little integrated that the economic historians almost forgot its existence until quite recently, with the result that they gave us a very one-sided picture of the medieval village community. In addition to all this, there were regular expulsions from the old social system – of 'dishonest men' for example. And this took place to such an extent that it is reckoned that they accounted for about 15 per cent of the total rural population, who thus led a very definitely marginal existence.[16] In the towns this group sometimes accounted – together with the poor and the incapacitated – for as much as 50 per cent of the total urban population.[17]

It must be pointed out that under various circumstances such under-strata can form repeatedly. They can exist for short or long periods. These elements were then joined by innumerable refugees and vagabonds from the Thirty Years War, crippled soldiers for example, and other uprooted elements who wandered over the countryside. Then in the nineteenth century came railway builders, often from Eastern Europe or Italy, who settled in village communities; then in the coal-mining districts there were miners, also brought in from abroad; and finally, in more modern times, there were the evacuees, refugees, displaced persons, deportees, people expelled from areas occupied by the German forces as collaborators with national socialism, and so on. For example, two separate Dutch community investigations carried out after the war listed such isolated sub-groups in the community as 'collaborators', and 'Members of the Dutch National Socialist Party'.[18] The same is true of the immigration of ethnic minorities, who are discriminated against by the other inhabitants of the village, as numerous American studies show.[19]

An extremely informative investigation in this respect was that conducted into the French community of Nouville by Lucien Bernot and René Blancard.[20] This investigation shows how under pressure from the new lower sub-groups the old-established and formerly distinct groups of independent peasants and dependent tenants tend to unite to defend themselves against this pressure. In this case too it is very clearly demonstrated that despite the smallness of the community (594 inhabitants only) and despite the general clarity of the situation, special circumstances prevent the development of integration. At the same time, the historical investigation shows that the situation must have existed for a long time, for almost two hundred years in fact. Two very different cultures, social forms and economic types clash here; namely, workers and peasants, who simply cannot unite. This is also expressed ecologically in that the different groups live apart from each other. It also expresses itself in two quite different attitudes to the world, to space and to time. Surprisingly a very stable development of the formal power structure is revealed: for a very long time (almost a century) the mayors of the community have all been chosen from the same family. The population is extremely fluid. The first factory, a glass works, was founded in 1776, and the second in 1887. In times of prosperity this means a constant influx of workmen, and not only from the immediate neighbourhood. Further, from the middle of the eighteenth to the middle of the nineteenth centuries, Nouville had an orphanage for illegitimate and abandoned children from Paris and Rouen. Because of these circumstances there was a steady influx into the community of complete strangers without any family ties; this was aggravated by the fact that the glass works preferred child labour. This, by the way, also means that the childhood of many of the glass workers was very definitely unhappy; which is a circumstance which must be taken into consideration when considering their strangely apathetic attitude and their mental isolation from the rest of the community. On the other hand there are the peasants, who are typically over-represented in the local council, because the working men have never succeeded in uniting against them.[21] Given all these circumstances, it is not surprising to find that the 'community' in Nouville is more remarkable for disunity than co-operation.[22] This unusual structural constitution makes its effects felt in every direction, with the result that even the daily behaviour of the population is affected by it. The truth is that two quite different systems are interlocked here, and they have never succeeded in attaining any integration.

We have dealt with this case in rather more detail because it gives a valuable insight into the variety of circumstances which can spontaneously and repeatedly cause new sub-peasant groups to arise in a rural community. It is thus far from being a uniform process whose course can be more or less clearly surveyed. On the contrary, such under-privileged groups can arise out of the most astonishing circumstances in any given community; something that no general survey can adequately convey, and which therefore requires numerous monographs. However, it must be borne in mind that we are not dealing here with a mere coincidence or some avoidable accident. On the contrary this development is definitely structurally predetermined just as the community is, among other things, also regarded as an expression of its own standards of value. Then the situation in which newcomers (irrespective of the reason for their arrival, provided only that they are 'different') are always regarded as less privileged, must of necessity be constantly repeated.

LIMITS TO INTEGRATION

When we review the literature about community studies which we have, we see that there are many reasons why a small community cannot become an 'integrated whole', although it may well be a unit of a local nature with social interactions and its own aims and standards of value. The reasons which prevent integration may well express themselves ecologically. Thus Richard Thurnwald refers to a type of living together which he calls chequered, in which various groups live separately side by side without interfering with each other.[23] Generally speaking he has primarily different ethnic groups in mind. It should be stressed here that this 'chequering' is something quite different from ecological segregation, which is so often encountered in ethnical minorities, for example, the Negroes in the Southern States of America. Here the people are settled at random; they interact, they work together, and they therefore of necessity have interests in common, but at the same time they remain culturally deeply separated, and thus no real community integration comes about. Similar circumstances can also be found in the American South West, where Ladinos (Spanish-speaking Americans), Mormons, Indians, Texans (who migrated there at the end of the twenties) and actual Anglo-Saxons have settled together. Thus we see in practice that various groups, which differ considerably, can settle down together side by side, mingled within the same locality without the development of an integral homogeneity, although they nevertheless form a community. Usually communities are not only differentiated by class distinctions, but also prevented thereby from developing any homogeneous integration. This can be seen clearly in connection with a dwarf community like Plainville, or like Anderen in the Dutch province of Drenthe, where the community falls into a number of sub-groups which do not overlap.[24] In addition still further cultural differences arise, for example in the English community of Gosforth, where the classes are still further divided by their manner of speech; this is the case in the Belgian community Château Gérard.[25] There can be sub-groups in a community anywhere, which are more or less respected according to the extent to which their behaviour approximates to the group standard. When, as is the case here, a community is defined, among other ways, by the existence of common ideas and standards of value, then this means that in principle there can be groups which live as sub-groups in a larger relationship without participating in or accepting these standards of value. Incidentally, this can also be the case without the community thereby becoming disorganized, as Homan showed in his analysis of Hilltown.[26]

Finally it must be pointed out that even biological reasons can prevent the development of integration. For instance, it is often the case that whilst children are naturally regarded by adults as belonging to the family, they are at the same time considered only in part subject to the laws of the community. Accordingly they enjoy great 'permissiveness' when they deviate from established standards of conduct. This seems to be a fundamental trait of Japanese community life, as John F. Embree has pointed out.[27] This expresses itself in a sort of 'diminished responsibility', and hence children in general, and often adolescents as well, are regarded as not completely integrated in the community. Because of this situation special institutions evolve whose object is to bring about and stress the complete transition from childhood and adolescence to adulthood. The consequences of this partial integration are clearly visible. For example there is often a relative indifference to pre-marital sexual intercourse amongst young people; whereas with the engagement, or the start of puberty, the sexes are at once separated from each other, and strictest sexual abstinence becomes the rule – something which can be seen very clearly in the Japanese community. But this is only one of many examples. This partial integration of children and adolescents is paralleled at the other end of the age scale by a far-reaching 'release' of old people from the community relationship. In recent years this problem has been examined from many angles. For us the relevant point here is that we have a group which is regarded as only part-integrated and this guarantees those in question a much greater degree of freedom from the bonds of community life.

The integration of the community

And, finally, there are the temporarily or permanently sick and isolated in the community, such as people in hospitals, lunatic asylums, prisons and penitentiaries of all kinds. They are also no longer integrated in the community relationship. Numerous other forms of incomplete integration could also be listed, and in conclusion we shall attempt to classify them.

In view of these circumstances we propose to adopt an expression of Herbert Kötter and say that the community as an association, or as an integral whole in the language of Redfield, can never be a preliminary assumption of research, but at best a result of it.[28] Kurt Utermann recently provided a good example of this in his investigation of a mining community in the northern Ruhr district, a community which developed from a rural community with 4,000 inhabitants around 1900, into a small town with 25,000 inhabitants. The particular circumstances of the Ruhr district meant that no sooner were shafts sunk than they quickly developed into large-scale undertakings – in this case employing 2,000 men within three years, and then 3,000 within five years. Further the mining industry employs a relatively large proportion of unskilled workers, who come partly from the Ruhr district, and also from the rest of the country and even from mining areas outside Germany. The workers in question were housed in large settlements somewhat removed from the old centre of the community, which began in consequence to develop into a sort of inner town. The extent to which the old peasant population was squeezed out by the newcomers can be seen from the fact that today the peasants represent only 8·4 per cent of the total population as compared with 60 per cent formerly. The main theme of the investigation was the consequences of this new relationship 'which develops from the fact that in such a community there are various spatially separated "districts" regarded as different from each other, and which despite a tendency towards amalgamation, do not form a unity'.[29] At the same time it is seen, in accordance with what has been said above, that it is not exclusively the class order which determines the community structure. On the contrary, 'the picture is dominated . . . by the multifarious co-existence of a number of groups which are not clearly separated from each other but which evince numerous transitions, rapprochements, adaptations and even amalgamation tendencies'.[30]

Utermann gives us a very penetrating picture of this great variety down to recent times with its various groups of newcomers, wherein, in addition to past and present, attention is directed to the future development of the social structure of this community. Instead of still further complicating this already involved situation by uncritically assuming a community integration, or equally uncritically talking of the total disintegration of the community by industrialization (uncritical because measured against the standard of a 'completely integrated community') the author speaks only of 'the unification of forces possible on the basis of such a community'.[31] Thus despite the extreme conditions in existence at present this does not exclude the possibility of a future integration. The central view remains that 'the community grows into a unity only gradually', in that an exact date at which this will take place cannot be given. The previously mentioned American investigation of Coal Town resulted in similar conclusions.

THE FORMATION OF NEW UNDERPRIVILEGED GROUPS

Eugene Lemberg and Lothar Krecker have collected numerous data concerning the appearance of new groups of under-privileged persons in various German rural communities resulting from the influx of evacuees, refugees and displaced persons after 1945. The interest was naturally concentrated in the first place on the refugees and the displaced persons themselves, and only secondarily – and it is here that the problem interests us – on the structural changes brought about in the communities into which these elements infiltrated. In view of the situation which existed at the time it would not have surprised us to see attention concentrated more on economic problems and not so much on the problem of community integration. However, a whole host of valuable information has come to light showing how numerous are the factors which prevent any direct integration of these new groups of underprivileged persons into the community.

In his preface Eugene Lemberg talks frankly of 'the class struggle' which results from the fact that even when the refugees and displaced persons do find jobs, they are usually on a lower social level in their new homes than they were in the places they came from.[32] However, we are using this expression only in order to underline the seriousness of the clash, which is, incidentally, repeated in many other fields, for example, culturally, religiously, educationally, and in language, dialect and customs. Thus the refugees and the displaced persons, who naturally do not share the same standards of value as their new community, are right from the start, no matter what they may do or not do, regarded as inferior. We can thus see very clearly that new underprivileged groups can arise repeatedly on a big scale in small communities. On the other hand, it is likewise very clear that in the course of time the circumstances can change fundamentally, and a great number of these immigrants become integrated into their new community, if only because they succeed in laying the basis of a new existence for themselves. We may therefore safely prophesy that at least the younger generation will be able more or less to integrate itself into the community; though for the older people the prospect is not so promising.

An important point, which undoubtedly aggravated matters, was that these fugitives often arrived in whole groups. For example, it is reported that a small Odenwald community 'reacted very violently in a kind of social defence against the settling of refugees who happened to hold different religious beliefs from the rest of the population'.[33] Further, in a community in the Weserland it was seen that the refugees formed a very definite social 'class', whose 'loyalties were directed elsewhere from the start'.[34] The influence of the newcomers was so strong in this particular case that in time it succeeded in changing the community itself. But here too there was serious tension, which at first was only relieved with the departure elsewhere of most of the refugees. On the other hand, perhaps one would be justified in expressing the view that the new substratum began to 'sediment', in that only those remained behind who were in any case incapable of making a fresh start, and were thus declassed not only temporarily but permanently (apathetic persons, widows, pensioners, etc.).

It also becomes clear that there are other circumstances which can make any community integration highly problematical, on the basis of the spontaneous formation of new underclasses or other groups. This, for example, is the case in Israel, where one wave of immigrants follows on the heels of the one before, and has done so since the days of the first Halijah, or immigrant wave. And the same is true, though in quite different circumstances, in India. There had always been a certain integration of the Mohammedan population in Hindu villages, and the inhabitants, in accordance with their own structural system, regarded them as a special caste. But after the war, when there was a clash between the two groups, this community integration broke down everywhere, and within a matter of hours; although in these cases one can say that the integration of the communities in question had not been encumbered by any outside influences such as urbanization or industrialization – or at least only to a very small extent by comparison with European villages.[35] This all shows very clearly that even when groups have lived side by side for very long periods, spatial proximity alone is not sufficient to create solidarity. When the inner system of a community is so deeply divided as it is in the question of mixed Hindu and Mohammedan communities, then bloody clashes can break out precisely on account of their spatial proximity. On the other hand, this need not necessarily be the case, as numerous examples prove in which even after the division of India, Hindus and Mohammedans continued to live together peaceably in the same mixed villages: just as there are mixed communities in Israel where Jewish settlers live side by side with Arabs. In a very interesting investigation by Gardner Murphy we are shown that the frustration-aggression pattern also applies here too, and from this we can judge the depth of the actual tensions which make community integration unlikely.[36]

Although the above cases present special problems which have been the centre of general attention in recent years, we can nevertheless say that over and above these exceptional developments, community structure is fundamentally of such a nature that with the development of its inner system it creates far-reaching differentiations which under certain circumstances prevent (but not always) community integration. In other words this means that even in a small community, neither spatial proximity nor joint interactions, nor the existence of common ideas, nor the bonds between the inhabitants will necessarily result in integration, because there are structural reasons operating in the opposite direction. This can be seen very clearly in connection with the factor of common ideas and standards of value, because this immediately creates big differences between those who live up to these standards and those who do not, those who live like animals – to quote the above-mentioned example of Plainville once again. Paradoxical though it may seem, the fact is that where common standards develop social discrimination necessarily develops too.

> Hans Linde concludes from his investigations that the communal relationship of economic life is not organic, that is to say, it is not uniform and inevitable, but only topographical; i.e. it is related because of its locality and site; from which it follows that the structure of the social aggregate, which presents itself as a sum only in statistical data, is not that of a community, and it should be regarded in principle as an agglomerative association of heterogeneous part-masses or groups.[37]

We agree with him completely, although we must add at once that this situation is not at all new as far as the village community is concerned, but has existed at least since the Middle Ages – all sentimental idealization of the small community to the contrary notwithstanding. On the other hand, we should like to stress that naturally this does not, under certain circumstances, necessarily prevent community integration. And, finally, we should like to make a few important observations on this subject without fully exploiting the subject as a whole here.

Once a joint settlement has taken place and joint action has developed under outside pressure, such social differences arise with the development of the internal system and a common standard of values, that the integration of the community is constantly threatened. If we wish to describe the nature of this danger at greater length, then we can say that it expresses itself in repeated acts of discrimination on the one hand, and vehement reactions to such discrimination on the other. Accordingly these developments take place in a framework of numerous social conflicts. But since a certain structural necessity is involved it is easy to suppose that purely in the social sphere such an integration is perhaps altogether impossible. On the other hand, as we have already seen, the structural nature of a global society does not exclude the possibility of a plethora of vital phenomena developing which are not attained by the structural processes themselves. It could even be that such phenomena and processes become particularly important for the full active life of the community, and especially for its development in time. We have now seen that the structurally conditioned conflicts in the community in the social dimension can, under certain circumstances, prevent the integration of the community. The question is now therefore whether there are other dimensions within the framework of these direct vital expressions of community life which are not primarily structurally conditioned and which therefore open up other spheres of integration apart from the social dimension.

THE ROLE OF SYMBOL IDENTIFICATION IN INTEGRATION OF THE COMMUNITY

We would like to suggest that an integration might nevertheless be possible, even if it cannot be attained – or only rarely – in the social sphere because of the diversity of the many interests involved. Possibly it is quite generally a fact that integration does not develop on its own, and that it must be a more or less deliberate act of projection from the social into some other dimension, for example the cultural. In that case perhaps an integration could be attained symbolically which is unattainable in social reality. The symbolism which is connected with the concept 'home', and which is a necessary consequence of the fact that most people still spend the greater part of their life in the same community, really does offer the possibility of an integration which can rise above social conflicts. Regarded as home the community is no longer an exclusively social structure, but essentially a part of culture which is withdrawn to some extent from social life and its priorities; and perhaps for this very reason it is in a position to bring about something which in the social sphere is largely impossible because of its structure.

Such socio-cultural symbolisms, and also actual collective and group identifications, may perhaps really be able to create a joint area where socio-economic reality with all its harshness is less significant. For example, a recent Norwegian study by Peter A. Munch shows how such group identifications are able to strengthen the contrasting tendencies of individual communities one from another very profoundly (out-group relationship), and also contribute to the self-sustenance of individual community culture (in-group relationship) against influences from outside. However, his study also shows that this encourages a tendency not only to exclude the marginal existences, but actually to thrust them still farther away, so that even this is not the last word on the matter.[38]

The realization of this state of affairs has recently led to the postulate that we must search for further cultural media of community integration. At this point we should like to indicate an essential difference between large and small communities. Whereas the feeling of being 'at home' with all its inherent symbolism may well prove quite adequate to bring about integration in a small community (in principle this may also apply to a small town) the great variety of life in a big town makes this medium too undifferentiated and too colourless, and therefore ineffective. For example, the cathedral at Cologne is an outward symbol for the community, and is, in fact, often regarded as such. But as a means of internal community integration this symbol is really too far removed from the realities of community life. But in the cultural dimension there are other media whose function is to create communications where the primitive forms of communication, by word of mouth and by rumour, are no longer adequate. One of these is the newspaper, a particular type of newspaper; namely the local paper. Of course, this is by no means all. On a higher level there are numerous other integrative media of a cultural nature. But there are very few media which are at all times available to everyone; perhaps only one, namely the local daily paper. It is here, therefore, that the process of integration could take place which cannot be brought about in the purely social sphere. But the development of this problem is a task in itself, which in conclusion can only be mentioned here in passing.

THE LOCAL NEWSPAPER AS A MEANS OF COMMUNITY INTEGRATION

Morris Janowitz in particular studied this problem quite recently in a very illuminating work,[39] and his investigations shed some welcome light on the matter. He shows[40] that a fundamental cause of the overestimation of the integrating force of the small community, and of the disorganization of the big community by sociologists of the older school lay in the fact that, without knowing it themselves, they were also marginal existences with a highly impersonal relationship to the society of their day. As a result of this situation they necessarily exaggerated the rootlessness of urban life and the inevitability of these developments. As against this, Janowitz now shows exactly what we have just suggested, namely that the local urban press is one of the social mechanisms which contribute towards the integration of the individual into the urban social structure. Thus one should not regard all means of mass communication as disintegrating factors in modern society. The actual question is now whether the local press encourages local community activities and identifications and helps to bring them into touch with non-local activities and identifications.[41] In his own investigation Janowitz confines himself to an examination of the local press of individual districts of Chicago, but this does not weaken the force of his arguments in any way. On the contrary, we feel it strengthens it. The actual background of such local newspapers is purely commercial in character. Almost all the local newspapers in question arose out of advertisement sheets at the neighbouring market centres. Then they developed and began to serve definite social, political and emotional needs which had not been originally foreseen. With this the local press now became a mechanism which 'sought to maintain the local consensus by stressing joint values rather than by resolving values which had come into conflict with each other'. On the whole, therefore, the local press seems to be less commercialized than the national dailies. The same factors which limit controversy also seem to operate against the effects of unlimited commercialism. The result is a more personal attitude towards the reader and a sympathetic awareness of the traditions of the community, which are clearly reflected in the text. The investigation also shows that there is a definite relationship between a strong degree of community integration and a big readership of the local press. As a result the local press is indissolubly connected with personal relationships which bind its personnel, the leading personalities of the community, and the readership together. Thus the local press occupies a position

half-way between the actual organs of mass communication, i.e.
the national dailies, and informal communication by word of
mouth and rumour.[42]

This extraordinarily interesting hypothesis is then examined
with detailed and methodical care on the basis of the available
data, as a result of which it is confirmed in full and at the same
time divided into a whole series of minor aspects which are a
matter of great interest for community sociology in general.
This is true of the analysis of the local press content, from which
we can see not only very interesting developments over the past
thirty years or so, but also the clear avoidance of controversial
matters; and also for the sociological analysis of the readership.
For example there are far more readers of the local press
amongst married than amongst single members of the community; and similarly even more readers amongst married
people with families than married people without. It is even
demonstrated that interest in local affairs increases with the
number of children in a family. Particularly noteworthy is the
fact that the interest in the local press steadily increases with
length of residence in the community, a circumstance which
must necessarily strengthen the chances of integration. This is
also confirmed by the fact that people with many neighbourhood contacts also proved to be correspondingly more interested
in the local press, and so did people whose friends lived in the
community, as opposed to those with personal relationships outside. This interest in the local press also increased with the
degree of emotional involvement with the community.[43]
Incidentally it must be stressed here that all these results provide
important corrections to many of the prejudices of urban
sociology. We do not propose to deal with this point in any
detail because we are not interested here in either the town or
the large city, but only in the community structure. However, it
is important to note that obviously the growth of large-scale
organization in modern urban culture does not mean a separation into impersonal individuals on the one hand and large-
scale social organizations on the other. Instead we see between
these two a whole series of intermediate social systems and
means of communication which have developed spontaneously.
This can also be seen with regard to the leading personalities of
the community, who are all the more influential the longer they

have lived there. On the other hand, 'social absenteeism' on the part of the leading personalities of a community means a direct decline in community integration. This is in exact accordance with the previously mentioned consequences of the migration of the factory owners from Yankee City as recorded by W. Lloyd Warner, and with the results obtained by George C. Homans in his investigation of Hilltown.[44]

THE SYSTEMATIC PROBLEM OF INTEGRATION

Apart from this special problem of the local newspaper as a means of community integration in the cultural dimension, the more general question also arises as to how the problem of community integration can be still further systematized and differentiated. As far as we know, the only attempt in this direction is that of Werner Landecker, which is based primarily on systematic considerations, but, because of its close relationship with the work of Robert C. Angell, is also based on empirical experience, and this factor makes his work of particular value for our purposes.[45] His preliminary interest lies in a typology of the possibilities of integration, which he classifies as follows: the integration of various cultural values; the integration between cultural values and individual behaviour, integration between persons either by communication or by the exchange of services. The cultural integration is concerned above all with conflicts of standards and inner contradictions in the cultural structure; the normative integration seeks to discover to what extent group standards actually influence behaviour; the communicative integration seeks to discover the limits for the exchange of opinions within a group; the functional integration seeks to estimate to what extent services within the group are based on reciprocity. With this we have four variables which at times represent a continuum varying from the highest possible degree of integration to its opposite. But that is only the preliminary general criterion, and in order to develop it effectively a structural analysis must also be made. In the case of the community this is represented, quite formally speaking, by the fact that integration expresses itself essentially in the relationship of sub-groups to a compound group of a higher order. This now opens up the following possibilities: the

integration of the compound group can be examined as a whole;
the integration of the sub-groups can be examined; or, finally,
the integration of the sub-groups in the compound group can be
examined. When these three structural possibilities are combined with the four variables which we previously mentioned
we obtain a valuable classification consisting of twelve possibilities, which Landecker develops in a most penetrating
fashion. At the same time it is pointed out that this by no means
exhausts all the available possibilities, and, that, in addition,
they present new problems for research, which must find out
how the relationship of the variables to each other develops in
individual cases.

HORIZONTAL AND VERTICAL INTEGRATION

Fruitful as this approach may seem, we agree with Landecker
when he points out that it by no means exhausts the problem,
particularly in relation to the community we feel that one or
two fundamental problems still remain open. These problems
are related in particular to the fact that in every global society
we have to deal not only with standards and functions, or the
relationship of sub-groups, to one another and to the compound
upper group, but that this group itself is a whole hierarchy of
functional groupings and social classes, i.e. a macrocosm of
groups in which the global society holds a social (not political)
sovereignty over all the elements which go to make it up; as was
said earlier on in connection with the work of G. Gurvitch.[46]
This opens up a new dimension of horizontal and vertical integration. Horizontal integration relates above all to the co-
operation of groups in the spatial order, and, accordingly, on
the same status level; vertical integration, on the other hand,
runs from below to above. In both directions there are greater
and lesser degrees, but only when the two aspects of integration
run simultaneously in both directions can we speak of any real
integration.

Roland L. Warren gives a good example, to which we have
already briefly referred, in his investigation into the local community activities in the German town of Stuttgart.[47] He shows
us very clearly that for example, the pursuit of special interests
binds the citizens of one community to similarly interested

citizens of other communities; and the pursuit of special interests separates the citizens of the same community from each other in accordance with their interests and the activities which result from them, and thus diminishes the horizontal integration. Finally, we can speak of a horizontal or vertical tendency according to whether the attitude of citizens in a community is determined by the special interests which separate them from each other, or by the common local interests which bind them together. Of course we are dealing here only with the relative predominance of the one tendency at one time and of the other tendency at another. As a result of his investigation in Stuttgart, Warren concludes that there was an excessive over-emphasis of the vertical integration as against the horizontal. When anyone takes part in a matter of common interest then his attention is first taken up by that group of chosen citizens in the community who share that interest with him, whilst horizontally he is drawn away from those interests which connect him with his neighbours or the other citizens of the community. The vertical tendency then leads the groups concerned to regard other groups as competitors and rivals, and to look upon the object or the ideology of their own group as the best. Consequently, a real 'discussion' between the individual groups rarely occurs. Each represents only its own standpoint. The result is that many functions are doubled, trebled and even further repeated, so that there is no longer any institution on a community basis which could bring the various groupings together to act in concert in any project in the interests of the community as a whole. As the same principle also operates in other relationships, it is easy to realize its significance where community integration is concerned.

Perhaps one might now suppose that such integration difficulties are typical only of larger towns, but as against that we should like to point to a concept recently formulated in Holland. Vertical integration in the previously mentioned sense is described as a 'columning' of social life, and the work of I. Gadourek on the community of Sassenheim proves that this is also, and indeed primarily, to be found on a community level. In Sassenheim the three fundamental forms of religious belief represented in the community – the Catholic, the Calvinist and the Dutch Reformed Church – provide the basis on which this columning takes place. On the other hand, from this standpoint it will perhaps no longer appear fortuitous that the author neglects the ecological aspect of the problem,[48] since obviously the vertical integration has spatially squeezed out the horizontal integration. As this situation is essentially independent of the size of a community, provided that the splitting up into the listed socio-cultural groups is operative, it can hardly be explained as a consequence of urban developments. In fact, here we see again how extremely problematical the integration of community life can become, particularly in a small community.

The interesting discussion of this concept of 'columnizing' as a type of vertical integration arose from the work of J. P. Kruijt, who investigated its special significance for the development of the national and thus the territorial unity of Holland. The structural importance of this columnization is expressed, *inter alios*, in the fact that it presents itself as an 'organizational columning'; that is to say, the various associations have a tendency to attach themselves to the main 'columns'. In practice the degree of this organizational columning seems to be steadily increasing, and the structural character of the development particularly expresses itself in the fact that this attitude has now extended even to Dutch Social Democracy and to the humanists (i.e. to the denominationally neutral), although originally it developed exclusively from the rivalry between the various denominations.[49]

CHAPTER X

WHY COMMUNITY INVESTIGATIONS?

The question as to why community investigations should be carried out at all can be answered in two ways. Firstly in a very general fashion wherein it is really sufficient to point to the existing community studies and the reasons which lie behind them. To some extent we shall do this in the next chapter, in which we shall give a brief history of community investigations and their background. In this connection we shall sometimes have to stress the particular intentions of the authors since we wish to characterize the various tendencies within this branch of sociological research. But in addition there is still a second and more fundamental way of answering the question 'Why?'. Then the answer must be given not by merely pointing to the facts, but in a more systematic fashion. Here a whole series of problems inevitably arises, and these have caused extensive discussions in recent years.

IS COMMUNITY SOCIOLOGY REALLY NECESSARY?

Albert J. Reiss Jr. has probably dealt most thoroughly with this problem in recent years. He questioned whether sociology really needs a special community theory, or whether the phenomena brought together under this head could not better be dealt with in a wider theoretical context.[1] He then dealt in an extremely penetrating fashion not only with the various ways in which the problem of the community has been approached, but also with the individual aspects of the community itself; at the same time he attempted to answer the question: how much in each individual case is actually of an exclusively community nature with regard to the phenomena in question. In the upshot he frequently concluded that many of these phenomena could just as readily be explained from more general associations of a more comprehensive social nature. With this, of course, it becomes highly problematical as to whether community sociology is really a specific branch of sociology whose subject is not already dealt with by other branches of the science. Personally we should even be prepared to go still further and point out that very many community investigations deal only with matters which could just as easily be dealt with elsewhere. However, we are not in complete agreement with Reiss, and we also consider that many of his observations are more trenchantly pointed – for methodological reasons – than is actually necessary. In many passages it is also quite clearly revealed that his own personal opinions are not altogether as radical as they would sometimes appear. On the other hand, there is no denying the fact that very interesting problems are raised by his whole for-mulation of the question; so much so that it is desirable for us to pay a little attention to the matter here.

Reiss very correctly stressed the ideological character of those opinions concerning the community which proceed more or less from the assumption that the rural community reveals a par-ticularly high degree of integration as against urban communi-ties; from the assumption that 'small' communities have a greater degree of stability than 'large' communities; and from the assumption that the large communities have squeezed out the smaller. As against this, of course, there is the opposite ideology which holds that the big community represents a cultural structure, whereas the small community is 'provincial' – and so on.[2] In all these cases the authors concerned express value judgements which have less to do with a description of what *is* than a de-scription of what, in their opinion, should be. This sort of thing can happen – as we have already pointed out – even with a man of such calibre as Robert Redfield; though his picture of the small community is less an ideological wish-concept, than a melancholy recollection of what is said to have been at one time a reality. The influence of these various ideologies have far-reaching consequences which can seriously hinder objective sociological research. Amongst those branches of research which are affected, are urban and big-city sociology, because if we proceed from the assumption that the village community has an unusually high degree of integration, then, conversely, when examining the town we will not fail to be struck in particular by the phenomena of disintegration. On the other hand, should we resolutely abandon the first assumption then we must necessarily gain a quite different and much more objective approach to the city.

Although Reiss has very properly avoided falling into these illusions, which derive from an old-time romantic outlook, it seems to us that he proceeds from another and no more justifiable assumption. The fact is that running quite clearly parallel with his justifiable criticisms, there is the unspoken assumption that in the highly-developed industrial societies of today, large-scale social structures of a global character have not only developed beyond the confines of the community, but have even replaced and squeezed out the community. This would then account for the fact that in attempting to grasp the specific in community life we generally arrive at total-social determinants. The question which then arises is whether there still is a special social system of determination which is peculiar to the community.

We do not deny the legitimacy of asking this question, the scope of whose problems has been insufficiently appreciated in so many community studies. In many cases they have even been expressly excluded; namely every time it is claimed that the reason for conducting community studies is that it is easier to tackle the problems of society as a whole, within a community framework. It is only too readily forgotten that this comes perilously close to a declaration of bankruptcy on the part of community sociology, since then the only reason for considering the community is a matter of convenience; namely, the more readily comprehensible nature of the given conditions. Further, there is a postulate at the basis of it all which is just as little self-evident. Just as quite generally in the investigation of human groups it has been shown that one cannot lightly draw conclusions from an analysis of small groups as to the state of larger groups, so it is true, and for the same reasons, that one cannot draw conclusions from the community which are necessarily valid for society as whole. And the fact that community conditions are more readily surveyable can prove a fatal trap, because it seems to be an essential characteristic of larger global societies that they are just not easily surveyable. With this, it would seem that there is a decisive difference between the two which should forbid extrapolation from the smaller scale to the larger. And the view that the community is the 'simpler' social form whilst society as a whole is merely the more complicated form would appear to be just as problematical. All our observations so far have gone to show how extremely complicated conditions can be, even in a small community.

Further, an example may be cited to show how different things are between a global society of a community type and a global society of a national character. Consider, for example, the totally different development of social class membership and of social rank in migration where a global society of the first type and one of the second are concerned. In changing from one community to another, both the social rank and, to a large extent also, the class membership must in some cases be re-established, whereas otherwise in migrations the factor of class membership remains much the same. For example, it makes a difference whether a doctor practises in town or country. In a village a doctor has a higher prestige and belongs to the prominent society; whereas in town a doctor is merely one amongst many. Precisely this illustrates the difference between a community and society as a whole, since the professional status which decides class membership remains the same in both cases, whereas the social position is greatly changed. With this we conclude without doubt that the global society community is essentially different from global societies of a higher order, so that one may also assume a specific system of determination here too. At the same time this leads to a conclusion that we have repeatedly stressed, namely that the community has not disappeared with the development of society. Although it is perhaps not so universal as the family, it has nevertheless managed to survive; and today the lives of most people are still lived out within the framework of the community. However, it must, of course, be pointed out that the determinants in larger societies of a global nature, national societies for example, have been greatly strengthened in comparison with former times. It is this which may, in any given case, make the decision so difficult between the competing determinant systems of the community on the one hand and the environmental society on the other.

Why community investigations?

With this, for the moment at least, we have answered the question as to whether the community has its own reality, and whether community sociology is a distinct branch of sociological investigation. Further, it also confirms the fact which has already been stressed, that we must not regard the development of global societies of a higher order as being a simple amalgam of individual communities. On the contrary, what happens is a step into a new dimension. With this of course an important motive behind community investigation loses its validity. It can no longer be claimed that community sociology carried out its work so that it can use the conclusions drawn from its analysis in order to obtain a better understanding of society as a whole. Of course, precisely this has often been done in the past, but it can only be said in reply that such community investigations have not dealt with specific community problems, but with problems relevant to society as a whole under cover of a community study; a proceeding which is, of course, perfectly legitimate, but not quite the same thing.

In the same connection we must also reject any very one-sided concentration on the 'problems' which are dealt with in a community study. Of course, when conducting such an investigation you can deal with the problems of poverty, alcoholism, prostitution, and so on; and, in fact, this was even the main tenor of the older studies of this kind, particularly in the nineteenth century. But there is no reason at all why this should be done, since the same problems can be dealt with in the same way on a national scale, unless one is particularly interested in the conditions in a large city, which represents a special type of community. Perhaps they will then take on a new aspect which will reveal itself particularly when we raise the question of the way in which the given conditions are connected with the structure of a given community. From this moment on, however, the results are no longer generally valid for national global societies, but only for the community in question. Here too, of course, there are general problems. There are structures which, as we have seen, are repeated. There are quite definite distributions in space, a circumstance one can see particularly clearly from the distribution of delinquency, and other phenomena, without thereby falling victim to the very doubtful theory of 'natural areas'. There are also typical processes which can

158

take place only within the framework of the community where, for example, the relation of the social classes is quite different from that in society as a whole. This can be seen very clearly with regard to the formation of political will in the community. Whereas this takes place on a national scale, in society as a whole, primarily within the framework of the political parties, the situation on a community level is quite different. As we have already pointed out, at election time, the candidates for the municipal council are usually put forward by the various political parties, but nevertheless it is not the political party which is decisive but the position of the candidate in the community, and the political parties too have to bow to this. Apart from these many structural characteristics which actually make the community into a reality of a very particular kind, it must be noted that from time to time many of the specific problems of a community and a region are included in a community study.

The treatment of community investigations from the standpoint of definite problems has recently been re-emphasized by Conrad M. Arensberg. He uses the community study as a method for investigating certain processes on a living object. 'It is a tool of social science and not an objective in itself.'[3] Although we agree with him that a community investigation must deal with its subject in its natural ambient, as against, for example, an experiment in a laboratory, we still maintain, on the basis of all the reasons we have put forward, that the community is, in addition, an object in itself. In fact we should like to point out that fundamentally Arensberg himself shares this view, as can clearly be seen from other studies he has made. He has also pointed out that a fundamental theory of the community must precede all community investigation if we wish to deal with a series of phenomena from a community standpoint, and perhaps compare them with other phenomena of a similar nature.[4] At the same time he justifiably points out that the word community has often been misused. Incidentally, and this is perhaps Arensberg's most important contribution in this respect, a community study cannot investigate a problem in its 'natural' ambient so long as it has not first succeeded in defining the exact extent of the community in question; something which is, for example, of extreme importance in sampling procedure, because only after this has been done is a statistical 'universe' obtained on the basis of which the sampling can be carried out.

In this way the typical living constellations in a community also become visible, something which can be obtained only very inadequately by the available means of identification such as local history, official statistics, and so on. This is one of the reasons which repeatedly give rise to community studies, because we are very far removed from the position of surveying the community in the whole extent of its inner life. Such a statement is all the more understandable when we consider the connection between a community and a region, a connection which reveals the enormous variety of community problems. At the same time, as Arensberg points out,[5] it is clear that community studies can offer a much more complete and internally cohesive picture of a community than any other branch of sociological investigation; not because the community is less complicated than larger relationships, but because on the basis of its closer proximity to us, with the help of local informants in the community, and with the application of numerous observation techniques, we can, under certain circumstances, obtain an unusually adequate 'model' of the community. Compared with these advantages the arguments of Julian H. Steward, who stressed the dangers resulting from the isolation of the community from its region or its district, are no longer valid. Even if at first we must identify the limits which separate the community from the outside world, this does not mean that we are not under certain circumstances interested precisely in the relations of the community to its hinterland – as for example the Darmstadt study shows – but only that at first we are primarily interested in the development of human relationships within the community.

With this we have already obtained an important development of motivation for the carrying out of community studies. However, we must stress that so far the most important motive has not been mentioned.

A. B. Hollingshead has stressed the ecological, typological and structural lines of approach,[6] and Arensberg has followed up with an analysis of individual processes. With the exception of these latter viewpoints, the general tendency so far seems to be of a structural nature, or limited to processes which take place between two structures. On the other hand, with the possible exception of John Dollard and his group, relatively little attention has been paid to the socio-psychological aspect of community investigation, although formerly this played a very important role and provided perhaps one of the most important motives for community study. Quite recently Jessie Bernard[7] stressed this point, thus taking up older ideas once again as they were developed at the beginning of the century by Charles H. Cooley[8] and E. Gettys,[9] and at the beginning of the thirties by others. Incidentally, the same ideas lie at the basis of the Chicago school, where they were largely introduced by Robert E. Park and Louis Wirth.[10] These ideas can easily be defined once one has admitted that the community is a determinational system of a special kind.

THE FUNCTION OF THE COMMUNITY IN THE DEVELOPMENT OF THE SOCIO-CULTURAL PERSON

Just as the family makes an essential contribution – perhaps even the most important of all – to the development of the socio-cultural personality of man, so also does the community. In this respect we must recognize that whilst the influence of the family is very profound, man is removed to another ambient very early on, and that this new ambient then has an analogical effect on the development of his socio-cultural personality. In addition to the play groups of the children there is, in particular, the neighbourhood and the community. Old-time sociology both in Europe and in the United States had, as has often been pointed out, a tendency to idealize the situation, and to refer to the family, the neighbourhood and the small community as 'primary' both in time and significance, and to consider them accordingly as 'primary groups' (Charles H. Cooley). The ideological nature of this conception was revealed the moment it was turned into a historical system of development, and because – by analogy with the development of the community to 'association' (F. Tönnies) – after the development of association the community was to disappear; the further contention was added that only in the community (family and community) could there be any really integrated social relationship. We have already seen how much these views are worth; and, as we know, they developed from an unworldly attitude on the part of academic intellectuals in the nineteenth century, men who had no connections with the economic system or with developments in our modern industrial society are understandable only against that background.

Although there is often a great deal of discussion about this problem, really practical investigations dealing specifically with the position of children and adolescents in the community are still relatively rare. It is a well-known fact which is confirmed in practice again and again that children usually successfully contribute to opening the neighbourhood. For example, the study conducted by Morris Janowitz showed that families with children (and particularly families with a number of children) tended to take a much more active part in community life by reading the local press. A recently published investigation conducted by Michael Young and Peter Willmott concerning family and kinship relations in London's East End also showed the direct relationship between families and the community:

> When a man has relatives in the community, then each of these relatives is a link with other people in the same district. The friends of his brothers are his acquaintances, and sometimes even his own friends. The neighbours of his grandmother are almost as well known to him as though they were his own neighbours. Properly understood, therefore, kinship is a bridge between the individual and the community.[11]

At the same time it is also shown that growing up together creates a strong bond, so that children tend automatically to join the gangs of children in their own neighbourhood, and these gangs thus perform an important social function.

These gangs are usually studied on account of their non-conformist attitude, and there is already a highly interesting body of criminological literature on this point, from the classic book of Frederick M. Thrasher, and *Street Corner Society* by William F. Whyte, to the recent book by the English author Barron Mays. The American Albert K. Cohen has also provided us with a very profound discussion of these problems.[12] Thrasher certainly warned us against any over-dramatization of the situation, as involved in the supposition that every boys' gang

is a criminal conspiracy. Apart from all this, very little is yet
known about children's play groups and adolescent gangs on a
community basis. Occasionally actual slum investigations throw
a little light on the matter, for example, the work of Betty M.
Spinley. She shows how an average boy in the slums grows up
taking part first in various play groups and then in street gangs
in his immediate neighbourhood. The gangs which develop in
this way have already taken on very definite forms, as William
F. Whyte in particular has shown. When youngsters are alone
they feel uncomfortable; and this feeling is so strongly marked
that they will not leave one such group until they are quite
certain of being accepted into another. The same thing is true of
other groups and of youth clubs, which all develop from the
neighbourhood factor in the streets.[13] Mays even shows that
football clubs also develop in this way and play against each
other, and he declares: 'Such teams spring from the normal life
of young people in a perfectly wholesome and natural way.
They meet a genuine need and have a real contribution to make
to the social education of those who take part.' Occasionally
such local attachments play a big role and youngsters often
return from far away after their parents have moved out of the
neighbourhood.[14] The investigation conducted by Madeleine
Kerr into the lives of the inhabitants of Ship Street, in a Liverpool slum, is just as thorough. It deals above all with certain
emotional instabilities on the part of the children growing up
there which makes them different from average children; and,
in addition, with feelings of exclusion amongst them as revealed
in numerous tests. Thus here too the direct neighbourhood is
regarded as a determinational system in that a particular type
of personality develops on the basis of existing conditions, a
type which is remarkable for an obvious ego weakness, and in
general by an insufficiently integrated personality structure.[15]

When we consider the difference between the development of
the neighbourhood factor in rich and poor areas we shall not be
surprised to find that these youth gangs are more often to be
found in the poorer ones. In the well-to-do areas young people
live a more isolated life and they find at school the group life
which the street does not offer them. More important, however,
is the fact that at the same time a special society of young people
develops in adult society (as A. B. Hollingshead has shown in

particular in his study of Elmtown) reflecting the community before they are aware of wider social and economic relationships. However, at the same time Hollingshead underlines that the life of young people sometimes develops in a sort of no-man's-land, because they have grown beyond the family without having as yet found their place in the adult world. Very often there is only the school available to bring about this transition. For the rest, youth welfare work on a community basis is still very undeveloped. This is becoming a real problem because as a result of the changed conditions of production in the modern world, young people enter business and industrial life much later than was at one time the case when, for example, in rural areas a child would be drawn gradually and almost imperceptibly into the working world of the adults. Today, on the other hand, there is a very strange intermediate period, the so-called teenage culture, which lies between childhood and adulthood. Very important social processes are taking place in this respect on a community level, though so far public consciousness has not by any means become sufficiently aware of them. The investigation into the youth of Elmtown shows us very clearly how youth groups and cliques form in exactly the same way as they do amongst adults. Whilst the adults strive to exercise some influence on the youth, the young people succeed in evading this interference again and again. 'The social pressure exercised in the young people's groups has a much greater and more subtle effect in the canalization of friendships within the framework of the limits recognized by the social system of the youth and of the adults than the hopes, fears and warnings of anxious parents.'[16] That all this, however, is in every respect a community affair is proved by the key factor that in the great majority of cases the cliques and friendships are formed exactly according to the class system of the community (three cases out of five), with which the young people are very well acquainted. In two cases out of five the cliques extended beyond a single class; but in only one case out of twenty-five did they extend beyond two classes.[17] The same thing applies in particular to 'dating' amongst boys and girls, as can be seen very clearly from the diagram reproduced on page 165.[18]

As soon as we accept the concept community with a lesser emphasis, that is, more neutrally and realistically, we shall have

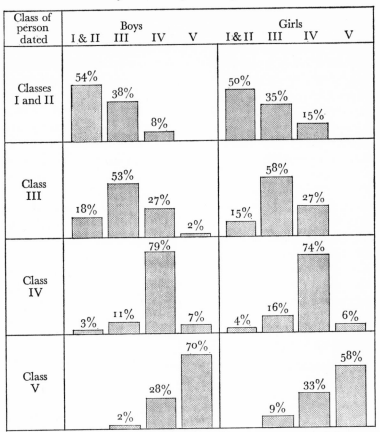

Class of person dated	Boys				Girls			
	I & II	III	IV	V	I & II	III	IV	V
Classes I and II	54%	38%	8%		50%	35%	15%	
Class III	18%	53%	27%	2%	15%	58%	27%	
Class IV	3%	11%	79%	7%	4%	16%	74%	6%
Class V			2%	28%	70%		9%	33%	58%

Appointments between boys and girls from the same and from different social classes in Elmtown. From A. B. Hollingshead *Elmtown's Youth.* New York, 1949, *page 231.*

(Reprinted with kind permission from John Wiley and Sons.)

no difficulty in recognizing the reality of the community as a determinational system of a specific kind, without at the same time falling into the partly sentimental and partly ideological historical philosophies which so often bedevil the concept. We then proceed from the principle that today, as in the past, a human being spends a very important part of his life in the community; even though we do not in the least deny that global societies of a higher order have also developed in addition. It is also a fact that the adult human being is involved in numerous other social and economic relationships apart from the community; but as a child and as an adolescent such relationships are completely foreign to him, and all social relationships, other than those of a purely family nature, are experienced by him without exception in a community form. In other words, this means that side by side with the family, the neighbourhood and the community determine the further development of the socio-cultural personality even in our highly developed industrial societies. From this follows the very great importance of those community investigations which see the community in relation to the growth of human beings, just as the central part of any community investigation must deal with the life cycle of the adolescent youth. Whilst anthropologically-influenced community studies invariably pay close attention to this point, this is not always the case with community studies in advanced industrial societies. In passing we must point out that this is certainly to some extent due to the unspoken misconception that the community as a determinational system of a specific kind, or as a primary group as it used to be called at one time, is gradually disappearing. The English community investigations mentioned here, which pay particular attention to the development of the socio-cultural personality and to the integration of the personality into the community, represent an important exception to this tendency.

With this we now have a new motive for community studies, and one which brings it into close relationship with family sociology; although on account of the global nature of its theme its operations extend far beyond the relatively narrow framework of family sociology. At the same time the approach has become more objective, and new special techniques of investigation have been developed which make it possible to measure the exact circle of the social relationships within which the development of the socio-cultural personality takes place. Amongst these new techniques is sociometry in particular, whose importance for the concrete measurement of neighbourhood for example, can hardly be overestimated. Much the same applies in general to the investigation of small groups. With its translation to the practical ambient of the community it has lost a great deal of its former artificial laboratory character. Further techniques of investigation which link up here concern themselves primarily with the development of indices of community participation, and so on, which naturally refer rather to the adult world and the problem of leadership within the framework of the community. In the same way, techniques for the analysis of interaction processes have also greatly increased our ability to recognize and understand concrete social processes within the community. Recently British investigators in particular have been applying psychological tests in community investigation, with success.

THE FUNCTION OF COMMUNITY SOCIOLOGY IN COMMUNITY PLANNING

What has been said so far probably indicates the essential motive for the conducting of community studies, but not necessarily the only one. On the contrary, in conclusion we should like to point out that there are still a number of secondary motives, some of which are indeed regarded by public opinion as the central reason for carrying out community investigations. We are thinking here of the contribution of community sociology both to social planning and to social policy within the framework of the community. A series of theoretical and practical activities have developed in connection with town, regional and national planning though so far they lack a proper sociological basis. Unfortunately this has given rise to a cheap-jack market for superficial community ideologies intent on utopian planning systems. The most charitable thing to hope is that they will never be imposed.

More serious in this connection are the ambitions of P. Chombart de Lauwe, for whom one of the most important motives for community investigation is the need to know 'the housing needs' of various social classes, and in particular of the working people, with the idea of putting the knowledge thus obtained to good purpose in the planning of working-class housing estates.[19] In Germany special studies into the housing needs of mine workers have been started with the same end in view.[20] As however the problems of planning quickly take us away from our own affairs into other spheres we do not propose to deal with them any further here. We will content ourselves with remarking that a certain danger lies in the fact that social

167

politicians and planners are usually obliged to act quickly, whereas adequate research takes time before it can be sure of the efficacy of its methods. In addition, as Ruth Glass has recently pointed out quite rightly,[21] the ideas behind such planning are actually more social reformist than sociological. It can easily be shown that the tradition of earlier English community investigators such as Charles Booth, and more later Sidney and Beatrice Webb, and B. G. Rowntree too, has had much less effect on British town planning than the rather vague ideas of men like Ebenezer Howard, Sir Patrick Geddes, Raymond Unwin, Victor Branford and others. All these philosophic, Utopian and reformist speculations have been more or less summed up in the ideas of Lewis Mumford and they have greatly affected both planning and public opinion, whilst unfortunately the more realistic and sober approach of community sociology remained almost neglected until fairly recently. This was confirmed once again a little while ago in a discussion on 'the New Town' which attracted a good deal of attention in Switzerland. To judge on the basis of the inadequate information so far available about the activities of these circles one can only say that all the goodwill in the world cannot make up for a lack of expert knowledge. The sphere of town planning still seems to be a stamping ground for sociological dilettantes. For this reason there is a deeply ingrained distrust in real sociological circles of all premature and hasty attempts to rush from theory into practice. Unfortunately the justification of this cautious attitude has been confirmed only too often in the past, even when the investigatory approach is so conscientiously planned as that of Michel Quoist when he studied a district in Rouen.[22] In this connection it can be seen very clearly how often the wish is the (thoroughly illegitimate) father of the thought; on the one hand the positive reform possibilities are invariably overestimated, whilst on the other the powerful influence of certain material factors is just as regularly underestimated.

The result of this is naturally a certain insecurity and hesitation in the relations of theory and practice in community sociology. It is obvious that this must make itself felt, and often very uncomfortably, in any study of the motivation of community investigation. It must naturally be admitted that highly urgent practical matters have always been in the foreground in this branch of an investigation. The very history of the development of community sociology from French and English sociopolitical sources in the nineteenth century, and its partial connection with town and regional planning in the twentieth century, clearly show us that practical matters have been of more than subordinate importance. Nevertheless, the sort of degeneration into pure pragmatism which has been indicated above cannot be either in the interests of the older development or of modern problems, because the shortening of perspectives to that which lies nearest, which is necessarily bound up with any form of pragmatism, means a direct threat to our knowledge and understanding. Above all, however, we must remember that pragmatism is impatient and clamours for a more or less immediate solution of any given difficulty and is unwilling to wait for the development of science. On the other hand, of course, research conducted for itself alone is similarly inadequate in face of the urgent needs of modern life. In the last resort we are thus faced with the need for compromise.

COMMUNITY SELF-SURVEY

Such a compromise has recently been arrived at in two particular ways: first of all rather unsystematically by means of 'community self-survey', to use the American expression for the concept; and secondly, and rather more systematically, within the framework of what is called 'action research', as it has developed from one or two suggestions made by Kurt Lewin primarily in the sphere of small-group investigation in America.

This so-called community self-survey is thus above all an attempt to arrive at a solution of the question of the relationship of theory and practice. When, for example, as Roland L. Warren points out, it is assumed that each community investigation must be part of an action programme, then this kind of analysis really does take on considerable significance.[23] Self-surveys carried out by citizens of a community with the assistance of experts have certainly proved an effective means of reducing tensions in the community. As a typical expression of Calvinistic self-examination it belongs essentially to the development of real community consciousness in the United States, whereas in

Europe there is as yet no real understanding of it and its implications. The few attempts on similar lines which have been made in Sweden were obviously very dilettante in character.[24] On the other hand, just consider how many difficulties could have been overcome in Germany immediately after the war, particularly in small communities with a large influx of refugees, displaced persons and evacuees if this method of self-survey had been adopted! The same method has proved itself fruitful in attempts to encourage backward ('underdeveloped') communities, both in highly-developed industrial societies and in technically backward and underdeveloped societies. In this case the aim was to encourage new initiative amongst a few individuals or amongst whole groups by providing and awakening a knowledge of all-important problems centrally connected with the life of the community. Here too the idea was to encourage a feeling of community participation which otherwise so often remains dormant because no real attempt is made to rouse it. And neglect on this score is due in particular to the absence of any general realization of how essentially important community participation is for the development of the adult human being. Only too often the well-known feeling of being helplessly in the grip of 'anonymous' powers, with all its paralysing effects on inner and outer development, is nothing more than a result of inadequate community participation.

In contrast to scientific community investigation, the aim of such self-surveys is primarily practical. In this respect it shares a decisive characteristic with other practical-therapeutic treatment techniques such as psycho-analysis. Whereas the purely scientific investigation comes to an end as soon as a definite relationship has been adequately understood, this new kind of analysis continues even after no further doubt remains with regard to the problems being analysed. The aim is to secure a 'fixation' of certain views by repetition and this is intended in the long run to bring about a change in behaviour. Thus in this connection the analytical self-survey technique is no longer an end in itself, but exclusively a means for the development of community participation on a highly practical and, above all, active form. This then brings us by easy stages to the concept of action research, which must not be confused with 'applied science', because its direct and essential aim is to arouse certain

activities by the development of certain knowledge and understanding. In other words, people will do something definite not
because they have been persuaded to do so by outside influence,
but because, on the basis of the knowledge and understanding
opened up to them, they desire to do it themselves. With this the
method of community self-survey acts as a lever for releasing
active participation not only in general matters of community
development, but also in highly practical individual questions.
Objective discussion helps to awaken a desire to develop the
community into a vital social body.

Similar problems have been dealt with in a rather more systematic form, by Kurt Lewin with special relation to minority
questions.[25] Had it been objected that this programme was
somewhat general in character, Ronald Lippitt soon gave it a
practical community basis by carrying out an experiment in
which the leaders of the community were trained to deal with
minority problems. At the same time special attention was
directed to the particular task of discovering ways and means of
changing deeply-rooted ideas and traditional behaviour by
means of systematic influence.[26] Incidentally, there are already
so many centres for the development of community activities
that it is impossible to mention them all here.[27] All these studies
stand or fall by the primary assumption that for the majority of
people the community is still the traditional vital sphere, and
that man's socio-cultural personality develops to full maturity
within the framework of its activities in a way that it could never
do exclusively within the limits of the family.

CHAPTER XI

A SHORT HISTORY OF
COMMUNITY RESEARCH

SOCIO-CRITICAL BACKGROUND OF THE OLDER
TYPE OF COMMUNITY INVESTIGATION

It is not and cannot be our intention to give here a full and detailed picture of the history of community sociology, because this would involve us in many subordinate branches of research which derive from very varied motives. This remains true even if, as suggested in our introduction to this book, we confine ourselves exclusively to the problem of the community structure in the broadest sense, i.e. with the deliberate exclusion of village and rural sociology, urban and large-city sociology, and the sociology of urban and rural relationships. In any case it seems to us that all these branches of investigation lack a proper basis unless the problem of the community is previously dealt with. Nevertheless, there are still sufficient problems left, as can be seen from the very fact that literature as such is now occupying itself in great detail with the problem of the community. For example, the community is the focus of attention in French realism, particularly in Emile Zola's works, and in Italian Verism, from Giovanni Verga's *Malavoglia*[1] (1881) to Carlo Levi's *Christ stepped at Eboli* (1945). The Polish village is the centre of events in the great epic of the Polish Nobel Prize Winner Vladislav Reymont[2] *The Peasants* (1904–9) and in another book by the same author, *The Promised Land* (1916), it is the textile town of Lodz.[3] We quote here only a few of the outstanding examples, but hundreds of romantic novels with a background of village life could be added.

We should not even have mentioned this point had it not been taken up quite recently by Theodor W. Adorno,[4] who draws a deliberate parallel between the work of Robert and Helen Lynd and their two volumes on Middletown, and the general literature of the period, in which

> the discovery of the American province plays a decisive role, particularly with regard to the uniformity of provincial life which immediately strikes all observers in the outward similarity of small towns, a similarity based on economic and technological conditions which do not exist in the same way in Europe, though the tendency in the same direction is unmistakable. And later on Adorno writes: The extraordinary effect achieved by the books of the Lynds arises from the fact that their search for the typical is conducted not only with a scientific but also with a socio-critical intention. They chose one of those towns in the American Middle West which are strikingly similar, and in their analysis they stressed the constant sameness, the standardization and the desolation of existence where it is lived without any historical tradition, exclusively according to economic laws, and under the conformist pressure exercised by an established society in which men live and earn their living.[5]

Now it is certainly true that there are many critical tendencies in the literary descriptions of community life in the United States in the twenties, but nevertheless it strikes us as rather one-sided to judge the whole production of this kind from the standpoint of this one motive. The profound inadequacy of such an attitude can be seen very clearly if – to take only one of the most prominent critics – we compare various novels by Sinclair Lewis, for example the highly critical *Main Street* (1920) or *Babbitt* (1922) on the one hand with *Cass Timberlane* (1945) on the other. But because Adorno finds nothing in community investigation beyond the attempt 'to discover from a model what may be valid on a large scale, but which can hardly be grasped empirically on the basis of society as a whole',[6] he necessarily misses the one thing which is open to structural-functional analysis. All that then remains, as far as he and others are concerned, is the usual social and cultural criticism from the angle of 'the totality of the actual social relationships' on the one hand, and the 'alienation' on the other; and this exaggerates matters to a greater degree than is good for any sober judgement.

If we often emphasize in what follows the socio-critical character of the early community studies, then this is to be understood in the realistic sense of Charles Booth, and by no means in the philosophic sense of the utopian town and social planners from Sir Patrick Geddes to Lewis Mumford, who represent more or less – translated into English – the viewpoint of Adorno. This is seen very clearly in connection with the work of the French sociologist Frederic Le Play (1806–82), who was primarily interested in the effects of industrialization and who examined the problem within the framework of the community. However, we must emphasize that the central subject of his study was the family, and that, like so many others, he turned his attention to the community because the family was most readily comprehensible against that background. Incidentally, there is a rapprochement here between sociological empiricism and community investigation, something which for many observers still seems to be the outstanding characteristic of the whole problem (for example, Adorno, to mention only one), whereas although it is important for a structural analysis of the community it is of only secondary importance compared with 'localization' of the community in the total development of human society. To some extent a distortion of perspective results, and the work of Robert and Helen Lynd is then regarded as the beginning of a more empirically slanted era of social investigation, whereas in reality, far from being a beginning, it represents the last document in a long series which began in France with Le Play and in England with Charles Booth. In all these cases the community was of interest only because it permitted certain definite problems (family, proletarianism and poverty, abandoned children, criminality, alcoholism, prostitution, and so on) to be studied in their natural surroundings. These problems were joined later on (up to the time of the Lynds) by other and less dramatic ones, such as the living habits of all social classes, the foundation of a home, the education of the young, the use of leisure, religious observance, community activity, information sources (the press and rumour), public health, the judicial system, the administration, etc. In all these cases questions of community structure arise only incidentally. Apart from one or two pioneers, this kind of analysis began with Robert E. Park and the Chicago school of sociology, and grew in an ever more specific sense from the end of the thirties.

Apart from the attempt to encourage a more realistic approach to modern social reality, the older community investigations aimed primarily at the development of a social policy based on social sciences. This has remained more or less true since the days of Le Play and down to the present day with the Economie et Humanisme group, which conducted a very interesting community study in Rouen.[7] We have already pointed out the dangers inherent in any intimate association of research and practice, and it is almost inevitable that the scientific side of an investigation will suffer if an investigator tends to judge what he actually finds in accordance with previously formed conclusions. This is true of all socio-politically slanted studies of this kind, whether they have a Right or Left wing bias.

THE EMPIRICAL INVESTIGATION OF CONTEMPORARY SOCIAL PROBLEMS

Suggestions first made in France were taken up in Britain, and the most important connecting point was the common desire to launch the empirical investigation of contemporary social problems (as against the development, say, in Germany, which, since the days of Wilhelm Heinrich Riehl has bogged down in a confusion of objective analysis with idealized standards). The first great representative of this development in Britain was Charles Booth (1840–1916), who carried out his investigations in the East End of London and documented his results in a monumental work in seventeen volumes published in the years 1892 to 1902.[8] He was also responsible for the training of a whole series of younger investigators, whose influence has lasted to some extent down to the present day, and who included Beatrice Potter, who later married Sidney Webb, with whom she wrote one of the most important works establishing empirical research methods in sociological investigation.[9] Later on the work of Charles Booth was continued by B. S. Rowntree, who took the town of York as the subject of his studies, which were primarily directed to the problem of poverty. His work is of particular interest to us because he repeated his first investigation of York (1901) approximately thirty-five years later (1936) and then together with G. R. Lavers fifty years later. With this he introduced the use of the comparative method by which the same community is taken as the subject of investigation at widely different times. Arthur Bowley systematically developed the method and conducted another investigation into the problem of poverty, this time in five medium-sized English industrial towns. The improvements in the empirical method of investigation introduced by Bowley were subsequently taken up by Sir Hubert Llewellyn Smith, a former collaborator of Charles Booth, who carried out a further wide-scale investigation into the living conditions of working people in London. The results of this investigation were published in nine volumes in the years 1930 to 1935. At about the same time Caradog Jones published his wide-scale study of Liverpool and Merseyside (1934-5), a work in which more and more systematic considerations replaced former descriptive methods. This development continued after the war, as witness the very interesting work of T. S. Simey and his colleagues on Liverpool, Manchester and Merseyside, in which structural questions played an increasing role. Ruth Glass, who is also an important representative of this school of thought, recently published an almost exhaustive bibliography of all these developments in Britain, and it is particularly valuable because it draws a very definite dividing-line between sociological research proper and the recrudescence of more practical political interests in connection with town planning. The most recent studies of this kind in Britain, in which the purely sociological character and the structural interest quite clearly dominate all subordinate interests of a practical political nature, include the study of a village in West Cumberland by W. M. Williams; the studies of Michael Young, Peter Willmott and Peter Townsend into the conditions prevailing in the slum districts in the East End of London; a study of kinship in a London suburb by Raymond Firth and Judith Djamour; the slum studies of Betty M. Spinley and Madeleine Kerr; and the Australian studies of O. A. Oeser and S. B. Hammond.[10] It is illuminating to note that the development in Britain today has reached the same stage as in the United States before the war, in that the particular strength of the British studies lies in their socio-psychological approach.

A short history of community research

In the United States, too, work in connection with the community goes back basically to socio-political interests, and it has resulted in very realistic descriptions of the slum areas in big towns. The men who carried out these investigations were publicly denounced as muck-rakers, and they included both journalists and novelists. Such studies have been more and more frequent since the eighties, but most of them were of a more or less unsystematic nature, and very often there was a tendency to stress the dramatic factor in order to cover up inadequacies in the collection of the basic material. As early as 1894 this led the University of Chicago to issue a small 'Catechism' in order to systematize the observation of social phenomena. This was followed in 1907 by the establishment of the Russell Sage Foundation, which devoted its activities from the beginning to a more methodical development of this branch of sociological research. Its success in this respect was vouched for by the subsequent publication of three important books over a period of forty years, each of which very convincingly documented the progress made in this sphere. A small volume by Marga F. Byington was published in 1911 entitled *What Social Workers should know about their own Communities*, and was directed entirely towards the needs of social welfare. Later Joanna C. Colcord wrote an extended introduction on the conducting of community investigations and this was also published by the Russell Sage Foundation (1939). And finally in 1955 the Foundation published a large and very systematic work by Roland J. Warren in which the whole material likely to be involved in a community investigation was thoroughly dealt with in no less than twenty chapters and approximately 1,800 questions. But the interests of the Russell Sage Foundation were not only methodological, but also practical; and from 1909 onwards (in co-operation with other bodies) it financed the Pittsburgh Survey, under the leadership of Paul Kellog, the results of which were subsequently published in six volumes. This study was primarily concerned with the conditions of the Pittsburgh steel workers, and the consequences of over-hasty industrialization. However, the scope of the study was kept very wide indeed, and other questions were also dealt with, including many relating to family developments. In 1914 Shelby M. Harrison, one of the original directors of the Russell Sage

177

Foundation, began the *Springfield Survey*, which was concerned with a comparatively small community of approximately 50,000 inhabitants. The material involved was collected under nine main headings, which clearly indicate the socio-political background of this branch of investigation: (1) the public, or elementary schools; (2) the welfare arrangements for lunatics, alcoholics and the feeble; (3) leisure time needs, and arrangements for satisfying them; (4) housing conditions; (5) public health and social hygiene; (6) public welfare and private charity; (7) conditions in industry; (8) criminality, and measures against it; and (9) urban administration. Incidentally a new concept was introduced for the first time, which has since become more and more characteristic of U.S. community studies, namely that they are used as a means of instructing social science students in the social problems of the day, and also in research techniques and the execution of such investigations. The present director of the Russell Sage Foundation, Donald Young, is, like his predecessors, intensely interested in all questions of sociological research and in the political development of the community. Today the main interest is directed to public health and hygiene, as can be seen from numerous interesting publications on the subject.

The development of this new branch of investigation in the United States has proceeded rapidly and intensively. A bibliography compiled by Allen Eaton and Shelby M. Harrison and published by the Russell Sage Foundation, lists no fewer than 2,775 titles or projects, including 154 full community studies and 2,621 specialized studies, all of which had been completed by the end of 1927. Journalistic 'reports' are expressly excluded from the list. During the course of this development, which is still going on uninterruptedly two factors which we think are of great importance for the immediate present crop up again and again. The first we have already mentioned, namely the teaching and training aspect of these studies. In this way sociology students are really provided with excellent training; whether they quite simply study certain problems on a community basis where they are more easily (and more economically) available than in wider spheres; or whether such studies are much more systematic (for example, the Detroit Area Study, which the University of Michigan has been conducting for years, and which offers numerous students the opportunity of carrying out their first scientific work in this field within the framework of a far-reaching project) and in addition, offer prominent and distinguished scholars an opportunity of carrying out specialized studies. Incidentally we mention the Detroit Area Study because it is typical of numerous other ones of a similar nature being carried out by various U.S. Universities, and the most prominent, whose publications have won world-wide attention, is the Chicago City Inventory, which specializes in large-scale urban research.

In view of what has been said above it is absolutely impossible to give an exhaustive account of these developments in the United States; first of all it is fed from too many sources, and secondly its results are so many and varied that they have become practically impossible to survey. Therefore only the most important aspects of this movement can be described here, and we propose quite deliberately to exclude everything which relates only to planning and reform. At this point the second factor we have mentioned appears very clearly, namely, that gradually more than merely 'social problems' in the general sense of social reform and social policy, are being dealt with, and they include sociological problems in the strictest sense of the word. From this, on the one hand, numerous specialized community studies have developed, including questions of criminality, racial relations, and, since the end of the twenties, unemployment and so on; and on the other hand there is the development of that special aspect of community research which is known as large-scale urban sociology, a sphere in which the Chicago School has produced excellent results. This means that the sociologists have now definitely taken the intiative; a circumstance which can be seen very clearly from the two volumes published by Robert and Helen Lynd on Middletown (1929 and 1937). However, they pay so little attention to purely sociological-structural matters, and the division of their material according to approximate living spheres is so obtrusive that one cannot describe their work as the beginning of something new, but only as the culmination of something old. Nevertheless, we have not the remotest intention of denying that specific sociological factors are beginning to appear; this will be seen very clearly if we take, say, the new Pittsburgh Survey of 1938 as a standard of comparison; an undertaking which was primarily conceived as a means and a basis for the reorganization of the welfare system. The really sociologically-based studies initiated by the University of Chicago began to appear in 1923, and have been published since in an uninterrupted series down to the present day.[11] Further, just before the war, there was another new departure which is generally speaking still characteristic today.

THE RISE OF THE STRUCTURAL PROBLEM

This last stage of development really started immediately after the conclusion of *Middletown*, when W. Lloyd Warner and his colleagues began the Yankee City study, covering a small New England town of 17,000 inhabitants near Cambridge (Massachusetts). Lloyd Warner's intention was not only to repeat the investigation of the two Lynds with improved research techniques, but, and in particular, to expose the social system of the community. His approach is thus strictly speaking structurally slanted. This can be seen very clearly from his detailed definition of the concept community in the first volume of the Yankee City study published in 1941:

The word community describes a number of people who share a certain attitude, certain interests, certain feelings and certain things on the basis of the fact that they belong to a social group. The scientific investigator describes the communities of primitive peoples as 'tribes', 'villagers' or 'clans'; the social scientist who occupies himself with present-day life, describes individual local groups as 'large-scale urban areas', 'towns', 'small towns', 'neighbourhoods', 'villages' and 'rural areas'. Now although the various kinds of advanced and primitive groups are superficially very different from each other, they are nevertheless fundamentally similar in kind. All of them are, for example, localized in a particular area, which to some extent they transform in order to maintain the physical and social life of the group; and all the individual members of the group have direct or indirect relations to each other. These social relationships are systematic, and their totality represents the social structure of the group. The structure of the group is maintained throughout the subsequent generations born under it, and it suffers only relatively little change. Apart from variations in the degree of autonomy prevailing in this group or that, and apart from the differences which distinguish this community from that, all these local groups are so essentially different from each other that the individuals living in them are never in any doubt as to which group they belong to, even when the other groups are outwardly only very little different from their own.[12]

Whilst Lloyd Warner and his colleagues concentrated their primary interest on the total structure of the community, about which they were able to draw a great many highly interesting conclusions, William F. Whyte, who was incidentally, like Lloyd Warner, originally a follower of the Chicago School, was more interested in sub-structures. In his *Street Corner Society* (1943) he investigated an Italian slum in 'Cornerville'. In contrast to the approach of the earlier investigators, who were, generally speaking, more interested in the phenomena of social disorganization, Whyte was quite clear in his mind that such a slum also had its own 'complex and well-established organization'.[13] In this way he discovered that each group had a 'hierarchical structure of social relationships which bind the individuals together, whilst the groups themselves stand in a similar relationship to each other'. This was true not only of organized groups such as political clubs and associations, but also of 'informal' groups. It is clear that his investigation was directed primarily to social sub-structures. Accordingly this outstanding work could be used by George C. Homans as valuable illustrative material for his theory of group structure.[14] Incidentally where Whyte is concerned, the analysis of the sub-structures serves as preliminary means for the understanding of the larger structures. The hierarchical organization of the groups makes it impossible for structurally widely separated groups to enter into direct relationships with each other. With this the significance of the function of intermediary groups emerges, particularly in the political order of the community.[15]

This review, in which the beginnings previously described have been more extensively developed, now brings us up to date. As the available material has already been used in our own study we do not propose to describe it in detail, as this would only repeat what is already known. On the other hand, and in conclusion, we propose to take a short glance at the situation in Europe, and particularly in Germany.

THE PRESENT SITUATION IN GERMANY AND ON THE CONTINENT OF EUROPE

It is very illuminating to note that the European continental tradition derives either from the social-reformist conception of Le Play, or from an apparently quite naturally accepted connection of community investigation with empirical social research, such as that seen in the work of Adorno. The result of this is only too often that such community studies reveal a great lack of theoretical orientation. This is illustrated very clearly in the French study *Auxerre* conducted by Charles Bettelheim and Suzanne Frère, which in many long passages is nothing more than an accumulation of material.[16] The German Darmstadt study also suffers to some extent from the same thing, in that inadequate theoretical terms of reference were adopted at the beginning of the investigation. Despite this, however, the study has provided us with two or three excellent volumes, particularly those dealing with the hinterland of Darmstadt and its rural communities (H. Kötter, K. G. Gruneisen and G. Teiwes), and with individual problems in the town itself; for example the volume by Gerhard Baumert on the family and the young. A new French study, on Nouville, developed highly interesting structural problems of community integration. But the village study carried out by G. Wurzbacher in Germany passed over many essential problems owing to a lack of methodological basis.[17] In community studies initiated and carried out by us in Switzerland from 1944 on we attempted to illuminate structural and cultural problems in particular, as evidenced in the investigation of a Zurich suburban community by Hansjürg Beck, the various urban investigations in Zurich by Max Leutenegger and Peter Atteslander, and a village study by Hans Weiss.[18] Later on we attempted the same thing in Germany, where a number of investigations were carried out and their results prepared for publication.[19]

Incidentally, any discussion of the situation in Europe must not ignore Holland and Scandinavia. Quite early on community study developed in Holland under the heading of 'sociography', a word which must not be understood, as it is in Germany, as embracing only a sort of descriptive inventory, but which focuses on 'problems', as evidenced by numerous interesting studies.[20] After the war A. N. J. den Hollander published a book in which he described the forms of settlement in the low lying Hungarian plains, and recorded that he found similar structural relationships in these communities to those existing in American border communities. This interest in structural questions continued and was dealt with again in the excellent study by I. Gadourek. In Sweden, on the other hand, this whole research tendency is more specialized and confined to the studies of small communities on the one hand, and urban and large-scale urban sociology on the other, so that the interest in structural questions seems to be secondary.[21] Other beginnings in Eastern Europe (Poland, Czecho-Slovakia and Roumania) have probably been stifled by post-war political developments there.

CHAPTER XII

METHODS OF COMMUNITY
INVESTIGATION

It goes without saying that the question of method becomes a matter of some urgency if – as has so often been done – community investigation and empiricism in sociology are closely connected with each other. For many people empiricism in sociology seems to have found its purest expression in such community investigations. However, we have already had occasion more than once to point out that this interpretation is too narrow; and therefore, to conclude our own investigation, we must return to this question once more, in order – if that is at all possible – to bring some clarity into the matter.

THE CHOICE OF COMMUNITIES TO BE INVESTIGATED

First of all we must stress in this connection too that there can be no empiricism without a preliminary theoretical reconnaissance. In other words, at least the concept of the community must first be defined before any particular community can be investigated. Previously in this study we have attempted to give such a complex definition of the concept community. Now we must see in what way this definition can be of value for community research. It is a matter of course therefore that before deciding whether a given object of investigation shall be chosen we must first decide whether it really is a local unity with social interactions and joint ties. In so far as this preliminary question has been decided it must then be decided whether the community which had been chosen is really suitable for the purposes of the proposed study. If, for example, one wishes to analyse certain questions which are characteristic of a peasant village, one naturally must not choose a definitely industrial village. Although we may reason-

184

ably assume that such a gross error is not likely to be committed, there are more subtle errors of the same nature which might well be. For example, the sort of thing that happened when G. Wurzbacher set out to investigate a German 'village within the orbit of industrial development', and then picked on a village which 'for decades before the turn of the century' had been a tourist centre. It ought to have been clear at once that such a community was not in the least suited for the purposes of the investigation.[1]

THE QUESTION OF COMMUNITY SIZE

In other words, a careful choice of the community to be analysed is the very first condition for any investigation of this sort. The choice of some special case must under all circumstances be avoided; unless, of course, the investigators happen to be interested in it. With this it will become quite clear that theoretical considerations (which can under certain circumstances be very detailed and circuitous) must first be dealt with before a decision is made as to the choice of the particular object to be investigated. Such considerations will immediately be complicated by questions of research techniques. If the intention is to approach so far as possible each family in a given community with an averaged sized staff of research assistants then the question of the community constitution, and, above this, the question of the size of the community, immediately arise. Experience shows that there are fairly definite limits to an undertaking of this kind. The limit is probably somewhere in the neighbourhood of 2,000 inhabitants. This size is determined in the first place by purely technical considerations and has no typological significance whatever, a point which is not always understood. In fact, only too often a decision determined by purely practical considerations is complicated by assumptions of a quite different nature; for example, assumptions concerning the supposed greater ease with which existing conditions can be studied. But, as we must stress emphatically, this is not a purely qualitatively relevant question, and it involves certain preliminary decisions of a structural nature affecting the integration of the community in question. Unless the utmost care is taken it can easily happen that what should remain to be proved is actually smuggled from the start into the definition of the object to be investigated, so that in the end, and after much labour and effort, the investigator will find that he has merely extracted from his material what he originally put into it.

Methodologically a very clear distinction must be drawn in the first place between the comprehensibility of the given conditions for an outside observer, and the inner comprehensibility of the community for the people living in it. In the one case the question is technical, and in the other it is structural. Whilst the former can be secured, that is not necessarily the case with the latter. In the best case it can be regarded as secured at the end of the investigation, but never at its beginning. The total of 2,000 is thus neither large nor small; it has been fixed merely because it represents the approximate size of a task which can be performed by a medium-sized staff of investigators, assuming that the investigation is really intent on getting some insight into the conditions of each individual family. If a staff of that size is not available then the maximum possible number of inhabitants must be set considerably lower; perhaps even as low as approximately 250. This figure is, in our view, about the lowest limit, because we must reckon with the possibility that the effect of the observer's operations on the object investigated will sometimes be so great that the result will be, so to speak, 'a posed picture'. Further, we must take into consideration the possibility that in very small communities, relatively trivial problems will sometimes bulk large enough to distort the situation to such an extent that the previously mentioned postulate, that under no circumstances must a special case be chosen, is nullified. This is especially the case where refugees or displaced persons have settled in a village. Even the presence of quite a small number of such elements can bring about a fundamental change in the situation; consider, for example, what can happen with the influx of elements of a different religious persuasion into a group which has previously been relatively homogeneous in the religious respect. Under certain circumstances special problems will immediately arise. On the other hand, larger communities are more able to absorb large numbers of outsiders without there being any fundamental disturbance of the community equilibrium. Further, from the beginning larger communities may well be more differentiated internally than

smaller communities. Consider the influence that the presence
of, say, twenty refugees or displaced persons can have on a small
community of, say, two hundred people; and then compare this
with the influence of, say, 2,000 refugees or displaced persons in
a community of, say, 20,000. Whereas in the former case the
influx can result in a complete transformation of the community;
in the latter case the influx can, under certain circumstances, go
almost unperceived and raise no real problems apart from the
purely technical ones of finding accommodation, work, and so
on, for the immigrants – problems which will, in any case, not
affect the constitution of the community.

PARTICIPATION IN COMMUNITY LIFE

We must now stress, however, that everything we have said so
far depends on the assumption that the investigators propose to
obtain an insight into each individual family in the community
concerned. However, such extremely close contact is not always
necessary, and in some cases it would prove altogether impossible, particularly where communities of a different culture are
concerned, because then an observer coming from outside
would only exceptionally find entrance into a family. And in
other cases such close contact would not even be desirable
because there might be a danger that the investigation itself
would transform the given conditions. In the first case we
should be dealing with a participant observation in the strictest
sense, whilst in the second case it would be a non-participant
observation, but nevertheless a direct observation to the extent
that the observer would be amongst the people to be observed,
but without establishing too close contact with them.[2] The
opinion is occasionally expressed that any close participation in
the lives of observed persons is in any case impossible with a
community of a different culture, but that, on the other hand,
such close contact is desirable for the observer of advanced
industrial cultures in order to obtain a really penetrating knowledge. However, we must warn readers against adopting this too
facile conclusion, because it is only too easy to indulge in
illusions about the degree to which it is possible to obtain close
participation even in one's own culture. And there is a further
danger involved, namely that an observer who is very close to

the conditions to be observed suddenly thinks that at last he knows everything, whereas what has really happened is that he had definitely got caught up in the system of prejudices which prevails in the group in question. Further, one should not go to the other extreme and underestimate the possibilities of the non-participant observer.

Social anthropology gives us far-reaching and convincing proof of the truth of these observations where primitive cultures are concerned. But it applies in exactly the same way to our own societies, as community studies conducted by outsiders, and sometimes even by foreigners in certain countries, have shown quite frequently. We need only mention the investigation conducted by the American H. H. Turney-High in Belgium, and that of the Czech I. Gadourek in Holland. In both cases the observer not only remained an outsider, he was even a foreigner. We should like to say that in the case of a non-participant direct observer the quality of being a foreigner is even an advantage, because he is not so endangered in his observations by the trap of the all-too-obvious; because, on the contrary, he calls everything he comes up against into question and takes nothing for granted. As soon as we decide on such an approach, the field of operations of the social investigator is very greatly widened. This means, in other words, that we can deal with much larger communities without necessarily having a particularly large staff of co-workers available. Conrad M. Arensberg provided a typical case when with a staff of four he did a year's field work in a community of 20,000 inhabitants.[3] That is more or less in accordance with our own experience so that it may perhaps be regarded as a normal case.

THE COMBINATION OF RESEARCH METHODS

The moment such numerical ponderables arise, however, there is immediately the question of choice. It goes without saying that in a community of that size it is out of the question to deal with everyone thoroughly. Thus the observer finds himself relying on the usual method of sampling, which can be of a more or less representative nature.[4] Incidentally, people often readily fall into the error of supposing that every kind of sampling must necessarily be, or at least should be, representative. It is an error if only for the reason that in view of the limited character of our means of obtaining knowledge we must always confine ourselves to part sampling and part choice in the plethora of material available. The question which then immediately arises is how to control and check the part results obtained from our choice against other criteria. It may then turn out that the results obtained from the sampling are in conformity with those obtained in a different connection. The same thing applies to the mutual control of the working results of the various co-workers involved. It is thus not always necessary to proceed from the beginning from a so-called representative sampling. Without denying that such a form of sampling can be useful, what we wish to point out here is that one can get on very well without it without necessarily arriving at non-representative results.

An essential condition for this, however, is that in conducting community studies one must on principle use a combination of various sampling and investigation methods which complement, control and check each other at least in part. Today, and particularly in Europe, investigators are too readily inclined to adopt representative sampling without first asking themselves whether it is really necessary or not. And this is often done irrespective of the fact that in most cases there are numerous sources of information available from which important results could be obtained, such as official statistics, official files, local history, the local newspaper, and so on. Under certain circumstances these may well be sufficient to provide an adequate picture of local conditions, as various examples have shown. This form of approach is largely dependent on the structure of the object to be investigated. If the community is really a global society on a local basis, then it will positively demand a great variety of research techniques which are adumbrated in the plethora of functional spheres which go to make up such a body. This is not the place to describe the various methods which can be used. However, it is important to make it quite clear that there is no particular research method for community studies; and that for the very simple reason that the most varied techniques can be adopted according to need, and also because new methods are being worked out and put into operation constantly, as can readily be seen from a glance at the literature on the subject.

Methods of community investigation

THE DEVELOPMENT OF A COMMUNITY STRUCTURAL MODEL

Much more important than the question of research techniques of observation and material collection is as Arensberg has pointed out,[5] the obtaining of a structural model of the community to be investigated. This remains true even when actual representative sampling is carried out. However, it must be realized that the technique of sampling cannot be merely mechanically operated; for example by taking a certain number of units from an existing list. On the contrary the objective logic of the investigation demands that the statistical model adopted is really in accordance with the actually existing constellation. Without this a sampling choice, however representative, can go completely awry. This is in accordance with the general principle that any form of statistical results can be obtained only at the end, after the model development is complete and the objective analysis has been carried out. Unless this is the case, then there is no framework in which the individual data can take on any significance.

We must point out in particular that an astonishing number of errors have been committed in Europe in this respect, particularly under the influence of certain sociographers, who seemed to believe that it was quite sufficient to gather together a volume of data more or less unsystematically arrived at in order to obtain an adequate insight into the structure of a community. Not only does such thoughtless empiricism, which is still far too widespread, make no contribution to the advance of research, but in the last resort it compromises the interests of all concerned. We therefore entirely agree with C. M. Arensberg, when in connection with this working method he strongly underlines the socio-anthropological approach, and indicates the way in which an investigator should proceed in order to obtain first a subjective model of the community as it appears in the minds of its inhabitants, and then to go on to obtain an objective model. With this approach the structure of the model becomes more important than the number of the people who reveal a certain attitude, or behave in a certain way; and more important too than the statistically 'representative' character of the sampling.[6] We must also point out that fundamentally a community as a global society on a local basis embraces a multiplicity of attitudes which have nothing whatever to do with this fundamental structure, whether it is perhaps a question quite simply of non-structured, or non-structurable, attitudes, or whether they are merely bound up with a determinational system which is essentially not of a community nature – for example, if they result from the determinational system of global societies of a higher order. This difficulty, which has been very properly stressed by A. Reiss, should mean that the technique of representative sampling ought to be adopted only at the very last, after the work of model building has been concluded and when all the other sampling techniques have been exhausted. And then the question will still arise as to whether such sampling is really worth while at all – in any case, one is not likely to learn anything from it that one has not already discovered previously; at the utmost one may hope to be able to estimate certain ponderables a little more accurately than before. All this applies of course only so long as one does not attempt to use a community sampling in order to come to conclusions concerning global societies of a higher order. This case, which is obviously regarded by many investigators as the usual thing, is however exactly the opposite: perhaps not an exception, but certainly not really typical. Further, it is then – as Julian H. Steward has pointed out – usual that only in very few cases does one keep to the limits of a community; generally speaking one takes a more or less large district, as was the case with the Darmstadt study.

In fact therefore the essential methodological problem of all community studies remains the development of a structural model of the community in question, and only within this framework can the individual traits from the various sources of information available be obtained and classified. With this the circle closes from the previously set out structural approach to the community as a global society of a specific kind to the methodological basic postulate of a model structure which takes advantage of the usual tried and trusted research techniques used in numerous other scientific spheres and applied here according to need.

AUTHOR'S EPILOGUE

'Community sociology'

Whilst family sociology established itself quite early on as a recognized special branch of sociology, that is by no means true of community sociology, although they both go back originally to the same time, and, to some extent, to the same sources. It can readily be said, for example, that the great French social reformer, Frédéric Le Play (1806–82) was interested both in the family and in the community although in dealing with the living conditions of the European working class he concentrated chiefly on the former problem (*Les ouvriers européens*, in six volumes, Paris 1855). Shortly after that the prominent English jurist and historian Sir Henry James Sumner Maine (1822–88) began to interest himself in the development of the village communities (*Village Communities in East and West*, London 1871), after having previously been concerned in an earlier book with the position of the family in the old and the new society (*Ancient Law*, first published in London in 1861 and subsequently in many further editions, and in particular in an edition with commentaries by F. Pollock first published in London in 1906, with a new edition in 1930). On this basis the French historian Numa Fustel de Coulanges (1830–89) developed his monumental work on the ancient polis, in which, similarly, special attention was paid to the relationship of the family and the community (*La cité antique*, first published in Paris in 1864, and subsequently republished over a score of times down to the present day). These sources served later sociologists for the development of speculative systems; for example, Ferdinand Tönnies (1855–1936), whose chief work, *Gemeinschaft und Gesellschaft* (first published in 1887 after a preliminary work in 1880–1) drew liberally on Maine and Fustel de Coulanges, although from the beginning he philosophically distorted their historical realism. With this he became responsible, particularly in Germany, for

193

numerous socio-ethical distortions of the concepts family
and community, which tended rather to hamper than to
further useful research; and, in addition, for the spread of
numerous stereotyped ideas and misconceptions, from which
present-day sociology is still striving to rid itself in a process of
self-cleansing.

Amongst these misconceptions, for example, is the belief that
in modern industrial societies the family must progressively
dissolve and disappear. The same thing is said about the community, which – and here the original speculative distortion of
the original problem can be seen very clearly – is regarded
largely as the small and 'village' community, whilst the growing
towns and cities were regarded as being a different kind of association from that of the small village community. Now although
family sociology in continental Europe quickly freed itself from
such philosophical futilities and turned its attention to objective
investigation, the situation with regard to community sociology
remained uncertain for quite a long time.

The first important steps in the development of community
sociology were taken in Britain and then followed up in the
United States. Originally, however, the main interest of such
community investigations was directed primarily towards urban
communities, and the background intention was strongly
socio-political, as the central role invariably occupied by the
problem of poverty sufficiently indicates. From this beginning,
however, a general structural analysis of the urban community
soon developed. Sociology now came into conflict with two
streams of thought, and at the same time with the developing
urban sociology on the other, a branch which was subsequently
joined by town and country planning. At the same time this
opened the way for the intervention of new philosophic-
reformist ideas which were just as unclear as the politico-
historical systems from Marx to Tönnies. In the Anglo-Saxon
countries in particular such men as Sir Patrick Geddes, Victor
Branford, Ebenezer Howard and others down to Lewis Mumford all contributed to confusing the real issues with their clever
utopian philosophies and their unrealistic culture criticism,
whilst objective research with its often circuitous strivings was
carried out more or less behind the scenes and did not attract
the public attention. Nevertheless from the eighties on in

Britain and the United States, decisive steps for the development of community sociology were taken, and usually – in accordance with its socio-political and social reformist background – referred to itself as the 'social survey movement'. In time this movement took on a clearer shape, and the individual phases of it were marked by the appearance of classic masterpieces of community sociology, such as the works of Charles Booth and of B. S. Rowntree in Britain, and then the Pittsburg Survey and the Springfield Survey in the United States. The culmination of this development was the publication of the two masterpieces of Robert and Helen Lynd on Middletown, a small town of the American Middle West, which represented a kind of résumé of all past experience. At the same time the purely theoretical aspect of community sociology developed more and more as the analysis of a social system governing a very important part of human social life, even though in modern large-scale societies there were other social formations in addition to the community, social formations of a much greater magnitude, such as the nation. Nevertheless, the fact remains that it is through the community that the human being is first introduced to social relationships extending beyond the confines of the family. The community is, in fact, an original social phenomenon, namely the local unity of a group of human beings who live their social, economic and cultural lives together, and jointly recognize and accept certain obligations and hold certain standards of value in common.

But this viewpoint could command acceptance only after the theory of primary groups, which had developed rapidly since the days of Charles H. Cooley, had been extended beyond the family to include the community. With this for the first time a structural-functional conception was opened up, after the socialization of man by his inclusion in groups of the family and community type, which were marked by a very definite structure, was recognized as an essential function of these groups in the formation of socio-cultural personality. However, first of all certain background attitudes of an evaluative nature had to be re-examined and dismantled, attitudes such as expressed themselves in particular in the occasionally very emphatic use of the term primary group – particularly observable in the United States in the work of Charles Ellwood. As soon as this was done a broad avenue opened up along which community sociology could develop independently and with confidence; a process to which social psychology and social and cultural anthropology made important contributions.

   With this it had now become possible to treat the problem of the community, independent of its particular aspects in rural and urban sociology, as one of the social elementary and total phenomena; thus a phenomenon which does not exhaust itself in the fulfilment of any particular objective, but which represents in a very real sense a 'totality of life' (Marcel Mauss). Community sociology actually is the supposition for all that, therefore it is all important to lay bare, first the structure of the community and then its function in the formation of socio-cultural personality. In dealing with the structural problem of community, all the stereotyped ideas and misconceptions of the old sociology have progressively dissolved; for example the idea that there can be integration only in small rural communities, whilst the towns, on the other hand, are hot-beds of social disorganization in our highly-developed industrial societies. At the same time the concept antinomy which seeks to confine social development into the pattern of community and society is also affected. In fact, an unprejudiced approach shows that even a small community can be structurally so differentiated that formidable obstacles are placed in the way of integration – no less in small communities than in large. Irrespective of this, the community remains as before the framework within which the human being is first introduced to social relationships beyond the confines of the family. This does not exclude the fact that later on still further relationships of a total social nature are opened up to him. However, it does mean that during the life of the average man the community still plays that important role which it has played since men first settled in any one particular spot. Thus the difference between today and the past is not that the community once played an essential role, which in the course of time it gradually lost, but in a different classification of the community. Whereas at one time it was the biggest visible social relationship altogether, today still bigger systems have developed beyond its confines, but without causing it to disappear on that account. The community still represents the most important intermediary social formation between the family and the larger social relationships such as the nation. And in the community the socialization of man is developed from the relatively narrow confines of the family and the home into larger relationships in which for the first time man is introduced to the social world in all its breadth and depth.

NOTES

INTRODUCTION

1. This was stressed in the United States a little while ago, where the technique of community investigation as such has made unusually great progress. In this connection the following important studies must be mentioned: August B. Hollingshead, 'Community Research: Development and Present Condition', in: *American Sociological Review*, XIII (1948), p. 145; Pauline V. Young. *Scientific Social Surveys and Research*, New York 1949, p. 491 et seq.; Julian H. Steward, *Area Research: Theory and Practice*, New York 1950; George H. Hillery Jr., 'Definitions of Community: Areas of Agreement', in: *Rural Sociology*, XX (1950), No. 2; Jessie Bernard, 'Social-Psychological Aspects of Community Study: Some Areas comparatively Neglected by American Sociologists', in: *The British Journal of Sociology* II (1951) No. 1; the same author expresses similar views in her book, *American Community Behaviour*, New York 1949. Earlier similar opinions: E. C. Lindeman, 'Community', in *American Encyclopaedia of the Social Sciences*, at first in New York 1930; Warner E. Gettys, 'The Field and Problems of Community Study', in *Fields and Methods of Sociology*, ed. Luther L. Bernard, New York 1934; Logan Wilson, 'Sociography of Groups', in *Twentieth Century Sociology*, ed. G. Gurvitch and W. G. Moore, New York 1945. A good résumé is provided also by Carl T. Taylor in 'Techniques of Community Study and Analysis as applied to Modern Civilized Societies', *The Science of Man in the World Crises*, ed. Ralph Linton, New York 1945, which deals in particular with the problems in rural areas. More recent fundamental discussion of this problem: Albert J. Reiss Jr., 'A Review and Evaluation of Research on Community. A Working Memorandum prepared for the Committee on Social Behaviour of the Social Science Research Council', Nashville (Tennessee) April 1945 (duplicated as typescript). Further, Conrad M. Arensberg, 'The Community Study Method', in *American Journal of Sociology* LX (1954). See also results of German community research in international comparison, in *Das Dorf im Spannungsfeld industrieller Entwicklung*, ed. Gerhard Wurzbacher, Stuttgart 1954; also 'American Communities', in *American Anthropologist* LVII (1955). More recently Irwin T. Sanders, *The Community*, New York 1958.

The rare community investigations undertaken in Germany after the war were largely interested in research as such, and therefore they usually kept the theoretical problems in the background. For example the competent leader of the great Darmstadt study, Nels Anderson. 'Die Darmstadt Studie', gives us an informal retrospective view, in *Kölner Zeitschrift für*

Soziologie und Sozialpsychologie, Special Number 1 : 'Soziologie der Gemeide', ed. Konig, Opladen 3rd ed. 1966. P. 149 notes that the theoretical volume is missing; the conceptual problems would presumably have been dealt with in this. Here Christian von Ferber also points to this deficiency: 'Die Gemeindestudie des Instituts für sozialwissenschaftliche Forschung, Darmstadt', p. 152, as also König, 'Die Gemeindestudie des deutschen Unesco-Instituts', p. 174, underlining the absence of a definition in the investigation mentioned. The other studies of a more fundamental nature are therefore usually rather uncertain. In particular Kurt Utermann must be mentioned, 'Aufgaben und Methoden der gemeindlichen Sozialforschung', in *Beiträge zur Soziologie der industriellen Gesellschaft*, ed. W. G. Hoffmann, Dortmund 1952; see also Utermann, 'Forschungsprobleme einer Gemeindeuntersuchung in nördlichen Ruhrgebiet', in 'Soziologie der Gemeinde'. In Hoffmann's comprehensive work there are also two interesting studies by Dietrich von Oppen and Helmuth Croon. See also Croon 'Sozialgeschichtsforschung und Archive', in *Der Archivar* VII (1954); 'Methoden zur Erforschung der gemeindlichen Sozialgeschichte', in *Westfälische Forschungen* VIII (1955) and 'Die Einwirkung der Industrialisierung auf die gesellschaftliche Schichtung der Bevölkerung im rheinisch-westfälischen Industriegebiet', in *Rheinische Vierteljahrsblätter* XX (1955). More recently Croon and Kurt Utermann, *Zeche und Gemeinde, Untersuchungen über den Strukturwandel einer Zechengemeinde, im nördlichen Ruhrgebiet*, Tubingen 1958. Quite unusually unclear and unusable is the work of Karl G. Specht, 'Mensch und räumliche Umwelt. Bemerkungen zur Geschichte, Abgrenzung und Fragestellung der Sozialökologie', in *Die Soziale Welt* IV (1953). Information concerning the work which has developed under the influence of Leopold von Wiese is given by Harriet Hoffmann, 'Die Beziehungslehre als sozialwissenschaftliche Forschungsmethode', in *Soziologische Forschung in unserer Zeit*, ed. K. G. Specht, Cologne 1951. As here both the conceptual preliminary conditions and also the research methods are very inadequately represented and very dilettantish, what has been obtained does not take us very much farther. A systematic outlook would have been all the more necessary when a special number was to be devoted to the question, as was done not so long ago in *Die Soziale Welt* V, 2 (1954). Instead of that all we get are a few, incidentally very incomplete, bibliographical notes in Harriet Hoffmann's, 'Amerikanische Community Forschung', and others. At least we are shown here that the community is an unusually complicated social system. Incomplete and lacking in outlook is Ernst Stauffer's 'Gemeindeforschung in Deutschland'. In *Wörterbuch der Soziologie*, ed. F. Bülow and F. Bernsdorf, Stuttgart 1944, the article 'Community' is much too brief, the article 'Gemeinde' deals too one-sidedly with the sociology of religion and the article 'Sozialökologie' is very confused. Cf. also König, 'Die Gemeinde im Blickfeld der Soziologie', in *Handbuch der kommunalen Wissenschaft und Praxis*, ed. Hans Peters, Berlin 1956; *idem*, 'Einige Bemerkungen zur Soziologie der Gemeinde', in 'Soziologie der Gemeinde'. The present book is essentially developed from these two works and a number of others. For the rest, see the bibliography and numerous other works quoted during the course of this study.

I. NATURE AND COMMUNITY

1. Cf. in this respect the thoroughly critical work of Amos H. Hawley, *Human Ecology. A Theory of Community Structure*, New York 1950; J. A. Quinn, *Human Ecology*, New York 1950; Marston Bates, in *Anthropology Today*, ed. A. L. Kroeber, Chicago 1953, and others.

2. See also with reference to the expression 'second birth', König, *Materialien zur Soziologie der Familie*, Berne 1946 (new edition in preparation).

3. In addition recently, Hans M. Peters, 'Gesellungsform der Tiere', in *Handbuch der Soziologie*, ed. W. Ziegenfuss, Stuttgart 1955, pp. 618–19. A good comprehensive work is Hans Hediger's, *Wildtiere in Gefangenschaft*, Basel 1942, with an extensive bibliography.

4. Maximilien Sorre, *Rencontres de la géographie et de la sociologie*, Paris 1957, p. 116.

5. Alfred Espinas, *Des sociétés animales*, first published in Paris 1877.

6. Adolf Portmann, *Animals as Social Beings*, London 1961, Chapter II.

7. ibid. p. 101.

8. ibid. p. 103.

9. ibid. pp. 98 et seq.

10. *idem, Zoologie und das neue Bild des Menschen*, Hamburg 1956, p. 135.

11. Daryll Forde, *Habitat, Economy and Society. A Geographical Introduction to Ethnology*, London 1952 (first published 1934), p. 465.

II. CERTAIN TERMINOLOGICAL DIFFICULTIES

1. Hawley, p. 65.

2. Theodor Geiger, 'Gemeinschaft' in *Handwörterbuch der Soziologie*, ed. A. Vierkandt, Stuttgart 1931, p. 173.

3. J. Grimm and W. Grimm, *Deutsches Wörterbuch*, IV, Vol. 1, Part 2, Leipzig 1891, p. 3264.

4. ibid. p. 3266.

5. ibid. p. 3223.

6. On this concept Max Huber, *Die Gemeinderschaften der Schweiz*, Breslau 1897; Eugen Huber, *Geschichte der schweizerischen Privatrechts*, Vol. IV, Basel 1893; Georg Cohn, *Gemeinderschaft und Hausgenossenschaft*, Stuttgart 1898; Arnold Altheer, *Das Gemeinderschaftsrecht des schweizerischen Zivilgesetzbuches*, Chur 1916 (Berner Diss.); Stéfane Poffet, *La communauté de frères et soeurs de l'ancien droit fribourgeois*, Paris 1935; August Egger, *Das Familienrecht, Kommentar zum schweizerischen Zivilgesetzbuch*, 2nd ed, Vol. 11, Zurich 1936.

7. See also Alfred Vierkandt, *Gesellschaftslehre*, 2nd ed., Stuttgart 1928, pp. 108 et. seq. It is only logical when, for example, Geiger (p. 170) observes that in the (modern) sense used here there can be a community only between people, and not between people and things, which was the main sense of the word in the old usage. Irrespective of the problem

which lies behind it, the question is extremely illuminating for the various meanings of the word formerly and now.

8. Grimm and Grimm, p. 3238.

9. Erich Becker, 'Entwicklung der deutschen Gemeinden und Gemeindeverbände im Hinblick auf die Gegenwart', in Hans Peters, Vol. I, p. 63

10. Characteristic of this mode of thought, for example, Robert M. MacIver, *Community*, New York 1930; *idem, Society,* New York 1937, as Gurvitch has already pointed out.

11. Grimm and Grimm, pp. 3227; 3241; 3266.

12. Gustav Mensching, *Soziologie der Religion*, Bonn 1947, pp. 180 et seq. The emphatic sense in which the word 'community' (*Gemeinschaft*) is used here can be seen from the following: 'To identify the sociological formation on the basis of religion we use the term "community", because here too it is a question of the establishment of the community-forms in the inner essential longing of the religious human being, and not of rationalistically motivated use-institutions in the sense of society' (pp. 23 et seq). As can be seen from the definition quoted, this concept of community has no place in sociology at all. This is also expressed in the fact that as a matter of course each concrete community, irrespective of degree of inner homogeneity, also has its outer organizational forms, in so far as it is a body and an administrative unit, and also in many other respects.

13. A similar tendency is noticeable today in E. A. Gutkind's *Community and Environment*, London 1953, and, in general, under the influence of L. Mumford, with many British town planners.

14. E. K. Francis, *In Search of Utopia, The Mennonites in Manitoba*, Altona, Manitoba 1955, pp. 278 et seq.

15. J. A. Pitt-Rivers, *The People of the Sierra*, London 1954.

16. Lucio Mendieta y Nuñez. *Théorie des groupements sociaux*, translated by A. Cuvillier, Paris 1957, pp. 110, 104 et seq.

III. PRELIMINARY DEFINITION OF COMMUNITY

1. Hillery.

2. Leopold von Wiese, *System der allgemeinen Soziologie*, 3rd ed., Munich 1955, p. 400.

3. Becker, art. cit. p. 92; *idem*, 'Die Selbstverwaltung als verfassungsrechtliche Grundlage der kommunalen Ordnung in Bund und Ländern', in: Hans Peters, Vol. I, pp. 125 et seq.

4. The expression 'full groups' is to be found in Karl Dunkmann, *Lehrbuch der Soziologie und Sozialphilosophie*, Berlin 1931, p. 189 (together with a reference to others who use the same expression), but, characteristically, coupled with the concept of 'autarchy'. The latter is not compensated for by the fact that Dunkmann is thinking above all of the 'Folk' as a full group, whilst the expression community is not used by him at all. But the Folk is also neither autarchic nor self-sufficient.

5. With regard to this point see also Forde, p. 466: 'No human community has lived in prolonged and absolute isolation. Man has both a greater effective mobility, and a wider distribution on the earth's surface

than any other species of animal. In his ability to acquire and to impart knowledge and belief, he is able not only to develop a particular cultural pattern and to transmit it from generation to generation within a particular society, but also, despite the confusion of tongues, to transfer such knowledge to other societies.'

6. This is also stressed by Steward. This point is returned to later in the text.

7. Robert Redfield, *The Little Community. Viewpoints for the Study of a Human Whole*, Uppsala and Stockholm 1955, p. 4.

8. This concept has been essentially taken over by Georges Gurvitch in his *Déterminismes sociaux et liberté humaine*, Paris 1955, pp. 192–5, although he himself does not wish to see it applied to the community. Thus although in this respect we deliberately avoid his use of the word we nevertheless largely accept his definition, in which he stresses the following factors: a global society embraces a whole hierarchy of functional groupings and social classes; thus it represents a microcosm of groups. In addition it possesses social (not political) sovereignty over all the elements which compose it; and sometimes, but not always, economic sovereignty. The global society has a structure; it is super-functional, that is to say, it does not exhaust itself in the functions it exercises, and can therefore not express itself adequately in any of its part organizations alone. Finally, it derives its life from an unorganized infrastructure which is pure spontaneity. Incidentally, it should be pointed out that Gurvitch at least applies this category to the *polis* of antiquity, so that our use of the expression does not fall completely outside the general framework.

9. Cf. König, 'Familie', in Bülow and Bernsdorf. This naturally by no means excludes the formation of leagues (for example, the Iroquois League), or 'amphictions', and assumes only a historical process and not a decision in principle concerning the 'composition' of society from individual 'parts'.

10. Hillery, p. 117.

11. See Wurzbacher, op. cit.

12. C. von Dietze, M. Rolfes, G. Weippert, *Lebensverhältnisse in kleinbürgerlichen Dörfern*, Hamburg and Berlin 1953.

13. For a detailed substantiation of this judgement see König, art. cit. in 'Sociologie der Gemeinde'.

14. Cf. Geiger, p. 175. Gurvitch comes to the same conclusion, and modern sociology in general.

IV. THE COMMUNITY IN THE DEVELOPMENT OF HUMAN SOCIETY

1. Cf. in this respect Forde, p. 50; George P. Murdock, *Our Primitive Contemporaries*, New York 1956 (first published in 1934), p. 93; Fritz M. Heichelheim, *Wirtschaftsgeschichte des Altertums vom Paläolithikum bis zur Völkerwanderung der Germanen, Slaven und Araber*, 2 vols., Leyden 1938, I, p. 31; Richard Thurnwald, *Werden, Wandel und Gestaltung von Staat und Kultur*, Berlin 1935, p. 65.

2. Thurnwald, p. 44.

3. ibid. pp. 41 et. seq.

4. Marvin Harris, *Town and Country in Brazil*, New York 1956, pp. 59 et seq.

5. Cf. Walter H. Terpenning, *Village and Open Country Neighbourhood*, New York 1931.

6. Alexandre Moret and Georges Davy, *Des clans aux empires. L'organization sociale chez les primitifs et dans l'Orient Ancien*, Paris 1923, pp. 48 et seq.

7. G. Glotz, *La Cité grecque*, Paris 1928, pp. 6 et seq.

8. ibid. p. 33.

9. ibid. p. 36.

10. Cf. on this point Berthel Huppertz, *Räume und Schichten bäuerlicher Kulturformen in Deutschland*, Bonn 1939, pp. 131 et seq.

11. Harry Goetz, 'Die ausländischen Gemeinden im Vergleich zu den deutschen', in Hans Peters, p. 598.

12. Max Weber. *Wirtschaft und Gesellschaft*, 4th ed., Tübingen 1956, p. 199.

V. THE COMMUNITY AS A GLOBAL SOCIETY ON A LOCAL BASIS

1. P. H. Chombart de Lauwe, *Découverte aérienne du Monde*, Paris 1948; *Photographic aériennes. L'études de l'homme sur la terre*, Paris 1951.

2. *idem*, Paris et l'agglomération parisienne, Vol. II, Paris 1952.

3. Cf. Ferber as an introduction.

4. Steward, p. 51.

5. I. Gadourek, *A Dutch Community*, Leiden 1956.

6. H. H. Turney-High, *Château Gérard, Time and Life of a Walloon Village*, Columbia (South Carolina) 1953.

7. Conrad M. Arensberg and Solon T. Kimball, *Family and Community in Ireland*, Cambridge (Mass) 1948 (first published in 1940), p. xxvii.

8. C. M. Arensberg, art. cit.

9. *idem*, 'American Communities', in *American Anthropologist*, LVII (1955).

10. *idem*, 'Ergebnisse der deutschen Gemeindestudie im internationalen Vergleich', in Wurzbacher.

11. Leon Festinger, Stanley Schachter and Kurt Back, *Social Pressures in Informal Groups*, New York 1950.

12. Charles P. Loomis and J. Allen Beegle, *Rural Social Systems*, New York 1950, p. 135.

13. ibid. pp. 137–44.

14. Albert Meister, *Coopération d'habitation et sociologie du voisinage*, Paris 1957.

15. H. W. Riecken and G. C. Homans, 'Psychological Aspects of Social Structure', in *Handbook of Social Psychology*, ed. Gardner Lindzey, Vol. II., Cambridge (Mass) 1954.

16. Egon Ernst Bergel, *Urban Sociology*, New York 1955, pp. 487 et seq.

17. ibid. p. 488.

VI. THE SOCIAL ECOLOGY OF THE COMMUNITY

1. For example, Emile Durkheim ran a special section for social morphology in the *Année sociologique* (Vol. II, p. 520) as early as 1897–8. Amongst other things the problem of the community, and in particular the problem of urban communities, was visible here. See also for this development, Maurice Halbwachs, *Morphologie sociale*, 2nd ed., Paris 1946 (first published in 1938). Today on the same subject Sorre.

2. Sorre, p. 135.

3. Marcel Mauss, 'Les Variations saisonières des sociétés Esquimaux', in the *Année Sociologique* IX (1904–5).

4. Richard Thurnwald, *Die Gemeinde der Banaro*, Berlin 1912.

5. Lucien Bernot and René Blancard, *Nouville. Un Village français*, Paris 1953. See also in this respect our own article in 'Soziologie der Gemeinde'.

6. Robert E. Park, *Human Communities*, Glencoe, Ill., 1952, pp. 17, 78 et seq.

7. Clear introduction by Young, pp. 430 et seq., 491 et seq.

8. Howard W. Odum's group occupies itself in particular with area research in the United States today. The best source of information at present is *American Sociology*, New York 1951, particularly pp. 353–60.

9. Park, pp. 88 et seq.

10. Chombart de Lauwe, p. 34.

11. Michael Quoist, *La Ville et l'homme: Rouen*, Paris 1952.

12. Beginning, say, with Milla A. Allihan, *Social Ecology: a Critical Analysis*, New York 1938. Harvey W. Zorbaugh gave the first systematically developed analysis of this concept in his contribution 'The Natural Areas of the City', to *The Urban Community*, ed. Ernest W. Burgess, Chicago 1926.

13. Very important on this Paul K. Hatt, 'The Concept of Natural Area', in *American Sociological Review* XI (1946).

14. Park, p. 18.

15. Developed in a different but related connection by Margret J. Hagood, 'Statistical Methods for Delineation of Regions Applied to Data on Agriculture and Population', in *Social Forces*, XXI (1943) and others.

16. Max Leutenegger, *Grossstadtsoziologie, Probleme der Stadt Zurich*, Zuricher Diss., 1953; *idem*, 'Die Sozialstruktur der Zuricher Innenstadt', in *Zuricher statistische Nachrichten* 1954, part 4. Recently a German book by Hermann Peters entitled *Biologie einer Grosstadt*, Heidelberg 1954, which naïvely ignores all these warnings and actually goes back to the ideas of districts as 'biocoenoses' in the biological sense; something not even Park had in mind when he spoke of the symbiosis of the individual districts of a town.

17. Hatt, pp. 489 et seq.

18. ibid. pp. 425 et seq.

19. Bergel, pp. 489 et seq.

20. Clifford R. Shaw and Henry D. McKay, *Juvenile Delinquency and Urban Areas*, Chicago 1942; *idem, Social Factors in Juvenile Delinquency*, Washington 1931.

21. See also David J. Bordua 'Theorie und Erforschung der Jugend-kriminalität in den U.S.A.', in *Kölner Zeitschrift für Soziologie und Sozial-psychologie*, Special No. 2, ed. P. Heintz and R. König, '*Soziologie der Jugendkriminalität*', Opladen 1957.

22. Robert K. Merton, 'Social Structure and Anatomy', in *Social Theory and Social Structure*, ed. R. K. Merton, 2nd ed. III, 1957; also König, 'Einige Bemerkungen zur Stellung des Problems der Jugend-kriminalität in der allgemeinen Soziologie', in 'Soziologie der Jugend-kriminalität'.

23. Hansjürg Beck, *Der Kulturzusammenstoss zwischen Stadt und Land in einer Vorortgemeinde*, Zurich 1952.

24. The American Walter Firey, reported on the importance of these social boundaries of the community in Germany too, in 'Grenzen als Faktoren in der Gemeindeplanung', in *Soziale Welt*, V (1954) 2, intro-ducing 'a concept of the community which is more comprehensive than unity in the juridical sense'. Cf. p. 114.

25. See also Ruth Glass, *The Social Background of a Plan: a Study of Middlesborough*, London 1948, pp. 18 et seq.

26. ibid. pp. 39 et seq.

27. Peter H. Mann, 'The Concept of Neighborliness', in *American Journal of Sociology*, LX (1954), p. 163. Similar problems arise early on in Bessie Averne McClenahan's book *The Changing Urban Neighborhood*, Los Angeles 1929. What is called 'nigh dwelling' is distinguished from neighbourhood in the sense of integrated neighbourhood. And latterly also the investigation group of T. S. Simey ed., *Neighbourhood and Com-munity*, Liverpool 1954, p. 106.

28. For example, Harold Orlans' *Stevenage. A Sociological Study of a New Town*, London 1952, pp. 97 et seq.

29. Arensberg, 'The Community Study Method', p. 124.

30. Gunther Ipsen, 'Die Gemeinde als Gemeinschaft', in *Jahrbuch für Kommunalwissenschaft* III (1936), p. 7.

31. Simey, p. 54.

32. ibid. p. 70.

33. ibid. p. 108.

34. ibid. p. 136.

35. Festinger *et al.*, pp. 34. et seq.

36. ibid. p. 151.

37. W. Lloyd Warner and Paul S. Lunt. *The Social Life of a Modern Community*, New Haven 1950 (first published in 1941), pp. 81 et seq.

38. W. Lloyd Warner and Leo Srole, *The Social Systems of American Ethnic Groups*, New Haven 1949 (first published in 1945).

39. Robert S. Lynd and Helen M. Lynd, *Middletown*, New York 1929; *idem, Middletown in Transition*, New York 1937.

VII. ATTEMPT AT A COMMUNITY TYPOLOGY

1. This division into ecological structural and typological approaches goes back to Hollingshead, pp. 139 et seq.

2. Stressed above all in the United States by Young, p. 496.

3. Steward, p. 51, expresses this as follows: 'The community approach is not yet sufficiently related to that of the various disciplines which study culture in these larger dimensions. It is also strikingly unhistorical in its modern applications. Many problems do not require historical study, but most of those pertaining to culture change and social relations, which are the concern of many community studies, would be illuminated by a historical "approach".' In the same sense also Arensberg, 'American Communities'. See also Oscar Lewis, *Life in a Mexican Village: Tepoztlan Restudied*, Urbana, Ill. 1951, pp. XII et seq. Similarly Horace Miner and others.

4. A good example in Europe was provided recently by Louis Chevalier, *La Formation de la population parisienne au 19 siècle*, Paris 1950. With regard to the concepts of social ecology used in the text see Emma Llewellyn and Audrey Hawthorn, 'Human Ecology', in Gurvitch and Moore. In the meantime an excellent ecological investigation has appeared in Paris: see Chombart de Lauwe, *Paris*.

5. Utermann, art. cit. in 'Soziologie der Gemeinde', see also Croon and Utermann.

6. Croon arts. cit.

7. Herman R. Lantz, *People of Coal Town*, New York 1958. Earlier the interesting English investigation of Norman Dennis, Fernando Henri Ques and Clifford Slaughter, *Coal is Our Life, An Analysis of a Yorkshire Mining Community*, London 1956.

8. R. D. MacKenzie, *The Metropolitan Community*, New York 1933; later Donald Bogue, *The Structure of the Metropolitan Community*, Ann Arbor, Mich., 1949; Wilbut C. Hallenbeck, *American Urban Communities*, New York 1951; Svend Riemer, *The Modern City*, New York 1952; Bergel; Amos H. Hawley, *The Changing Shape of Metropolitan America*, Glencoe, Ill. 1956.

9. Pierre Michel, *Pfaffenhofen. L'évolution des rapports fonctionels entre un petit centre urbain et la campagne voisine*, Centre de Documentation Universitaire, Paris 1954.

10. See also König, 'Banlieues, déplacements journaliers, migrations de travail', in *Villes et campagnes*, ed. G. Friedmann, Paris 1953.

11. Forde, p. 464.

12. For example, quite early on, C. C. Zimmermann, *The Changing Community*, New York 1938.

13. Hans Bobek, Albert Hammer and Robert Ofner, *Beiträge zur Ermittelung von Gemeindetypen*, Klagenfurt 1955, p. 37.

14. P. A. Sorokin and C. C. Zimmermann, *Principles of Rural Urban Sociology*, New York 1929.

15. Louis Wirth, 'Urbanism as a Way of Life', in his *Community Life and Social Policy*, Chicago 1956 (first published in *American Journal of Sociology*, 1938).

16. Max Weber, 'Die Stadt', chapter VIII of *Wirtschaft und Gesellschaft*, 4th ed., Tübingen 1956.

17. Werner Sombart, 'Städtische Siedelung' in Vierkandt.

18. Leopold von Wiese, 'Ländliche Siedelungen', ibid. pp. 522 et seq.
19. The following still provide the best information concerning the latest developments: Loomis and Beegle; J. H. Kolb and Edmund G. Brunner, *A Study of Rural Society*, New York, 1950.
20. Paul Hesse, *Grundprobleme der Agrarverfassung*, Stuttgart 1949.
21. H. A. Finke, 'Soziale Gemeindetypen', in *Geographisches Taschenbuche*, Stuttgart 1953, pp. 509–12.
22. A similar viewpoint, stability-unstability, was at the centre of a series of community investigations carried out by the Agricultural Department of the U.S. Government of which six were published: *Culture of Contemporary Rural Community*, Rural Life Studies, Nos. 1 to 6, United States Department of Agriculture, Washington D.C. 1941–3.
23. M. Schwind, 'Typisierung der Gemeinden nach ihrer sozialen Struktur als geographische Aufgabe', in *Berichte zur deutschen Landeskund*, Vol. 8, Stuttgart 1950.
24. Hans Linde, 'Grundfragen der Gemeindetypisierung', in *Forschungs- und Sitzungsberichte der Akademie für Raumforschung und Landesplanung*, ed. Kurt Brüning, Vol. III, 'Raum und Wirtschaft', Bremen-Horn 1952.
25. ibid. p. 75.
26. ibid. p. 68.
27. Bobek *et al.* p. 36.
28. ibid. p. 40.
29. Linde, p. 66.
30. Bobek *et al.* p. 53.
31. ibid. p. 35.
32. ibid. p. 82.

33. Wurzbacher, *op. cit.* is, in particular, based on Paul Hesse. However, the most important community investigations of this kind are represented by the nine monographs of the Darmstadt Study, which also owe a good deal to Paul Hesse. See also H. Kötter, *Struktur und Funktion von Landgemeinden im Einflussbereich einer deutschen Mittelstadt*, Darmstadt 1952; K. G. Grüneisen, *Landbevölkerung im Kraftfeld der Stadt*, Darmstadt 1952; G. Teiwes, *Der Nebenerwerbslandwirt und seine Familie*, Darmstadt 1952; G. Baumert, *Jugend der Nachkriegszeit*, Darmstadt 1952; Baumert and E. Hünninger, *Deutsche Familien nach dem Kriege*, Darmstadt 1954; I. Kuhr and G. Koepnik, *Schule und Jugend in einer ausgebombten Stadt*; *Mädchen einer Oberprima*, Darmstadt 1952; K. A. Lindemann, *Behörde und Bürger*, Darmstadt 1952: A. Mausolff, *Gewerkschaft und Betriebsrat im Urteil der Arbeitnehmer*, Darmstadt 1952. Earlier, the community investigation occasioned by us and directed by Hansjürg Beck. Similarly under our auspices, Hans Weiss, *Ein schweizerisches Industriedorf*, Cologne 1958; also Manfred Sieben, *Die Prüfung der Validität von Untersuchungsmethoden zur Analyse von Genossenschaften. Eine Befragung in zwei ländlichen Gemeinden*, Kölner Diss. 1955; idem, 'Welche Faktoren bewirken das Wachstum von Genossenschaften?', in *Archiv für öffentliche und freigemeinwirtschaftliche Unternehmen*, III/4 (1958). Just appeared, Renate Mayntz *Soziale Schichtung und soziale Wandel in einer Industriegemeinde*, Stuttgart 1958.
34. Hollingshead.

35. Kötter, p. 70.
36. ibid. p. 21.
37. König, in *Villes et campagnes*, p. 194.
38. Beck.
39. Alexander Rüstow, *Ortsbestimmung der Gegenwart*, Vol. 1, Zurich, 1950, p. 262.
40. Lewis Mumford, *The Culture of Cities*, New York 1938. The cultural aspect as an estimate of value is less stressed in Zimmermann.
41. Elisabeth Pfeil, *Grossstadtforschung*, Bremen 1950, p. 105.
42. Colin Clark, *The Conditions of Economic Progress*, London 1940. In this connection see also König, *Soziologie heute*, Zurich 1949.
43. Robert C. Angell, 'The Moral Integration of American Cities'. Supplement to the *American Journal of Sociology*, July 1951.
44. Morris Janowitz, *The Community Press in an Urban Setting*, Glencoe, Ill. 1952.
45. Angell, pp. 119–22.
46. Gustav Krall, Leopold Rosenmayr, Anton Schimka and Hans Strotzka, 'Wohnen im Wien', results and conclusions of an investigation into housing conditions in Vienna, in *Der Aufbau*, Monograph No. 8, Vienna 1956.

VIII. THE STRUCTURAL ASPECT OF THE COMMUNITY

1. Lynd and Lynd, p. 23.
2. With reference to the 'informal groups' in the community see Warner and Lunt, pp. 301 et seq and pp. 350 et seq. Almost at the same time, Charles P. Loomis, *Social Relationships in Seven Rural Communities*, Washington D. C. 1940.
3. Hollingshead, p. 143.
4. Warner, Whyte, Arensberg, Eliot D. Chapple and others. Cf. also as an introduction Peter Heintz, 'Neue Forschungsergebnisse der Soziologie der Gruppenführung', in *Schweiz*, 4. Zeitschrift für Volkswirtschaft und Statistik, 90th year, 1954.
5. Cf. König, 'Einleitung zu einer Soziologie der sog. rückständigen Gebiete', in *Kölner Zeitschrift*, VII/1 (1955).
6. Wolfgang Teuscher, 'Klassenstruktur und Initiative in einer sich wandeldende ländlichen Gemeinde', in 'Soziologie der Gemeinde'.
7. Sieben, op. cit.
8. Renate Pflaum-Mayntz. 'Politische Führung und Politische Beteiligung als Ausdruck gemeindlicher Selbsgestaltung', in Wurzbacher, p. 271. 'After all that has been said, the population demands particularly active community-interested persons, keen on community and local interests, as leaders of the local administration; and the parties comply with this demand by doing their best to win over suitable candidates. Today, as in former times, there are a number of personalities in the community who can be described as natural leaders, or – if one cares to use a new and uncompromised term – as 'social activists'. These are men whose character and mode of life causes them to be looked up to in their home locality, and

to whom the villagers go for advice and assistance, to settle disputes, to draw up a petition, to represent an interest, or perhaps merely in connection with the purchase of a pig. The inhabitants of the locality, and sometimes even the inhabitants of larger areas, unanimously recognize such personalities and their unofficial special position in the community.'

9. ibid. p. 267.

10. Renate Mayntz, 'Lokale Parteigruppen in der kleinen Gemeinde', in *Zeitschrift für Politik*, 1955, 1. p. 67.

11. ibid. p. 64.

12. ibid.

13. Warner and Lunt, pp. 349 et seq., pp. 110 et seq.

14. Loomis and Beegle, pp. 134 et seq.

15. Heintz, p. 87. Cf. also W. Lloyd Warner and J. O. Low, *The Social System of the Modern Factory*, New Haven 1947, pp. 180 et seq.

16. Warner and Low, pp. 134 et seq.

17. Pflaum-Mayntz, for example, repeatedly pp. 274–9, where the sociological importance of the administrative division of competence between the managing director and the mayor is specially stressed. Quite unhelpful for this problem is Lindemann's work in which there are merely one or two observations concerning the personalizing tendencies in the administration (p. 61). But there is the correct comment: 'The character of the administration is hardly changed thereby.' New views in this respect were obtained in Germany through the American Roland L. Warren; see comments in the text.

20. Pflaum-Mayntz, p. 272.

21. Loomis and Beegle, p. 135.

22. Lynd and Lynd, *Middletown in Transition*, p. 329.

23. Floyd Hunter, *Community Power Structure*, Chapel Hill, N.C., 1953, Floyd Hunter, Ruth C. Schaffer and Cecil G. Sheps, *Community Organization: Action and Inaction*, Chapel Hill, N.C., 1956.

24. Beck, pp. 115 et seq.

25. ibid. pp. 120 et seq.

26. R. Pflaum, 'Die Vereine als Produkt und Gegengewicht soziale Differenzierung', in Wurzbacher, p. 158.

27. ibid. pp. 174 et seq. Incidentally, exactly the same expression is to be found in Floyd Hunter's book, p. 86 – 'training grounds for many of the men who have become power leaders'.

28. Pflaum, p. 178.

29. ibid, p. 179.

30. Hunter, p. 84; a very penetrating analysis.

31. Roland L. Warren, 'Bürgerschaftliche Tätigkeiten in einer deutschen Grossstadt', in *Kölner Zeitschrift* IX, 3 (1957), p. 246.

32. ibid. p. 44.

33. ibid. p. 445.

34. George C. Homans, *The Human Group*, New York 1950, chapter XV, pp. 334–68, specially pp. 353 et seq.

35. Hunter, p. 104.

36. ibid. p. 112.

37. Turney-High, pp. 107 et seq.
38. W. M. Williams, *The Sociology of an English Village: Gosforth*, London 1956, p. 123.
39. ibid. p. 125.
40. See also König, *Soziologie heute*, p. 73.
41. E. Digby Baltzell, *Philadelphia Gentlemen*, Glencoe, Ill. 1958.
42. John Dollard, *Caste and Class in a Southern Town*, 2nd ed., New York 1949 (first published in 1937).
43. Hortense Powdermaker, *After Freedom. The Portrait of a Community in the Deep South*, New York 1939.
44. Allison Davis, Burleigh B. Gardner and Mary R. Gardner, *Deep South. A Social Anthropological Study of Caste and Class*, Chicago 1941.
45. St. Clair Drake and Horace R. Cayton, *Black Metropolis. A Study of Negro Life in a Northern City*, New York 1945.
46. W. Lloyd Warner and collaborators, *Democracy in Jonesville*, New York 1949; *Social Class in America*, Chicago 1949 and *Structure of American Life*, Edinburgh, 1952.
47. B. Hollingshead, *Elmtown's Youth*, New York 1949, p. 148.
48. ibid. pp. 204 et seq.
49. ibid. pp. 441 et seq.
50. James West, *Plainville USA*, New York 1945, pp. 115 et seq; see also the diagram on p. 117.
51. John Y. Keur and Dorothy L. Keur, *The Deeply Rooted. A Study of a Drenthe Community in the Netherlands*, Assen 1955, pp. 148 et seq.
52. ibid, p. 102.
53. Turney-High, chapter VI.
54. See Williams. Cf. also Appendix V, tables 1–5, and the whole of chapter V.
55. For example Hollingshead, art. cit., p. 143.
56. Cf. Richard Centers, *The Psychology of Social Classes*, Princeton, N.J. 1949.
57. Theodor Geiger, Soziale Umschichtungen in einer dänischen Mittelstadt, 2nd vol., Copenhagen 1951, p. 12.
58. Williams, p. 88.
59. ibid. pp. 107–9.
60. Homans, p. 180.
61. ibid. pp. 281 et seq.
62. Robert Redfield and Alfonso Villa Rojas, *Chan Kom, a Maya Village*, Washington D.C., 1934; Robert Redfield, *A Village that Chose Progress*, Chicago 1950.
63. Arensberg, 'The Community Study Method', p. 123; in which the earlier word 'rurban' is adopted, from 'rural-urban' to indicate the development trend.

IX. THE INTEGRATION OF THE COMMUNITY

1. Robert Redfield, *The Little Community*, p. 3.
2. For example, Max Rumpf, *Deutsches Bauernleben*, Stuttgart 1936;

Hans F. Günther, *Das Bauerntum als Lebens-und Gemeinschaftsform*, Leipzig–Berlin 1939, and others.

3. Lewis.

4. R. Redfield, *Tepoztlàn – A Mexican Village*, Chicago 1930.

5. Lewis, p. 432.

6. Redfield, *The Little Community*, p. 135.

7. ibid. p. 135.

8. ibid, p. 144.

9. Cf. König, 'Die Begriffe Gemeinschaft und Gesellschaft bei Ferdinand Tönnies', in *Kölner Zeitschrift* VII 3. (1955), p. 402.

10. Homans, p. 90.

11. ibid. p. 110.

12. West, pp. 115 et seq.

13. Hans Linde, 'Zur sozialökonomische Struktur und soziologischen Formation des deutschen Dorfes', in *Das Dorf und die Aufgabe ländlichen Zusammenlebens*, Rural Social Problems Series, ed. W. Abel, Hannover 1954, p. 6.

14. Ipsen, p. 5.

15. Linde, p. 9.

16. Alexandre Vexliard, *Introduction à la sociologie du vagabondage*, Paris 1956.

17. See also, Eberhard Gothein, *Verfassungs – und Wirtschaftsgeschichte der Stadt Köln vom Untergang der Reichsfreiheit bis zur Errichtung des Deutschen Reiches*, Cologne 1916.

18. Keur and Keur, pp. 150 et seq; Gadourek, p. 79.

19. See also E. K. Francis, 'Minderheitsforschung in Amerika', in *Kölner Zeitschrift*, IX 4 (1957).

20. Bernot and Blancard.

21. ibid. pp. 242–4.

22. ibid. p. 46.

23. Thurnwald, p. 285.

24. West; Keur and Keur.

25. Williams; Turney-High.

26. Homans, pp. 334 et seq.

27. John I. Embree, *A Japanese Village: Suye Mura*, London 1946.

28. Herbert Kötter, 'Die Gemeinde in der ländlichen Soziologie', in 'Soziologie der Gemeinde', p. 15.

29. Utermann, 'Soziologie der Gemeinde', p. 119.

30. ibid. p. 122.

31. ibid. p. 128.

32. Eugen Lemberg and Lothar Krecker, *Die Entstehung eines neuen Volkes aus Binnendeutschen und Ostvertriebenen*, Marburg 1950, p. 9.

33. Martin Egger, 'Die Integration eines Dorfes im sozialen Wandel', in 'Soziologie der Gemeinde' p.71.

34. Teuscher, p. 111.

35. S. C. Dube, *Indian Village*, London 1955, pp. 34 et seq.

36. Gardener Murphy, *In the Minds of Men. The Study of Human Behaviour and Social Tensions in India*, New York 1953, chapters VII and VIII.

37. Linde, p. 68.
38. Peter A. Munch, *A Study of Cultural Change. Rural-Urban Conflicts in Norway*, Oslo 1956, pp. 82 et seq., 90 and 99.
39. Janowitz.
40. ibid. p. 18, note 1; also pp. 17 et seq.
41. ibid. p. 21.
42. ibid. p. 21.
43. ibid, see in particular chapter IV.
44. ibid. see in particular chapter VII.
45. Werner Landecker, 'Types of Integration and their Measurement', in *American Journal of Sociology*, LVI (1950) and 'Integration and Group Structure', in *Social Forces* XXX (1951–2).
46. Cf. chapter III, note 8.
47. Roland L. Warren, 'Eine sozialpsychologische Analyse der bürgerlichen Tätigkeiten in Stuttgart', in *Kölner Zeitschrift* IX 4.
48. This despite a different opinion expressed by us formerly, see in this respect König, review of a book by I. Gadourek in 'Soziologie der Gemeinde', p. 196.
49. See also J. P. Kruijt, 'Levensbeschouwing en Groep-solidariteit in Nederland', in *XII de Jaarboek van de Nederlandse Sociologische Vereiniging* (1957) and 'Sociologische beschouwingen over zuilen en verzuiling', in *Socialisme en Democratie*, Special Number 1957.

X. WHY COMMUNITY INVESTIGATIONS?

1. Reiss, p. 2.
2. ibid. p. 8.
3. C. M. Arensberg, 'The Community Study Method', p. 110.
4. ibid. p. 111.
5. ibid. p. 114.
6. Hollingshead, art. cit.
7. J. Bernard, art. cit.
8. Charles H. Cooley, *Human Nature and the Social Order*, New York 1902.
9. Gettys.
10. Cf. the collection of many studies by Park; today the same with regard to Louis Wirth.
11. Michael Young and Peter Willmott, *Family and Kinship in East London*, London 1957, pp. 81 et seq.
12. Frederic M. Thrasher, *The Gang*, revised edition, Chicago 1936; William F. Whyte, *Street-Corner Society. The Social Structure of an Italian Slum*, Chicago 1943 (5th edition 1949); John B. Mays, *Growing up in the City*, 2nd edition, Liverpool 1956 (first published in 1954); Albert K. Cohen, *Delinquent Boys. The Culture of the Gang*, Glencoe, Ill, 1955. For further literature see Heintz and König.
13. B. M. Spinley, *The Deprived and the Privileged*, London 1953, pp. 68 et seq.
14. Mays, p. 47.
15. Madeline Kerr, *The People of Ship Street*, London 1958.

16. Hollingshead, op. cit.
17. ibid. p. 212.
18. ibid. p. 231.
19. Chombart de Lauwe, *Paris*, Vol. 1, p. 19.
20. Elisabeth Pfeil, *Die Wohnwünsche der Bergarbeiter*, Tübingen 1954.
21. Ruth Glass, 'Urban Sociology in Great Britain', in *Current Sociology*, IV, 4 (1955), p. 12.
22. Quoist.
23. Roland L. Warren, *Studying your Community*, New York 1955, p. 307.
24. See also Harald Swedner, 'Die Untersuchung kleiner Gemeinden in Schweden', in 'Soziologie der Gemeinde'.
25. Kurt Lewin, 'Action Research and Minority Problems' in *Resolving Social Conflicts*, Selected Papers on Group Dynamics, New York 1948, chap. XIII.
26. Ronald Lippitt, *Training in Community Relations*, New York 1949.
27. See also here J. Bernard, *passim*.

XI. A SHORT HISTORY OF COMMUNITY RESEARCH

1. Giovanni Verga, *Die Malavoglia*, translated and provided with an epilogue by König, Zürich 1945.
2. W. Reymont, *Die Bauern*, new edition, Dusseldorf 1956.
3. *idem, Das gelobte Land*, German translation, 1916.
4. Cf. Theodor W. Adorno and Walter Dirks, *Soziologische Exkurse*, Frankfurt 1956, chapter X.
5. ibid. p. 135.
6. ibid. p. 145.
7. Quoist.
8. Amongst the older literature on the subject, see Andreas Walter, *Soziologie und Sozialwissenschaften in Amerika*, 1926; see also for what follows, Young, Part I, chapters I and II; E. Gordon Erikson, *Urban Behaviour*, New York 1954, pp. 8 et seq. See also Glass, chapter IV, which has a more comprehensive bibliography.
9. Beatrice and Sidney Webb, *Methods of Social Study*, London 1932.
10. Williams; Young and Willmott; Peter Townsend, *The Family Life of Old People*, London 1957; Raymond Firth and Judith Djamour, *Two Studies of Kinship in London*, London 1956; Spinley; Kerr; O.A. Oeser and S. B. Hammond, *Social Structure and Personality in a Rural Community*, London 1954 and *Social Structure and Personality in a City*, London 1954.
11. Cf. Young, p. 89.
12. Warner and Lunt, p. 16.
13. Whyte, p. VIII.
14. Homans, chapters VII and VIII.
15. Whyte, p. 271.
16. Charles Bettelheim and Suzanne Frère, *Une Ville française moyenne: Auxerre en 1950. Etude de structure sociale et urbaine*, Paris 1950.
17. Kötter; Grüneisen; Teiwes; Baumert; Baumert and Hünniger; Bernot and Blancard; Wurzbacher.

18. Beck; Leutenegger, op. cit. and art. cit.; Peter M. Atteslander, 'Dynamische Aspekte des Zuzuges in die Stadt', in *Kölner Zeitschrift* VII/2 (1955); Weiss; *op. cit.*, 'Die Industrialisierung auf dem Lande', in 'Soziologie der Gemeinde' and 'Ausbreitung städtischer Lebensformen auf dem Lande', in *Internationales Gewerbearchiv*, 1958.

19. Sieben.

20. S. Groenman, *Methoden der Soziographie*, 2nd edition, Assen 1953; 'Die Gemeindeforschung in den Nederlanden', in *Soziale Welt*, V 2 (1954); on community investigation and town planning *Sociale Opbouw op territoriale grondslag* (Community Organization), Utrecht 1958. A. N. J. den Hollander, *Nederzettingsvormen en – problemen in de groote Hongaarsche laagvlakte*, en Europeesch 'Frontier' gebied, Amsterdam 1947. Concerning the concept 'sociography' in Dutch and German usage, see König in the article 'Social Morphology', in *Lexikon der Soziologie*, Frankfurt 1958.

21. Swedner.

XII. METHODS OF COMMUNITY INVESTIGATION.

1. Wurzbacher, pp. 21 et seq. See also König, art. cit. in 'Soziologie der Gemeinde', p. 178.

2. *Praktische Sozialforschung*, ed. König, Vol. II, 'Observation and Experiment', 4th ed., Cologne 1965, p. 35.

3. Arensberg, 'The Community Study Method', p. 115.

4. See also *Praktische Sozialforschung*, Vol. I, 'Das Interview', 5th edition, Cologne 1965.

5. Arensberg, 'The Community Study Method', p. 113.

6. ibid.

INDEX

Action research, 169, 170
Adorno, 172
Angell, 96, 97, 134, 150
Areas, Natural, 61, seq.
Arensberg, 71, 77, 85, 126, 159, 160, 188, 190
Arkansas settlement, 53
Association, 7 seq., 14

Baltzell, 116
Beck, 68, 105
Beegle, 52, 74
Bernard, 161
Bernod, 137
Biocoenology, 9
Biocoenosis, 9
Blancard, 137
Block-Overseer system, 71, 72
Bobek, 85, 91
Booth, 174, 175
Bowley, 176

Caste, 115, 116
Chateau-Gerard, 140
Chombart de Lauwe, 62, 167
Clark, 96
Class, 115 seq.
Class classification, 120 seq.
Cliques, 101, 106, 112
Community,
    Biotic, 131
    Culture, 10, 11, 12
    Definition, 1 seq., 180
    External system, 133
    Internal system, 133
    Investigation, 172 seq., 184 seq.
    Planning, 167, 168
    Self-survey, 169
    Social system, 29
    Social totality, 23, 24
    Sociology, 154 seq., 193 seq.
    Spheres, 56 seq.
    Structure, 3, 5, 6, 114, 190
    Typology, 76 seq.
Cohen, 162
Croon, 77

Darmstadt investigation, 68, 93
Delinquency, 66
Detroit Area Study, 178, 179
Dollard, 116, 161
Durkheim, 66
Ecology,
    definition, 9, 10
    social, 59 seq.
Elmtown, 164, 165
Embree, 140
Empirical investigations, 175 seq.
Eskimoes, 60
Festinger, 74
Finke, 88
Forde, 13, 82
Francis, 20

Gadourek, 152, 188
Galpin, 26
Gangs, 162
Geiger, 123
Gemeinde, 1, 14 seq.
Gemeinderschaft, 1, 14 seq.
Gemeinschaft, 1, 14 seq.

216

The International Library of
Sociology
and Social Reconstruction

Edited by W. J. H. SPROTT
Founded by KARL MANNHEIM

ROUTLEDGE & KEGAN PAUL
BROADWAY HOUSE, CARTER LANE, LONDON, E.C.4

CONTENTS

PRINTED IN GREAT BRITAIN BY HEADLEY BROTHERS LTD
109 KINGSWAY LONDON WC2 AND ASHFORD KENT

GENERAL SOCIOLOGY

Brown, Robert. Explanation in Social Science. *208 pp. 1963. (2nd Impression 1964.) 25s.*

Gibson, Quentin. The Logic of Social Enquiry. *240 pp. 1960. (2nd Impression 1963.) 24s.*

Homans, George C. Sentiments and Activities: Essays in Social Science. *336 pp. 1962. 32s.*

Isajiw, Wsevelod W. Causation and Functionalism in Sociology. *About 192 pp. 1968. 25s.*

Johnson, Harry M. Sociology: a Systematic Introduction. *Foreword by Robert K. Merton. 710 pp. 1961. (4th Impression 1964.) 42s.*

Mannheim, Karl. Essays on Sociology and Social Psychology. *Edited by Paul Keckskemeti. With Editorial Note by Adolph Lowe. 344 pp. 1953. (2nd Impression 1966.) 32s.*

Systematic Sociology: An Introduction to the Study of Society. *Edited by J. S. Erös and Professor W. A. C. Stewart. 220 pp. 1957. (3rd Impression 1967.) 24s.*

Martindale, Don. The Nature and Types of Sociological Theory. *292 pp. 1961. (3rd Impression 1967.) 35s.*

Maus, Heinz. A Short History of Sociology. *234 pp. 1962. (2nd Impression 1965.) 28s.*

Myrdal, Gunnar. Value in Social Theory: A Collection of Essays on Methodology. *Edited by Paul Streeten. 332 pp. 1958. (2nd Impression 1962.) 32s.*

Ogburn, William F., and **Nimkoff, Meyer F.** A Handbook of Sociology. *Preface by Karl Mannheim. 656 pp. 46 figures. 35 tables. 5th edition (revised) 1964. 40s.*

Parsons, Talcott, and **Smelser, Neil J.** Economy and Society: A Study in the Integration of Economic and Social Theory. *362 pp. 1956. (4th Impression 1967.) 35s.*

Rex, John. Key Problems of Sociological Theory. *220 pp. 1961. (4th Impression 1968.) 25s.*

Stark, Werner. The Fundamental Forms of Social Thought. *280 pp. 1962. 32s.*

FOREIGN CLASSICS OF SOCIOLOGY

Durkheim, Emile. Suicide. A Study in Sociology. *Edited and with an Introduction by George Simpson. 404 pp. 1952. (4th Impression 1968.) 35s.*

Socialism and Saint-Simon. *Edited with an Introduction by Alvin W. Gouldner. Translated by Charlotte Sattler from the edition originally edited with an Introduction by Marcel Mauss. 286 pp. 1959. 28s.*

Professional Ethics and Civic Morals. *Translated by Cornelia Brookfield. 288 pp. 1957. 30s.*

Gerth, H. H., and **Mills, C. Wright.** From Max Weber: Essays in Sociology. *502 pp. 1948. (6th Impression 1967.) 35s.*

Tönnies, Ferdinand. Community and Association. *(Gemeinschaft und Gesellschaft.) Translated and Supplemented by Charles P. Loomis. Foreword by Pitirim A. Sorokin. 334 pp. 1955. 28s.*

SOCIAL STRUCTURE

Andreski, Stanislaw. Military Organization and Society. *Foreword by Professor A. R. Radcliffe-Brown. 226 pp. 1 folder. 1954. Revised Edition 1968. 35s.*

Cole, G. D. H. Studies in Class Structure. *220 pp. 1955. (3rd Impression 1964.) 21s.*

Coontz, Sydney H. Population Theories and the Economic Interpretation. *202 pp. 1957. (2nd Impression 1961.) 25s.*

Coser, Lewis. The Functions of Social Conflict. *204 pp. 1956. (3rd Impression 1968.) 25s.*

Dickie-Clark, H. F. Marginal Situation: A Sociological Study of a Coloured Group. *240 pp. 11 tables. 1966. 40s.*

Glass, D. V. (Ed.). Social Mobility in Britain. *Contributions by J. Berent, T. Bottomore, R. C. Chambers, J. Floud, D. V. Glass, J. R. Hall, H. T. Himmelweit, R. K. Kelsall, F. M. Martin, C. A. Moser, R. Mukherjee, and W. Ziegel. 420 pp. 1954. (4th Impression 1967.) 45s.*

Kelsall, R. K. Higher Civil Servants in Britain: From 1870 to the Present Day. *268 pp. 31 tables. 1955. (2nd Impression 1966.) 25s.*

König, René. The Community. *224 pp. 1968. 25s.*

Lawton, Dennis. Social Class, Language and Education. *192 pp. 1968. 21s.*

Marsh, David C. The Changing Social Structure in England and Wales, 1871-1961. *1958. 272 pp. 2nd edition (revised) 1966. (2nd Impression 1967.) 35s.*

Mouzelis, Nicos. Organization and Bureaucracy. An Analysis of Modern Theories. *240 pp. 1967. 28s.*

Ossowski, Stanislaw. Class Structure in the Social Consciousness. *210 pp. 1963. (2nd Impression 1967.) 25s.*

SOCIOLOGY AND POLITICS

Barbu, Zevedei. Democracy and Dictatorship: Their Psychology and Patterns of Life. *300 pp. 1956. 28s.*

Crick, Bernard. The American Science of Politics: Its Origins and Conditions. *284 pp. 1959. 32s.*

Hertz, Frederick. Nationality in History and Politics: A Psychology and Sociology of National Sentiment and Nationalism. *432 pp. 1944. (5th Impression 1966.) 42s.*

Kornhauser, William. The Politics of Mass Society. *272 pp. 20 tables. 1960. (2nd Impression 1965.) 28s.*

Laidler, Harry W. History of Socialism. Social-Economic Movements: An Historical and Comparative Survey of Socialism, Communism, Co-operation, Utopianism; and other Systems of Reform and Reconstruction. *New edition in preparation.*

Lasswell, Harold D. Analysis of Political Behaviour. An Empirical Approach. *324 pp. 1947. (4th Impression 1966.) 35s.*

Mannheim, Karl. Freedom, Power and Democratic Planning. *Edited by Hans Gerth and Ernest K. Bramstedt. 424 pp. 1951. (2nd Impression 1965.) 35s.*

Mansur, Fatma. Process of Independence. *Foreword by A. H. Hanson. 208 pp. 1962. 25s.*

Martin, David A. Pacificism: an Historical and Sociological Study. *262 pp. 1965. 30s.*

Myrdal, Gunnar. The Political Element in the Development of Economic Theory. *Translated from the German by Paul Streeten. 282 pp. 1953. (4th Impression 1965.) 25s.*

Polanyi, Michael. F.R.S. The Logic of Liberty: Reflections and Rejoinders. *228 pp. 1951. 18s.*

Verney, Douglas V. The Analysis of Political Systems. *264 pp. 1959. (3rd Impression 1966.) 28s.*

Wootton, Graham. The Politics of Influence: British Ex-Servicemen, Cabinet Decisions and Cultural Changes, 1917 to 1957. *316 pp. 1963. 30s.*
Workers, Unions and the State. *188 pp. 1966. (2nd Impression 1967.) 25s.*

FOREIGN AFFAIRS: THEIR SOCIAL, POLITICAL AND ECONOMIC FOUNDATIONS

Baer, Gabriel. Population and Society in the Arab East. *Translated by Hanna Szöke. 288 pp. 10 maps. 1964. 40s.*

Bonné, Alfred. State and Economics in the Middle East: A Society in Transition. *482 pp. 2nd (revised) edition 1955. (2nd Impression 1960.) 40s.*
Studies in Economic Development: with special reference to Conditions in the Under-developed Areas of Western Asia and India. *322 pp. 84 tables. 2nd edition 1960. 32s.*

Mayer, J. P. Political Thought in France from the Revolution to the Fifth Republic. *164 pp. 3rd edition (revised) 1961. 16s.*

Trouton, Ruth. Peasant Renaissance in Yugoslavia 1900-1950: A Study of the Development of Yugoslav Peasant Society as affected by Education. *370 pp. 1 map. 1952. 28s.*

CRIMINOLOGY

Ancel, Marc. Social Defence: A Modern Approach to Criminal Problems. *Foreword by Leon Radzinowicz. 240 pp. 1965. 32s.*

Cloward, Richard A., and Ohlin, Lloyd E. Delinquency and Opportunity: A Theory of Delinquent Gangs. *248 pp. 1961. 25s.*

Downes, David M. The Delinquent Solution. A Study in Subcultural Theory. *296 pp. 1966. 42s.*

Dunlop, A. B., and McCabe, S. Young Men in Detention Centres. *192 pp. 1965. 28s.*

Friedländer, Kate. The Psycho-Analytical Approach to Juvenile Delinquency: Theory, Case Studies, Treatment. *320 pp. 1947. (6th Impression 1967.) 40s.*

Glueck, Sheldon and **Eleanor.** Family Environment and Delinquency. *With the statistical assistance of Rose W. Kneznek. 340 pp. 1962. (2nd Impression 1966.) 40s.*

Mannheim, Hermann. Comparative Criminology: a Text Book. *Two volumes. 442 pp. and 380 pp. 1965. (2nd Impression with corrections 1966.) 42s. a volume.*

Morris, Terence. The Criminal Area: A Study in Social Ecology. *Foreword by Hermann Mannheim. 232 pp. 25 tables. 4 maps. 1957. (2nd Impression 1966.) 28s.*

Morris, Terence and **Pauline,** assisted by **Barbara Barer.** Pentonville: A Sociological Study of an English Prison. *416 pp. 16 plates. 1963. 50s.*

Spencer, John C. Crime and the Services. *Foreword by Hermann Mannheim. 336 pp. 1954. 28s.*

Trasler, Gordon. The Explanation of Criminality. *144 pp. 1962. (2nd Impression 1967.) 20s.*

SOCIAL PSYCHOLOGY

Barbu, Zevedei. Problems of Historical Psychology. *248 pp. 1960. 25s.*

Blackburn, Julian. Psychology and the Social Pattern. *184 pp. 1945. (7th Impression 1964.) 16s.*

Fleming, C. M. Adolescence: Its Social Psychology: With an Introduction to recent findings from the fields of Anthropology, Physiology, Medicine, Psychometrics and Sociometry. *288 pp. 2nd edition (revised) 1963. (3rd Impression 1967.) 25s. Paper 12s. 6d.*
The Social Psychology of Education: An Introduction and Guide to Its Study. *136 pp. 2nd edition (revised) 1959. (4th Impression 1967.) 14s. Paper 7s. 6d.*

Halmos, Paul. Towards a Measure of Man: The Frontiers of Normal Adjustment. *276 pp. 1957. 28s.*

Homans, George C. The Human Group. *Foreword by Bernard DeVoto. Introduction by Robert K. Merton. 526 pp. 1951. (7th Impression 1968.) 35s.*
Social Behaviour: its Elementary Forms. *416 pp. 1961. (2nd Impression 1966.) 32s.*

Klein, Josephine. The Study of Groups. *226 pp. 31 figures. 5 tables. 1956. (5th Impression 1967.) 21s. Paper, 9s. 6d.*

Linton, Ralph. The Cultural Background of Personality. *132 pp. 1947. (7th Impression 1968.) 16s.*

Mayo, Elton. The Social Problems of an Industrial Civilization. With an appendix on the Political Problem. *180 pp. 1949. (5th Impression 1966.) 25s.*

Ottaway, A. K. C. Learning Through Group Experience. *176 pp. 1966. 25s.*

Ridder, J. C. de. The Personality of the Urban African in South Africa. A Thematic Apperception Test Study. *196 pp. 12 plates. 1961. 25s.*

Rose, Arnold M. (Ed.). Human Behaviour and Social Processes: an Inter-actionist Approach. *Contributions by Arnold M. Rose, Ralph H. Turner, Anselm Strauss, Everett C. Hughes, E. Franklin Frazier, Howard S. Becker, et al. 696 pp. 1962. 70s.*

Smelser, Neil J. Theory of Collective Behaviour. *448 pp. 1962. (2nd Impression 1967.) 45s.*

Stephenson, Geoffrey M. The Development of Conscience. *128 pp. 1966. 25s.*

Young, Kimball. Handbook of Social Psychology. *658 pp. 16 figures. 10 tables. 2nd edition (revised) 1957. (3rd Impression 1963.) 40s.*

SOCIOLOGY OF THE FAMILY

Banks, J. A. Prosperity and Parenthood: A study of Family Planning among The Victorian Middle Classes. *262 pp. 1954. (2nd Impression 1965.) 28s.*

Burton, Lindy. Vulnerable Children. *about 272 pp. 1968. 35s.*

Gavron, Hannah. The Captive Wife: Conflicts of Housebound Mothers. *190 pp. 1966. (2nd Impression 1966.) 25s.*

Klein, Josephine. Samples from English Cultures. *1965. (2nd Impression 1967.)*
1. Three Preliminary Studies and Aspects of Adult Life in England. *447 pp. 50s.*
2. Child-Rearing Practices and Index. *247 pp. 35s.*

Klein, Viola. Britain's Married Women Workers. *180 pp. 1965. 28s.*

McWhinnie, Alexina M. Adopted Children. How They Grow Up. *304 pp. 1967. (2nd Impression 1968.) 42s.*

Myrdal, Alva and **Klein, Viola.** Women's Two Roles: Home and Work. *238 pp. 27 tables. 1956. Revised Edition 1967. 30s. Paper 15s.*

Parsons, Talcott and **Bales, Robert F.** Family: Socialization and Interaction Process. *In collaboration with James Olds, Morris Zelditch and Philip E. Slater. 456 pp. 50 figures and tables. 1956. (2nd Impression 1964.) 35s.*

THE SOCIAL SERVICES

Ashdown, Margaret and **Brown, S. Clement.** Social Service and Mental Health: An Essay on Psychiatric Social Workers. *280 pp. 1953. 21s.*

Goetschius, George W. Working with Community Groups. *About 256 pp. 1968. about 35s.*

Goetschius, George W. and **Tash, Joan.** Working with Unattached Youth. *416 pp. 1967. 40s.*

Hall, M. Penelope. The Social Services of Modern England. *416 pp. 6th edition (revised) 1963. (2nd Impression with a new Preface 1966.) 30s.*

Hall, M. P., and **Howes, I. V.** The Church in Social Work. A Study of Moral Welfare Work undertaken by the Church of England. *320 pp. 1965. 35s.*

Heywood, Jean S. Children in Care: the Development of the Service for the Deprived Child. *264 pp. 2nd edition (revised) 1965. (2nd Impression 1966.) 32s.*

An Introduction to Teaching Casework Skills. *190 pp. 1964. 28s.*

Jones, Kathleen. Lunacy, Law and Conscience, 1744-1845: the Social History of the Care of the Insane. *268 pp. 1955. 25s.*

Mental Health and Social Policy, 1845-1959. *264 pp. 1960. (2nd Impression 1967.) 28s.*

Jones, Kathleen and **Sidebotham, Roy.** Mental Hospitals at Work. *220 pp. 1962. 30s.*

Kastell, Jean. Casework in Child Care. *Foreword by M. Brooke Willis. 320 pp. 1962. 35s.*

Nokes, P. L. The Professional Task in Welfare Practice. *152 pp. 1967. 28s.*

Rooff, Madeline. Voluntary Societies and Social Policy. *350 pp. 15 tables. 1957. 35s.*

Shenfield, B. E. Social Policies for Old Age: A Review of Social Provision for Old Age in Great Britain. *260 pp. 39 tables. 1957. 25s.*

Timms, Noel. Psychiatric Social Work in Great Britain (1939-1962). *280 pp. 1964. 32s.*

Social Casework: Principles and Practice. *256 pp. 1964. (2nd Impression 1966.) 25s. Paper 15s.*

Trasler, Gordon. In Place of Parents: A Study in Foster Care. *272 pp. 1960. (2nd Impression 1966.) 30s.*

Young, A. F., and **Ashton, E. T.** British Social Work in the Nineteenth Century. *288 pp. 1956. (2nd Impression 1963.) 28s.*

Young, A. F. Social Services in British Industry. *about 350 pp. 1968. about 45s.*

SOCIOLOGY OF EDUCATION

Banks, Olive. Parity and Prestige in English Secondary Education: a Study in Educational Sociology. *272 pp. 1955. (2nd Impression 1963.) 32s.*

Bentwich, Joseph. Education in Israel. *224 pp. 8 pp. plates. 1965. 24s.*

Blyth, W. A. L. English Primary Education. A Sociological Description. *1965. Revised edition 1967.*

1. Schools. *232 pp. 30s.*
2. Background. *168 pp. 25s.*

Collier, K. G. The Social Purposes of Education: Personal and Social Values in Education. *268 pp. 1959. (3rd Impression 1965.) 21s.*

Dale, R. R., and **Griffith, S.** Down Stream: Failure in the Grammar School. *108 pp. 1965. 20s.*

Dore, R. P. Education in Tokugawa Japan. *356 pp. 9 pp. plates. 1965. 35s.*

Edmonds, E. L. The School Inspector. *Foreword by Sir William Alexander. 214 pp. 1962. 28s.*

Evans, K. M. Sociometry and Education. *158 pp. 1962. (2nd Impression 1966.) 18s.*

Foster, P. J. Education and Social Change in Ghana. *336 pp. 3 maps. 1965.* (*2nd Impression 1967.*) *36s.*

Fraser, W. R. Education and Society in Modern France. *150 pp. 1963. 20s.*

Hans, Nicholas. New Trends in Education in the Eighteenth Century. *278 pp. 19 tables. 1951.* (*2nd Impression 1966.*) *30s.*
Comparative Education: A Study of Educational Factors and Traditions. *360 pp. 3rd (revised) edition 1958.* (*4th Impression 1967.*) *25s. Paper 12s. 6d.*

Hargreaves, David. Social Relations in a Secondary School. *240 pp. 1967. 32s.*

Holmes, Brian. Problems in Education. A Comparative Approach. *336 pp. 1965.* (*2nd Impression 1967.*) *32s.*

Mannheim, Karl and **Stewart, W. A. C.** An Introduction to the Sociology of Education. *206 pp. 1962.* (*2nd Impression 1965.*) *21s.*

Musgrove, F. Youth and the Social Order. *176 pp. 1964. 21s.*

Ortega y Gasset, José. Mission of the University. *Translated with an Introduction by Howard Lee Nostrand. 86 pp. 1946.* (*3rd Impression 1963.*) *15s.*

Ottaway, A. K. C. Education and Society: An Introduction to the Sociology of Education. *With an Introduction by W. O. Lester Smith. 212 pp. Second edition (revised). 1962.* (*5th Impression 1968.*) *18s. Paper 10s. 6d.*

Peers, Robert. Adult Education: A Comparative Study. *398 pp. 2nd edition 1959.* (*2nd Impression 1966.*) *42s.*

Pritchard, D. G. Education and the Handicapped: 1760 to 1960. *258 pp. 1963.* (*2nd Impression 1966.*) *35s.*

Simon, Brian and **Joan (Eds.).** Educational Psychology in the U.S.S.R. *Introduction by Brian and Joan Simon. Translation by Joan Simon. Papers by D. N. Bogoiavlenski and N. A. Menchinskaia, D. B. Elkonin, E. A. Fleshner, Z. I. Kalmykova, G. S. Kostiuk, V. A. Krutetski, A. N. Leontiev, A. R. Luria, E. A. Milerian, R. G. Natadze, B. M. Teplov, L. S. Vygotski, L. V. Zankov. 296 pp. 1963. 40s.*

SOCIOLOGY OF CULTURE

Eppel, E. M., and **M.** Adolescents and Morality: A Study of some Moral Values and Dilemmas of Working Adolescents in the Context of a changing Climate of Opinion. *Foreword by W. J. H. Sprott. 268 pp. 39 tables. 1966. 30s.*

Fromm, Erich. The Fear of Freedom. *286 pp. 1942.* (*8th Impression 1960.*) *25s. Paper 10s.*
The Sane Society. *400 pp. 1956.* (*3rd Impression 1963.*) *28s. Paper 12s. 6d.*

Mannheim, Karl. Diagnosis of Our Time: Wartime Essays of a Sociologist. *208 pp. 1943.* (*8th Impression 1966.*) *21s.*
Essays on the Sociology of Culture. *Edited by Ernst Mannheim in co-operation with Paul Kecskemeti. Editorial Note by Adolph Lowe. 280 pp. 1956.* (*3rd Impression 1967.*) *28s.*

Weber, Alfred. Farewell to European History: or The Conquest of Nihilism. *Translated from the German by R. F. C. Hull. 224 pp. 1947. 18s.*

SOCIOLOGY OF RELIGION

Argyle, Michael. Religious Behaviour. *224 pp. 8 figures. 41 tables. 1958. (3rd Impression 1965.) 25s.*

Knight, Frank H., and **Merriam, Thornton W.** The Economic Order and Religion. *242 pp. 1947. 18s.*

Stark, Werner. The Sociology of Religion. A Study of Christendom.
Volume I. Established Religion. *248 pp. 1966. 35s.*
Volume II. Sectarian Religion. *368 pp. 1967. 40s.*
Volume III. The Universal Church. *464 pp. 1967. 45s.*

Watt, W. Montgomery. Islam and the Integration of Society. *320 pp. 1961. (3rd Impression 1966.) 35s.*

SOCIOLOGY OF ART AND LITERATURE

Beljame, Alexandre. Men of Letters and the English Public in the Eighteenth Century: 1660-1744, Dryden, Addison, Pope. *Edited with an Introduction and Notes by Bonamy Dobrée. Translated by E. O. Lorimer. 532 pp. 1948. 32s.*

Misch, Georg. A History of Autobiography in Antiquity. *Translated by E. W. Dickes. 2 Volumes. Vol. 1, 364 pp., Vol. 2, 372 pp. 1950. 45s. the set.*

Schücking, L. L. The Sociology of Literary Taste. *112 pp. 2nd (revised) edition 1966. 18s.*

Silbermann, Alphons. The Sociology of Music. *Translated from the German by Corbet Stewart. 222 pp. 1963. 28s.*

SOCIOLOGY OF KNOWLEDGE

Mannheim, Karl. Essays on the Sociology of Knowledge. *Edited by Paul Kecskemeti. Editorial note by Adolph Lowe. 352 pp. 1952. (3rd Impression 1964.) 35s.*

Stark, W. America: Ideal and Reality. The United States of 1776 in Contemporary Philosophy. *136 pp. 1947. 12s.*
The Sociology of Knowledge: An Essay in Aid of a Deeper Understanding of the History of Ideas. *384 pp. 1958. (3rd Impression 1967.) 36s.*
Montesquieu: Pioneer of the Sociology of Knowledge. *244 pp. 1960. 25s.*

URBAN SOCIOLOGY

Anderson, Nels. The Urban Community: A World Perspective. *532 pp. 1960. 35s.*

Ashworth, William. The Genesis of Modern British Town Planning: A Study in Economic and Social History of the Nineteenth and Twentieth Centuries. *288 pp. 1954. (3rd Impression 1968.) 32s.*

Bracey, Howard. Neighbours: On New Estates and Subdivisions in England and U.S.A. *220 pp. 1964. 28s.*

Cullingworth, J. B. Housing Needs and Planning Policy: A Restatement of the Problems of Housing Need and "Overspill" in England and Wales. *232 pp. 44 tables. 8 maps. 1960. (2nd Impression 1966.) 28s.*

Dickinson, Robert E. City and Region: A Geographical Interpretation. *608 pp. 125 figures. 1964. (5th Impression 1967.) 60s.*
The West European City: A Geographical Interpretation. *600 pp. 129 maps. 29 plates. 2nd edition 1962. (3rd Impression 1968.) 55s.*
The City Region in Western Europe. *320 pp. Maps. 1967. 30s. Paper 14s.*

Jennings, Hilda. Societies in the Making: a Study of Development and Redevelopment within a County Borough. *Foreword by D. A. Clark. 286 pp. 1962. (2nd Impression 1967.) 32s.*

Kerr, Madeline. The People of Ship Street. *240 pp. 1958. 23s.*

Mann, P. H. An Approach to Urban Sociology. *240 pp. 1965. (2nd Impression 1968.) 30s.*

Morris, R. N., and Mogey, J. The Sociology of Housing. Studies at Berinsfield. *232 pp. 4 pp. plates. 1965. 42s.*

Rosser, C., and Harris, C. The Family and Social Change. A Study of Family and Kinship in a South Wales Town. *352 pp. 8 maps. 1965. (2nd Impression 1968.) 45s.*

RURAL SOCIOLOGY

Haswell, M. R. The Economics of Development in Village India. *120 pp. 1967. 21s.*

Littlejohn, James. Westrigg: the Sociology of a Cheviot Parish. *172 pp. 5 figures. 1963. 25s.*

Williams, W. M. The Country Craftsman: A Study of Some Rural Crafts and the Rural Industries Organization in England. *248 pp. 9 figures. 1958. 25s. (Dartington Hall Studies in Rural Sociology.)*
The Sociology of an English Village: Gosforth. *272 pp. 12 figures. 13 tables. 1956. (3rd Impression 1964.) 25s.*

SOCIOLOGY OF MIGRATION

Eisenstadt, S. N. The Absorption of Immigrants: a Comparative Study based mainly on the Jewish Community in Palestine and the State of Israel. *288 pp. 1954. 28s.*

Humphreys, Alexander J. New Dubliners: Urbanization and the Irish Family. *Foreword by George C. Homans. 304 pp. 1966. 40s.*

11

SOCIOLOGY OF INDUSTRY AND DISTRIBUTION

Anderson, Nels. Work and Leisure. *280 pp. 1961. 28s.*

Blau, Peter M., and **Scott, W. Richard.** Formal Organizations: a Comparative approach. *Introduction and Additional Bibliography by J. H. Smith. 326 pp. 1963. (2nd Impression 1964.) 28s. Paper 15s.*

Eldridge, J. E. T. Industrial Disputes. Essays in the Sociology of Industrial Relations. *about 272 pp. 1968. 40s.*

Hollowell, Peter G. The Lorry Driver. *272 pp. 1968. 42s.*

Jefferys, Margot, with the assistance of Winifred Moss. Mobility in the Labour Market: Employment Changes in Battersea and Dagenham. *Preface by Barbara Wootton. 186 pp. 51 tables. 1954. 15s.*

Levy, A. B. Private Corporations and Their Control. *Two Volumes. Vol. 1, 464 pp., Vol. 2, 432 pp. 1950. 80s. the set.*

Liepmann, Kate. Apprenticeship: An Enquiry into its Adequacy under Modern Conditions. *Foreword by H. D. Dickinson. 232 pp. 6 tables. 1960. (2nd Impression 1960.) 23s.*

Millerson, Geoffrey. The Qualifying Associations: a Study in Professionalization. *320 pp. 1964. 42s.*

Smelser, Neil J. Social Change in the Industrial Revolution: An Application of Theory to the Lancashire Cotton Industry, 1770-1840. *468 pp. 12 figures. 14 tables. 1959. (2nd Impression 1960.) 42s.*

Williams, Gertrude. Recruitment to Skilled Trades. *240 pp. 1957. 23s.*

Young, A. F. Industrial Injuries Insurance: an Examination of British Policy. *192 pp. 1964. 30s.*

ANTHROPOLOGY

Ammar, Hamed. Growing up in an Egyptian Village: Silwa, Province of Aswan. *336 pp. 1954. (2nd Impression 1966.) 35s.*

Crook, David and **Isabel.** Revolution in a Chinese Village: Ten Mile Inn. *230 pp. 8 plates. 1 map. 1959. 21s.*
The First Years of Yangyi Commune. *302 pp. 12 plates. 1966. 42s.*

Dickie-Clark, H. F. The Marginal Situation. A Sociological Study of a Coloured Group. *236 pp. 1966. 40s.*

Dube, S. C. Indian Village. *Foreword by Morris Edward Opler. 276 pp. 4 plates. 1955. (5th Impression 1965.) 25s.*
India's Changing Villages: Human Factors in Community Development. *260 pp. 8 plates. 1 map. 1958. (3rd Impression 1963.) 25s.*

Firth, Raymond. Malay Fishermen. Their Peasant Economy. *420 pp. 17 pp. plates. 2nd edition revised and enlarged 1966. (2nd Impression 1968.) 55s.*

Gulliver, P. H. The Family Herds. A Study of two Pastoral Tribes in East Africa, The Jie and Turkana. *304 pp. 4 plates. 19 figures. 1955. (2nd Impression with new preface and bibliography 1966.) 35s.*
Social Control in an African Society: a Study of the Arusha, Agricultural Masai of Northern Tanganyika. *320 pp. 8 plates. 10 figures. 1963. 35s.*

Hogbin, Ian. Transformation Scene. The Changing Culture of a New Guinea Village. *340 pp. 22 plates. 2 maps. 1951. 30s.*

Ishwaran, K. Shivapur. A South Indian Village. *about 216 pp. 1968. 35s.*
Tradition and Economy in Village India: An Interactionist Approach. *Foreword by Conrad Arensburg. 176 pp. 1966. 25s.*

Jarvie, Ian C. The Revolution in Anthropology. *268 pp. 1964. (2nd Impression 1967.) 40s.*

Jarvie, Ian C. and **Agassi, Joseph.** Hong Kong. A Society in Transition. *about 388 pp. 1968. 56s.*

Little, Kenneth L. Mende of Sierra Leone. *308 pp. and folder. 1951. Revised edition 1967. 63s.*

Lowie, Professor Robert H. Social Organization. *494 pp. 1950. (4th Impression 1966.) 42s.*

Maunier, René. The Sociology of Colonies: An Introduction to the Study of Race Contact. *Edited and translated by E. O. Lorimer. 2 Volumes. Vol. 1, 430 pp. Vol. 2, 356 pp. 1949. 70s. the set.*

Mayer, Adrian C. Caste and Kinship in Central India: A Village and its Region. *328 pp. 16 plates. 15 figures. 16 tables. 1960. (2nd Impression 1965.) 35s.*
Peasants in the Pacific: A Study of Fiji Indian Rural Society. *232 pp. 16 plates. 10 figures. 14 tables. 1961. 35s.*

Smith, Raymond T. The Negro Family in British Guiana: Family Structure and Social Status in the Villages. *With a Foreword by Meyer Fortes. 314 pp. 8 plates. 1 figure. 4 maps. 1956. (2nd Impression 1965.) 35s.*

DOCUMENTARY

Meek, Dorothea L. (Ed.). Soviet Youth: Some Achievements and Problems. *Excerpts from the Soviet Press, translated by the editor. 280 pp. 1957. 28s.*

Schlesinger, Rudolf (Ed.). Changing Attitudes in Soviet Russia.

1. The Family in the U.S.S.R. *Documents and Readings, with an Introduction by the editor. 434 pp. 1949. 30s.*

2. The Nationalities Problem and Soviet Administration. Selected Readings on the Development of Soviet Nationalities Policies. *Introduced by the editor. Translated by W. W. Gottlieb. 324 pp. 1956. 30s.*

Reports of the Institute of Community Studies

(*Demy 8vo.*)

Cartwright, Ann. Human Relations and Hospital Care. *272 pp. 1964. 30s.*
Patients and their Doctors. A Study of General Practice. *304 pp. 1967.40s.*

Jackson, Brian. Streaming: an Education System in Miniature. *168 pp. 1964.* (*2nd Impression 1966.*) *21s. Paper 10s.*
Working Class Community. Some General Notions raised by a Series of Studies in Northern England. *192 pp. 1968. 25s.*

Jackson, Brian and **Marsden, Dennis.** Education and the Working Class: Some General Themes raised by a Study of 88 Working-class Children in a Northern Industrial City. *268 pp. 2 folders. 1962.* (*4th Impression 1968.*) *32s.*

Marris, Peter. Widows and their Families. *Foreword by Dr. John Bowlby. 184 pp. 18 tables. Statistical Summary. 1958. 18s.*
Family and Social Change in an African City. A Study of Rehousing in Lagos. *196 pp. 1 map. 4 plates. 53 tables. 1961.* (*2nd Impression 1966.*) *30s.*
The Experience of Higher Education. *232 pp. 27 tables. 1964. 25s.*

Marris, Peter and **Rein, Martin.** Dilemmas of Social Reform. Poverty and Community Action in the United States. *256 pp. 1967. 35s.*

Mills, Enid. Living with Mental Illness: a Study in East London. *Foreword by Morris Carstairs. 196 pp. 1962. 28s.*

Runciman, W. G. Relative Deprivation and Social Justice. A Study of Attitudes to Social Inequality in Twentieth Century England. *352 pp. 1966.* (*2nd Impression 1967.*) *40s.*

Townsend, Peter. The Family Life of Old People: An Inquiry in East London. *Foreword by J. H. Sheldon. 300 pp. 3 figures. 63 tables. 1957.* (*3rd Impression 1967.*) *30s.*

Willmott, Peter. Adolescent Boys in East London. *230 pp. 1966. 30s.*
The Evolution of a Community: a study of Dagenham after forty years. *168 pp. 2 maps. 1963. 21s.*

Willmott, Peter and **Young, Michael.** Family and Class in a London Suburb. *202 pp. 47 tables. 1960.* (*4th Impression 1968.*) *25s.*

Young, Michael. Innovation and Research in Education. *192 pp. 1965. 25s.*

Young, Michael and **McGeeney, Patrick.** Learning Begins at Home. A Study of a Junior School and its Parents. *about 128 pp. 1968. about 18s. Paper about 8s.*

Young, Michael and **Willmott, Peter.** Family and Kinship in East London. *Foreword by Richard M. Titmuss. 252 pp. 39 tables. 1957.* (*3rd Impression 1965.*) *28s.*

14

The British Journal of Sociology. *Edited by Terence P. Morris. Vol. 1, No. 1, March 1950 and Quarterly. Roy. 8vo., £2 10s. annually, 15s. a number, post free. (Vols. 1-16, £6 each; Vol. 17, £2 10s. Individual parts 37s. 6d. and 15s. respectively.)*

All prices are net and subject to alteration without notice

15

1267 H.B.